ILL-ADVISED

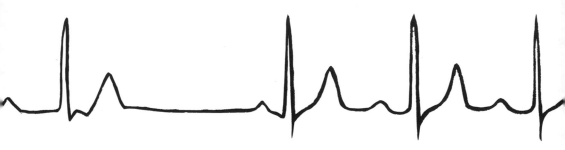

University of Missouri Press
Columbia and London

ILL-
ADVISED

Presidential Health
and Public Trust

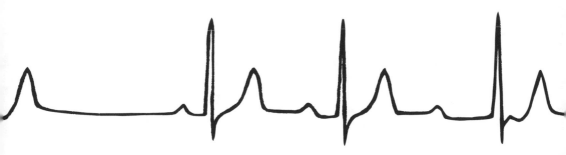

ROBERT H. FERRELL

5 4 3 2 1   96 95 94 93 92

Library of Congress Cataloging-in-Publication Data
Ferrell, Robert H.
    Ill-advised : presidential health and public trust / Robert H. Ferrell.
        p.   cm.
    Includes bibliographical references and index.
    ISBN 0-8262-0864-9 (alk. paper)
    1. Presidents—United States—History. 2. Presidents—United States—
Health. I. Title.
E176.1.F47   1992
973'.099—dc20   92-18527
                                                                    CIP

∞™ This paper meets the requirements of the
American National Standard for Permanence of Paper
for Printed Library Materials, Z39.48, 1984.

Designer: Danah Coester
Typesetter: Connell-Zeko Type & Graphics
Printer and Binder: Thomson-Shore, Inc.
Typefaces: Palatino and Aura

For
BRIGADIER GENERAL THOMAS W. MATTINGLY, M.C. (RET.)

CONTENTS

PREFACE

The pages that follow deal with one of the most distressing developments in American national politics during the past century: the
willingness of presidents of the United States or their physicians,
and sometimes presidents in collaboration with their physicians, to
cover up their illnesses.

It is a deplorable situation, these cover-ups, for public trust gets
lost in the bargain. After all, voters presume they are electing people
whose health is up to the heavy requirements of the nation's most
important office. They need to know, down to the smallest personal
detail, when the subject of their trust is incompetent to carry it out.

But look at what has happened over the years. The first cover-up
began one morning early in May 1893 when the president of that time,
Grover Cleveland, noticed a sore spot on the roof of his mouth. The
story moves forward to October 2, 1919, when another exigency arose;
President Woodrow Wilson collapsed in a bathroom in the private
quarters of the White House, suffering a debilitating stroke. He, his
personal physician, his wife, and his secretary decided they would
disguise his illness, and did so for months. A few years later, Wilson's
successor, Warren G. Harding, died in the Palace Hotel in San Francisco just when he seemed to have turned a corner in his illness and
was getting better. This raised a question, quickly resolved, about the
need to cover up the incompetence of his physician, Dr. Charles E.
Sawyer. A generation later, Franklin D. Roosevelt collapsed and died
at Warm Springs, Georgia, a few months after his countrymen in complete ignorance of his pitiful physical condition reelected him to a
fourth term.

The most interesting case of a president whose illnesses were not
always matters of public knowledge was that of Dwight D. Eisenhower.
On the face of things a cover-up of Eisenhower's illnesses has not
seemed possible. It would have been so ill-advised in an era just a few
years after the death of Roosevelt. Too, it seems impossible considering Eisenhower's personality, a great public figure who had risen to
general of the army in fair part because of his openness, his lack of

guile. Moreover, when he suffered a major heart attack in 1955 his words to his press secretary were "tell them everything," and his doctors released more detail, sometimes embarrassingly personal detail, than had ever occurred when a president was ill.

The present book looks closely at Eisenhower's case because it seems impossible that anyone could have concealed anything. Also, because much new information on his health care has recently become available. Indeed, more is now known about Eisenhower's illnesses than those of any other president.

I have chosen to deal with John F. Kennedy's and Ronald Reagan's cover-ups in less detail, partly because what happened is fairly close to the present and not everything may have come out, also because, paradoxically, their situations seem obvious, hardly subtle, and do not deserve as much attention as the fascinating cases of their predecessors.

ACKNOWLEDGMENTS

For assistance in pursuing what has been a series of medical detective stories, I am grateful to Gretchen Worden of the Muetter Museum of the College of Physicians of Philadelphia, who brought out articles and correspondence about the secret operation on Cleveland and showed the holdings of her extraordinary museum, and to Thomas A. Horrocks of the college's library. A few years ago Arthur S. Link and associates at the Papers of Woodrow Wilson in the Firestone Library of Princeton University explained President Woodrow Wilson's illness in 1919–1921 and made available their special materials on the subject, including the diary of Dr. Cary T. Grayson. My appreciation to the Ohio Historical Society for use of microfilm of the papers of President Harding's personal physician, Dr. Charles E. Sawyer. I am indebted to Verne W. Newton and staff at the Franklin D. Roosevelt Library, likewise Daniel D. Holt, James W. Leyerzapf, Hazel Stroda, and Kathleen Struss of the Eisenhower Library. It has been a pleasure to use papers in the Library of Congress, the Southern Historical Collection of the University of North Carolina at Chapel Hill, the American Heritage Center of the University of Wyoming, and the Francis A. Countway Library of Medicine of the Harvard Medical School (here my appreciation to Elin and Richard Wolfe and to the biographer of Dr. Paul Dudley White, Dr. Oglesby Paul).

Brenda L. Heaster gave me the transcript of her 1989 taped interview with Dr. Howard G. Bruenn, President Roosevelt's cardiologist. Jan Kenneth Herman, editor of *Navy Medicine*, similarly made available the transcript of his interview the following year, only part of which he has published. February 16, 1992, Dr. and Mrs. Bruenn kindly provided luncheon in their Riverdale, New York, apartment and spoke glowingly of memories of President Roosevelt.

A very special thanks to Brigadier General Thomas W. Mattingly, Eisenhower's cardiologist from 1952 until the president's death in 1969. Dr. Mattingly a few years ago deposited his massive medical history of Eisenhower in the presidential library in Abilene, Kansas. Brought together under the auspices of the U.S. Army Medical Corps, and written with Lieutenant Colonel Olive F. G. Marsh and several of the physicians associated with Eisenhower's health care, it is a definitive account. Dr. Mattingly offered hospitality in Davidson, North Carolina, and read drafts of chapters and pointed out errors of fact. It would have been impossible to write the present book without his help. He has advised a separation of narrative and judgment; he willingly admits his textual corrections, but the judgments, he says, with a twinkle, nonetheless firmly, are not his.

Drs. Mark N. Goren and J. A. Creek were very helpful. The former answered many technical questions. The latter, a distinguished diagnostician, read the entire manuscript and pointed out places to enlarge and emphasize.

Colonel Richard C. Snyder gave permission of the Snyder family to use and quote from papers of his father in Abilene and Laramie.

I am much indebted to William B. Pickett of Rose-Hulman Institute of Technology in Terre Haute, Indiana, whose forthcoming biography of Eisenhower has often taken him to Abilene. It was his telephone call that persuaded me to examine the Mattingly medical history.

The staff of the University of Missouri Press once more made everything easy: Beverly Jarrett, director and editor-in-chief; Jane Lago, managing editor; Kathryn Conrad, publicity manager; and especially Polly Law, editor, who possesses a keen eye for error, and a fine sense of what will or will not work.

Again the help of Lila and of Carolyn, who prepared everything for the scanner.

ILL-
ADVISED

1

Cleveland, Wilson, and Harding

O f the seven medical cover-ups in the White House during all the years from President George Washington to President George Bush, the first three possessed differing rationales but the same general purpose, which was to keep the inquisitive noses of the American people out of what, according to the people in the White House, was not their business. President Grover Cleveland underwent a serious operation and covered it up because of the country's shaky financial condition. Woodrow Wilson suffered a massive stroke that turned him into a shell of a man, but he refused to acknowledge his pitiful physical state for fear he would have to leave the presidency. Warren G. Harding's personal physician, Dr. Charles E. Sawyer, who was grossly incompetent, gave no attention to the fact that his patient was in heart failure, and when four other physicians finally discovered this dismal situation they said nothing about it.

For presidents of the United States there of course have been many medical awkwardnesses that did not involve cover-ups, and one should mention this fact in passing with a sense of gratitude that in the last quarter of the nineteenth century the practice of medicine in the United States, and indeed worldwide, emerged from the dark ages and began to take on the accouterments of a science. In the early decades of government under the Constitution, from the first president's inauguration in 1789 at least down to the Civil War, medical science was essentially medical art. In those ancient times the doctor was not much better than an Indian medicine man and in some cases worse (Indian remedies were not all that farfetched). Anyone who felt like being a doctor could study with a practicing physician or take an easy course and learn how to sew up a wound, to amputate an inconvenient arm or leg, and to "physic" a patient to expel such "humors" that might reside within him or her. (These three accomplishments seem to have dominated the medical craft.) The entire medical course at the University of Pennsylvania in the early nineteenth century consisted of two series of lectures of sixteen weeks each. Actually, in many areas of the United States it was not even necessary to work with a physi-

1

cian or take a course or two; in the state of Ohio until passage of the state's Medical Practice Act of 1896, anyone could be a doctor who registered at the nearest probate court. And so it could happen, and did, that when Washington retired from his presidential duties and suffered from a severe sore throat, his physicians bled him, dehydrated him with cathartics and emetics, and in a day he died.

Sometimes presidents assisted in their own demises. Excited by the prospect of his inaugural address, and filled with the desire to make as many references to Roman proconsuls as he could, William Henry Harrison in 1841 wrote out an address longer than any of his predecessors had attempted and had the bad judgment to deliver it without wearing an overcoat. An old man, he fell ill with pneumonia, complicated by a chronic intestinal inflammation. He entrusted himself to the doctors, who did their worst, prescribing suction cups, stinging ointments, cathartics of calomel and castor oil, followed by more calomel, rhubarb, and ipecac, then opium, camphor, and brandy, topped off with a Seneca Indian recipe of crude petroleum and Virginia snakeweed. These medicines they administered within eight days; Harrison died one month after his inauguration. Just a few years later President Zachary Taylor stood out in the broiling sun next to what was to become the Washington Monument and, perhaps out of boredom with the dedicatory speeches, partook of a large bowl of cherries and ice that had been made from contaminated water. He became ill from typhoid fever, which the doctors treated with brandy and opium, and in a few days died of "severe bilious intermittent fever with congestion."

The assassinations of James A. Garfield and William McKinley were followed by medical attentions as the patients "lingered," to use the nineteenth-century term, and in the case of Garfield, who lingered two and a half months, it is clear that there was gross medical negligence. His doctors probed for the bullet when they should have let it alone, as it was not hurting anything. They only infected the patient from their unsterilized instruments and insertion even of their fingers; they converted the entry cavity from a finger-length three and a half inches to a pus-oozing canal twenty inches deep. In his weakened state Garfield died when the splenic artery, torn by the bullet, initially limited by an aneurysmal sac about the size of an egg yolk that formed a protective bypass around the wound, at last ruptured. McKinley's case was somewhat different and perhaps showed only poor medical judgment rather than incompetence. After he was shot in Buffalo, his physicians carried him to a small emergency hospital, a dimly lit place on the grounds of the Pan-American Exposition where a local surgeon operated; thereafter, they took him to a private house. An excellent general hospital was nearby. Fortunately for him, and unlike Garfield, he died in a few days.

One turns, however, to the cover-ups.[1]

1.

The case of Cleveland, who in May 1893 came down with what his physicians diagnosed as cancer of the mouth, requiring a hasty operation, was an outright cover-up. It did not become known in any detail until many years later, in 1917, when one of the participating surgeons, Dr. William W. Keen, published an account.

The presidency of Cleveland seems an unlikely time for a cover-up—one might ask what were the affairs of moment, national or international, that might have made his illness an issue? Why would anyone have seen it as a great overriding problem, other than members of Cleveland's family and the incumbent himself? Affairs of the United States government, not to mention those of the family of nations, somehow would go on. It was a time of small government, a modestly sized bureaucracy in Washington, which did not often touch the lives of Americans. Matters in the capital were so modest that when a telephone was installed in the White House—newly invented, it had been shown at the Centennial Exposition in Philadelphia in 1876—Cleveland in the evenings answered calls himself. In this bygone era the economic life of the country, agricultural and industrial, lay largely outside government supervision, the social development of the nation was no government issue, and the nation's intellectual life bore almost no connection with what went on in Washington. As for foreign relations, little was happening. Senator George F. Hoar of Massachusetts observed, "When you saw uncommon activity in our grave, reverend, and somewhat sleepy Committee on Foreign Relations . . . it was circumstantial evidence, not that there was any great trouble as to our foreign relations, but that a presidential election was at hand."

But as Cleveland's second term opened in March 1893, there was one real issue in Washington and that was the currency, which was approaching a state of chaos. The reason for covering up Cleveland's illness lay in the currency crisis and what Cleveland proposed to do about it and what his vice-president, Adlai E. Stevenson, grandfather of the later Democratic presidential candidate, might have done about it if Cleveland had died and he, Stevenson, had become president. The election cry of the time, free and unlimited coinage of silver and gold at the ratio of sixteen-to-one, disguised the currency question. To Cleveland and businessmen with whom he associated in New York between his two nonconsecutive presidential terms the very future of the United States rested on a strong, stable currency. The nation was moving toward industrial dominance of the world. In the 1880s steel production surpassed that of Great Britain and Germany. Further progress lay in the balance, over the issue of sixteen-to-one. From arrival in Europe of great quantities of bullion from the New World in the sixteenth century, until discovery of vast deposits of silver in the American West in the latter nineteenth century, supplies of silver and gold remained roughly in this ratio, and the governments used both metals to back their currencies. But then, with the American discoveries, the value of silver plummeted, moving the ratio of stocks toward thirty-two-to-one. European governments demonetized silver, dumping silver stocks on the world market, further cheapening silver. The United States did not do so because of pressure from silver-mining states, and from the nation's farmers who were in debt and hoped the falling value of silver would cheapen the currency and get them out of debt. Cleveland wanted the country to base its currency on gold. He wanted Congress to repeal the inflationary Sherman Silver Purchase Act of 1890. Only the nation's redoubtable chief executive—a huge bulk of a man possessing several layers of fat below his chin, round-faced, heavily mustached—seemed to stand between order and disaster. Stevenson appeared an inflationist, a "silverite." He, so his enemies whispered, had no backbone at all.[2]

With this as background the president on the morning of May 5, 1893, noticed a rough spot on the roof of his mouth. At first he thought it a canker sore and gave it little attention, but when it persisted he asked an army physician in Washington, Dr. Robert M. O'Reilly, to have a look. O'Reilly was concerned, sent a piece of tissue to the Army Medical Museum, predecessor of the present-day Armed Forces Institute of Pathology, and learned that it was probably cancerous. Dr. William H. Welch of Johns Hopkins University confirmed the diagnosis. The ulcer was as large as a quarter, extended from the molar teeth to within a third of an inch of the middle line, and was encroaching on the soft palate, with evidence of diseased bone.

The president's personal physician and close friend, Dr. Joseph D. Bryant, associate professor of surgery at Bellevue Hospital Medical College in New York, went down to Washington and after examination of the malignant area proposed an immediate operation. Cleveland assented but insisted on absolute secrecy because of the financial crisis.

Arrangements for the operation proceeded with haste. It was decided to hold the operation aboard his friend Elias C. Benedict's yacht, the *Oneida*, on which Cleveland had spent much time, having sailed in it over fifty thousand miles. The yacht of Commodore Benedict was the ideal place for what was to occur. He could take a train from Washington to Newark, cross the Hudson, be met by a carriage, and drive ostentatiously to the *Oneida*. No one would think twice. The president would need about five weeks to recover, so Dr. Bryant calculated. Cleveland hence prepared a proclamation summoning Congress to meet in a special session on August 7 to consider repeal of the Sherman Act. On the day of its publication, June 30, he entrained for New Jersey.

Years later Dr. Keen related what happened. "I reached New York City in the evening," he wrote, "went to Pier A, and was taken over to the yacht," which was lying at anchor at a considerable distance from the Battery.[3] There he joined Dr. John F. Erdmann who was Dr. Bryant's assistant, Dr. O'Reilly, Dr. Edward G. Janeway of New York, and Dr. Ferdinand Hasbrouck, a New York dentist. It was certainly a group of competent individuals, although they had never worked as a team. The group included Dr. Keen for perhaps two reasons. One, he was a renowned neurosurgeon, a pioneer in the surgery of cauterizing blood vessels with electricity during brain operations; his expertise guaranteed that the team could perform the most modern techniques. Two, he could "assume responsibility, in part, in the event of a fatality."[4]

The president, Dr. Bryant, and Secretary of War Daniel S. Lamont, the only member of the cabinet who was in on the secret (Bryant wrote him that "it is wise that a cabinet officer be available on that occasion"), arrived later from Washington, drove to Pier A, and likewise were taken out to the yacht.[5] Upon arriving the president sat down in a deck chair and lit a cigar, and the company sat around smoking and talking until nearly midnight. Cleveland was full of his presidential troubles, not the least of which was the overwhelming number of office seekers—that bane for every chief executive at the beginning of a term, especially with a change of party. Once he burst out, "Oh, Doctor Keen, those office seekers! Those office seekers! They haunt me even in my dreams!" Eventually the group broke up and everyone retired for the night. Cleveland took no medication and slept soundly.

Early the next morning, July 1, 1893, the *Oneida* proceeded at half speed up the East River. The men aboard had a leisurely breakfast. Cleveland drank a cup of coffee and ate a piece of toast, something no surgeon today would allow because of the risk of the patient vomiting and choking under anesthesia. Meanwhile, the salon was cleared of everything but the organ, which was fastened down, and Dr. Bryant told the captain with some anxiety, "If you hit a rock, hit it good and hard, so that we'll all go to the bottom."[6] The doctors prepared their equipment—oxygen, two storage batteries for cautery, an electric light, strychnine in case of shock, digitalis for the heart, and morphine. They then propped the president in a chair against the interior mast—there was no operating table.

The operation worried the physicians, for two reasons. One was the danger that the president might have a stroke. Dr. Keen had lost a patient from a stroke on the table, and Cleveland was just the age and build; fifty-six years old, he weighed perhaps two hundred and fifty pounds. He had a strong pulse, and there seemed little arteriosclerosis—abnormal thickening and hardening of the walls of the arteries. But he was worn out physically and mentally by four months of worry over the economic crisis and, as he had mentioned, the importunities of the office seekers.

Then they expected and duly had trouble with the anesthetic. At the outset Hasbrouck gave the patient nitrous oxide gas. Bryant did not want to take any chances. "It is my intention," he had written Lamont, "to try and do the job with the use of laughing gas. It has the merit of being entirely safe, altho' it will prolong matters somewhat." But the anesthetic had to be augmented with ether, and the heavier a patient the more ether is necessary. Cleveland being a great consumer of beer further complicated matters because of the related chemical composition of alcohol and ether: the more a person drinks the more resistant he or she is to ether. Moreover, ether is highly volatile, and its use with the primitive electrical equipment for cauterization could have caused an explosion. O'Reilly administered the ether and must have sighed with every drop. The anesthetists did manage to reduce the amount of ether used by "cocainizing" the parts to be removed.

But everything went according to plan, with a splendid if, in its details, horrifying result. The operation was a very serious one, for which Bryant was something of an expert. He had published a paper on the history of two hundred and fifty cases, in which one of every seven patients had died, usually from hemorrhage during the procedure or infection soon after. He had performed only two such operations himself.[7] But with a considerable fortitude, not to mention that of the patient, he went ahead. Hasbrouck, the dentist, first pulled two healthy upper teeth. After the ether took effect the surgeons, employing a cheek retractor, cut the president's cheek bone free from his jaw, which created a flow of blood amounting to a tumblerful. They stopped it with cold water, pressure, and at one point the galvanocautery, tying only a single blood vessel. They then chiseled loose the front of the jaw, divided the bone beneath the palate, and using forceps removed it in eight pieces. They found that the cancer, "a gelatinous mass, evidently a sarcoma" (in fact it later appeared to be a carcinoma), extended into the sinus cavity above the roof of the mouth and below the eye.[8] Keen considered it fast-growing. He wanted to remove the entire left upper jaw, together with the sinus and floor of the bony eye socket. But this would have left the president with a sagging eye and double vision. The team decided not to go farther. Keen went along, perhaps thinking the case hopeless; after all, this was cancer of the jaw. Just eight years before, former President Ulysses S. Grant had died of throat cancer, a sort of medical first cousin to what they were now encountering. As a result the president afterward looked normal. This greatly assisted the subsequent effort to keep the operation secret.

At 1:55 P.M. all was done. "What a sigh of intense relief we surgeons breathed when the patient was once more safe in bed," Keen wrote, "can hardly be imagined!" Cleveland received a small injection of morphine to keep him down for a while after the anesthetic began to wear off.

Dr. Erdmann was with the president when he began to awake. With his mouth full of cotton he demanded of Erdmann, "Who the hell are you?" The doctor told the patient who he was and why he was there. The president asked where he came from and he said, "Chillicothe."

"Oh," said Cleveland, "do you know Mr. Nibge there?"
"Yes, he's the druggist," said the doctor.
"Well," asked the president, "is he so poor that he needs a job from me?"
"No," said Erdmann.
"Then he won't get one," growled Cleveland.[9]

July 3 the president was walking, and two days later when the *Oneida* arrived at Buzzards Bay he walked from the launch to his summer place, Gray Gables. On July 17 a second brief operation was necessary to remove tissue that looked suspicious, but it proved nothing serious. Six weeks later, by September, Bryant was able to record, "All healed."

How to keep the operation secret? The problem of secrecy had its solution by lying. Dr. Bryant held press conferences at Buzzards Bay and gave every assurance the reporters might have asked: "The President is all right," he proclaimed. "From what is he suffering?" a reporter asked. "He is suffering from rheumatism and somewhat from his teeth, just as it was reported this afternoon; that's all." The next day he reiterated that the president was all right. According to the *New York Times* reporter:

> President Cleveland is tonight feeling slightly better than he did this morning. His knee is lame and his left foot swollen so that he is obliged to wear a big shoe. He spent the greater part of the day playing checkers with Mrs. Cleveland, and enjoying the beautiful weather. Doctor Bryant says the President is absolutely free from cancer or malignant growth of any description. No operation has been performed, except that a bad tooth was extracted.[10]

Secretary Lamont said the same thing—that the president's difficulties were trivial, and he was suffering from a sore tooth.

Upon receiving these intelligences, the reporters momentarily did not know what to do. They were staying at a hotel near the railroad station and had walked a mile and a half over to an old barn on the Gray Gables property where Lamont talked to them. As they walked back they argued heatedly; half of them believed what they had been told, and the others did not. They agreed, however, to stand together on whatever account they sent out, and back at the hotel they arrived at a consensus that fortunately agreed with the official version. Next day without a dissenting voice they telegraphed their stories.

But it was a problem to keep things quiet. Even though several weeks would elapse before the president had to return to Washington and face interviews and talks and other work incident to the reassembling of Congress, it was necessary to see officials at Gray Gables—he could not remove himself from the business of government. The attorney general, Richard Olney, called and found the president changed in appearance, having lost much weight, and his mouth so stuffed with antiseptic wads he could hardly talk. On this occasion Cleveland himself hardly cooperated. "My God, Olney," he said, "they nearly killed me!" He spoke little, was obviously depressed, and Olney believed he thought he would not recover. Charles S. Hamlin went up on July 23 to deliver statistics on the silver question, and afterward wrote in his diary that he had "found Lamont and Dr. Bryant there. President appeared not well at all: had his mouth evidently packed with some kind of bandage—could not therefore speak distinctly. Seemed to me to have some serious trouble with his mouth—looked thoroughly tired out."[11]

The dentist, Hasbrouck, eventually let the cat out of the bag. He had landed at New London on July 2, missing an operation scheduled that day in Greenwich. When he returned he explained to the irate physician who had asked for his services as an anesthetist, Dr. Leander P. Jones, that he had attended the president of the United States. By chance Jones was the family physician of the New York correspondent of the *Philadelphia Press*, Elisha J. Edwards, who wrote under the name "Holland." Some weeks later, happening on Edwards, and in knowledge that all was well with the president and that Congress would repeal the Sherman Act, Jones told Edwards about the operation. Edwards confronted Hasbrouck, who confirmed everything. On August 29, Edwards's story appeared.

Lying again solved the problem. Secretary Lamont said Edwards's story was a total fabrication. The president's friend, L. Clarke Davis, editor of the *Philadelphia Public Ledger,* printed a marvelous piece of nonsense. The Edwards story "has a real basis of a toothache," he related. If it had any other basis, "Mr. Cleveland's closest friends do not know it. I have seen the President at intervals since he first came to Buzzards Bay this summer, passing hours and days in his company and in the boat fishing with him. I passed all of last Monday with him, fishing, and I have never seen him in better health—never stronger, physically or mentally, and I consider him in both respects the healthiest man I know."[12] Bryant, furious, never spoke to Hasbrouck again, nor wrote him, and sent his $250 fee by messenger.

Meanwhile another New York dentist, Dr. Kasson C. Gibson, repaired to Gray Gables and working in a makeshift dental laboratory fashioned an artificial jaw out of vulcanized rubber, which made the president's face appear normal and his speech unimpaired.

In the years that remained to Cleveland, it is possible that the knowledge that he had had cancer placed a pall upon his life. He served out his second term, then retired to Princeton, New Jersey (he refused to go back to Buffalo where the press in 1884 first discovered his liaison with Mrs. Maria Halpin, which nearly cost him the presidency). He lived there eleven years, long enough to clash with his eventual successor, Woodrow Wilson, for Wilson was president of Princeton University and Cleveland served on the board of trustees. He hated Wilson, although he acknowledged his talents. He said that if Wilson were to go into politics, he would go far but would wreck the Democratic Party. It was said, and Cleveland's biographer Allan Nevins agreed, that although he always was a bit on the irritable side, ready to take on opponents, through the years after the operation he was more irritable with little patience for antagonists. On occasion in 1893–1897 he spoke of mortality, of how much he had to do before the darkness overtook him.

Still, this is all surmise. What one can conclude is that in a time of great public crisis, or seeming crisis (one must think that the country's currency problems were perhaps not as large as Cleveland and friends believed, that debtors as well as creditors deserved attention from the federal government), a president of the United States hid his illness from the American people. The twentieth century's belief in total disclosure of presidential illness certainly did not govern during the nineteenth.

Incidentally, in long retrospect it is now clear that Cleveland did not need such a hurried, almost frantic, operation as he underwent in 1893; he did not suffer from an immediately life-threatening cancer. During the years after the operation, as mentioned, a conspiracy of silence surrounded it. But after repeal of the Sherman Silver Purchase Act, and certainly after Cleveland's death in 1908, why the silence? It is possible that the doctors had begun to suspect that they had misdiagnosed their patient. If he had had, as Keen and the others believed, a fast-growing cancer of the mouth, it must have seemed to them that even with their wide-ranging operative procedure, in which they took out everything they could see in two operations, the chances of survival for fifteen years would not have been great; most cancers of the mouth, they knew, were likely to recur, if not in the same place, then through metastasis. Dr. Bryant died in 1914, never having revealed what he and the others had done. He wrote up an account of the operation in 1905 or 1906, but gave it to Lamont, who kept it.[13] Keen did not publish his account until 1917, and then not in a prestigious medical journal, where it should have been, but in, of all places, the *Saturday Evening Post*. It was all very curious. By the time he published his article Keen was eighty years old and still practicing at the Jefferson Medical College in Philadelphia. He was also director of the Muetter Museum, a part of the College of Physicians of Philadelphia, and after his article appeared the museum's attendants set up an exhibit case displaying the two teeth and eight pieces of upper jaw removed during the operation aboard the *Oneida*. Until his death in 1932 he refused to allow anyone to examine his personal notes about the operation. For years afterward his successors at the museum adhered to this policy. To the Cleveland items in the case they added Keen's death mask, and his face in repose seems to guard the other specimens.

In 1967 museum authorities at last relented, allowing Dr. Charles L. Morreels, Jr., of Johns Hopkins to examine the notes, and Morreels disclosed that the doctors and pathologists in 1893 were none too sure the growth was malignant. In 1975 the museum consented to an investigative panel of medical experts headed by Dr. Gonzalo E. Aponte, which among other activities examined tissue preserved from 1893. The panel found that Cleveland's lesion was a "verrucous carcinoma," a low-grade tumor. Admittedly, this variety of carcinoma was not identified until many years after Cleveland's operation. It is often found among individuals who use tobacco immoderately, and there seems to be some connection with consumption of alcohol. (Cleveland was an inveterate cigar smoker and, as mentioned before, drank a lot of beer.) It is not a fast-growing tumor, nor does it metastasize. In those respects, the hurry Cleveland's doctors insisted upon was entirely unnecessary. Still, the modern-day treatment of choice for verrucous carcinoma remains that of a century ago, namely, wide local excision. Cleveland assuredly had that.[14]

2.

Of the presidential cover-ups over two hundred years of American national government, the case of Wilson, president from 1913 until 1921, was serious indeed. For the last year and a half of Wilson's administration, from the time of his massive stroke of October 2, 1919, down to his departure from office on March 4, 1921, he was incompetent to hold the presidency. At the outset, for a month, he was so ill that he could not handle any matters of state. For three more months he saw hardly anyone other than his doctor (and such medical consultants as his doctor brought in), his wife, and his private secretary. For the remainder of his term he could hardly focus his mind on any piece of public business beyond, say, ten minutes or so, after which he tired.

Nor was this abysmal physical condition public knowledge. At the beginning of his illness his doctor announced that he had had a nervous breakdown, which was hardly the case. At last on February 10, 1920, a reporter from the *Baltimore Sun* interviewed one of the president's attending physicians, Hugh H. Young of Johns Hopkins, who said the trouble was cerebral thrombosis.

Secretary of State Robert Lansing, incensed by this state of affairs, told a friend the public was entitled to know Wilson's trouble and that the reticence of the family and administration was a fraud upon the public.[15] It was a terrible time for the president to fall ill. No time is a good time for presidential illness, but if Cleveland had taken ill at a crucial time in his country's national life, so assuredly had Wilson. The League of Nations Covenant, the proposed new world government, lay before the Senate for advice and consent. The Old Order of international affairs, in which great powers cut and pared at the territories of small nations as if they were Dutch cheeses (to use the phrase of the Spanish minister Alberoni), was to give way to the New Order, in which every international argument had adjudication or at least conciliation. Wilson himself had announced the New Diplomacy, successor to the Old. The nations of Europe had paid the highest prices for ending the Old Order; the American nation had lost only fifty thousand of its young men during the short time, a scant year and a half, in which the country was at war. Still, even that price was high and there was every reason to engage the American people in the affairs of the world, educate them perhaps in what was necessary to make foreign affairs go properly, thereby protecting their own affairs. After all the effort, and all the need, Wilson sickened just at the point where his country and the tired governments and peoples of Europe needed leadership.

Behind this tragedy, personal and public, lay the fact that because of a medical history of strokes and arteriosclerosis Wilson never should have been nominated in 1912. Firm-jawed, stern-eyed, he looked the very picture of health. He moved rapidly with whatever he was about, his face serious and purposeful in public. To intimates he was the soul of fellowship and a great mimic—the public mask turned into a series of contortions as he spoke the words of people he was imitating, or he mimed his way through their antics. He was the father of three adoring daughters and two adoring wives (his first wife had died in August 1914). But his health was often on the edge. He had suffered an initial stroke in 1896, when he suddenly lost control of his right hand, well before becoming president of Princeton in 1902, not to mention president of the United States. In 1904 there was another relatively mild stroke, again affecting his right hand and lasting several months. In 1906 there was still another episode when he awoke one morning blind in his left eye. After examination by the distinguished Philadelphia ophthalmologist, Dr. George E. de Schweinitz, it became evident even to Wilson that he was suffering if not strokes then hardening of the arteries, "premature old age," the dreaded disease that accompanied his father's last years.

He gradually recovered from these illnesses, save that after the episode of 1906 he never had more than peripheral vision in his left eye. Ambition urged him onward, first to the governorship of New Jersey, then to the presidency. Knowing nothing about his medical past, the people of New Jersey, then of the United States, elected him as their leader in belief that he was in perfectly good health.[16]

During Wilson's years as president the White House physician was Rear Admiral Cary T. Grayson, and one might properly ask what qualities recommended Grayson for this difficult post. The answer has to be that luck conspired to give him the appointment. The slight, modest officer possessed little medical background for watching over the health of the president of the United States. After he graduated from the College of William and Mary, he obtained his medical degree from the University of the South, a small institution that offered a degree in one year. After joining the Medical Corps of the U.S. Navy, he became assistant White House physician during the last part of Theodore Roosevelt's administration. At the very beginning of the Wilson administration, during the inaugural luncheon held in the White House, Wilson's sister fell on one of the steps and cut her forehead. Grayson stitched the cut and came to the attention of the new president who chose him from a large group of applicants for the post of personal physician to the chief executive.

An added attraction was the fact that Grayson, like the president, was a native of Virginia. Wilson had been born in Staunton. Grayson hailed from a village so small that his friend the president was accustomed to tease him about it—Wilson told the doctor that he, the president, had passed through the vicinity and was gazing in the direction of the village but was unable to see it because a freight car stood in the way.

After becoming the president's physician, Grayson further recommended himself by introducing Wilson to a Washington widow,

Mrs. Edith Bolling Galt. The president's wife Ellen had died of Bright's disease, making Wilson apparently inconsolable. But when Mrs. Galt came to tea one day everything changed. The president fell head over heels in love, and it was all his advisers, including Colonel Edward M. House, who of all individuals was closest to the president, could do to keep him from marrying the widow until December 1915 when it seemed a decent interval had passed.

As carefully as he could, Grayson watched over Wilson and recommended a program of leisure that for a while proved possible and doubtless assisted the health of his patient. He knew that his presidential charge was incapable of working much more than three or four hours a day. To outsiders the fact was not evident, and to insiders it might have seemed that the president could do things quicker than ordinary mortals. He advised, and the president followed, a regimen of leisure and entertainment—long automobile rides in the country surrounding Washington, or golf games, and attendance at Keith's Theater on G Street between Fourteenth and Fifteenth near the treasury building where the president laughed heartily at the vaudeville acts. Sundays he attended church and rested. Summers passed without much attention to public business. Wilson did not see a great many visitors in his office, doubtless at Grayson's advice, and this added to his leisure time and subtracted in untold ways from conversations with cabinet officers and other activities pertaining to the government of the United States. The president found military matters uninteresting and did not deal much with them, almost assuming they could manage themselves—this even after August 1914.

Then came American entrance into the war in 1917, a circumstance that Grayson had not planned for. Suddenly, almost in a moment, the nation entered the war, and President Wilson's burdens increased immeasurably. During the war, and perhaps because of Grayson's advice, probably because of inertia (the president already had spent four years of leisurely activity in the White House), Wilson did not pick up many of the burdens that came to his office. The consequent muddle in economic mobilization was in fair part due to lack of presidential leadership. The similar military disorganization received little of his attention. Economic and military mobilization finally went in the right directions, but hardly because of Wilson's leadership. The president appeared to be spending his time planning for peace and bringing the Allied statesmen, from a distance and against their wills, around to his own point of view. In a short time the war was over, and

Wilson's health had held. The inevitable followed when the president went to Paris and personally negotiated with Allied statesmen and personally advocated his own plan for peace, the League of Nations Covenant. After little consultation with the Senate, he brought the Covenant home and presented it with the injunction that if the senators rejected it they would break the heart of the world. The inevitable was not merely the defeat of the Covenant but the collapse of the president.

A good deal more than Wilson's illness was at stake in the defeat of the Covenant. If Wilson had been in his imperious prime, able to bargain and cajole, push and bend senators to his will, as in the first two or three years of his administration when the New Freedom legislation was passing Congress, he still might not have been able to handle the Senate in 1919–1920. The Covenant contained its own problems. It was foreign to all American experience, which in international affairs meant the gradual buildup of international law, the slow accumulation of precedents through practice as well as law, the occasional conciliation and sometimes arbitration of issues of secondary importance. Wilson was advocating a new instrument of order with which his countrymen had no acquaintance, and this was a large proposition to shove down the throats of senators already irritable because of the way he had ignored them during the war. Too, American participation in the war had boiled up too suddenly, the nation had been unprepared mentally as well as physically, and this meant that a war fought out of suddenly marshaled nervous energy could end in a collapse of national spirit, which in fact happened. Much more than Wilson's illness lay behind defeat of the Covenant in the fight between the president and the Senate. Still, whatever good effect Wilson might have had on the result was lost when his health collapsed.

The straw that broke the patient's back was the speaking tour out to the West Coast in the late summer of 1919, in which Wilson sought to stir the American people to support the Covenant. The president made no preparation for the many speeches he would have to make, and before long was complaining to Grayson of headaches and insomnia. On the return trip he became so nervous after a speech at Pueblo, Colorado, that Grayson arranged to stop the train and allow the president to walk into the surrounding country, calming his nerves, the doctor hoped. Next morning on the train, after a sleepless night, the president collapsed, shaking, distraught, in tears. "I don't seem to realize it," he said, "but I seem to have gone to pieces. The Doctor is right. I am not in condition to go on. I have never been in a condition like this, and I just feel as if I am going to pieces."[17] The train sped back to Washington where in a few days he suffered the stroke.

The subsequent chaos in management of the government has often been described. The president should have resigned immediately. Instead Grayson did not reveal that he had suffered a stroke. This was no strange disease but an ordinary stroke, and any adult American knew what that could mean. Grayson and such other doctors as he brought into the case felt it was a confidential matter. The president's private physician told Secretary of the Interior Franklin K. Lane that the president had suffered a nervous breakdown.[18]

On the day after the stroke, Secretary of State Lansing met in the cabinet room with the president's private secretary, Joseph P. Tumulty, and said that he had called to suggest that in view of the president's incapacity they should call in the vice-president to act in his stead as soon as possible. He read from the Constitution: "In case of the removal of the President from office, or of his death, resignation, or inability to discharge the powers and duties of the said office, the same shall devolve on the Vice President." Tumulty coldly turned to Lansing and said, "Mr. Lansing, the Constitution is not a dead letter with the White House. I have read the Constitution and do not find myself in need of any tutoring at your hands of the provision you have just read."

Tumulty asked Lansing who should certify to Wilson's disability, and the secretary of state intimated it would be the job either of Tumulty or Grayson. "You may rest assured," said the alarmed private secretary, "that while Woodrow Wilson is lying in the White House on the broad of his back I will not be a party to ousting him. He has been too kind, too loyal, and too wonderful to me to receive such treatment at my hands." Just then Grayson appeared in the cabinet room and Tumulty turned to him and continued, "And I am sure that Doctor Grayson will never certify to his disability. Will you, Grayson?" The doctor said he would not. Tumulty then said that if anybody "outside of the White House circle" attempted to certify to Wilson's disability, he and Grayson would repudiate it. He added a remarkable threat for a private secretary: if the president were in a condition to know of the preceding conversation, "he would, in my opinion, take decisive measures."[19]

Lansing at this moment made a mistake. He should have certified to Wilson's disability himself, but he waited until a cabinet meeting on the following Monday and asked the members what to do. They summoned Grayson who spoke of the president's health in general terms, not describing a stroke, and then, like Tumulty, threatened the cabinet. The doctor informed them that just before he left the president, Wilson had asked why the members wanted to see Grayson and by whose authority they were meeting. The implication was not lost on the group. What they should have done was stood up to Grayson and, if he was behind him, Wilson. Instead they meekly assured the doctor of their concern for the president's welfare.

In his illness Wilson was a pathetic figure. He grew a long white beard and appeared scarcely presidential. He was accustomed to sit outside the White House along a covered walkway, bundled in blankets, taking the sun, oblivious to what was happening outside the White House grounds. He was trundled around in a makeshift wheel chair, a chair crudely supplied with wheels. After he improved a bit he shaved off his beard but was nonetheless pathetic in his crippled condition: he had lost much of the use of his left arm and leg and walked with difficulty. Servants removed rugs from rooms and halls through which he passed, and onlookers could hear the tapping of his cane as he slowly made his way.

All the while he secluded himself. The highest public officials could not get to him. Secretary of State Lansing had to pass notes to Mrs. Wilson, who perhaps took them to the president. Notations to papers came back in Mrs. Wilson's handwriting, not the president's. Vice-President Thomas R. Marshall never saw the president until the day Wilson left office, March 4, 1921. The president did almost no work; he dictated no letters to his stenographer, Gilbert F. Close.[20] Tumulty replied to letters that required answers and wrote state papers and proclamations.

During this saddening period the president's cabinet met by itself for five and a half months, twenty-one times, in sessions called by Lansing, and at last on April 14, 1920, the president called a meeting. Secretary of Agriculture David F. Houston testified to what happened.

> I arrived several minutes late. The President was already seated behind a desk at the far end of the room. I noted that I was ushered into his presence by the White House aide, and was announced by him to the President. This struck me as singular, and I wondered why it was done. The President looked old, worn, and haggard. It was enough to make one weep to look at him. One of his arms was useless. In repose, his face looked very much as usual, but, when

he tried to speak, there were marked evidences of his trouble. His jaw tended to drop on one side, or seemed to do so. His voice was very weak and strained. I shook hands with him and sat down. He greeted me as of old. He put up a brave front and spent several minutes cracking jokes. Then there was a brief silence. It appeared that he would not take the initiative. Someone brought up the railroad situation for discussion. The President seemed at first to have some difficulty in fixing his mind on what we were discussing. Doctor Grayson looked in the door several times, as if to warn us not to prolong the discussion unduly for fear of wearying the President. The discussion dragged on for more than an hour. Finally, Mrs. Wilson came in, looking rather disturbed, and suggested that we had better go.[21]

According to the White House usher, Irwin H. (Ike) Hoover, "If there was ever a man in bad shape he was." Hoover saw no comparison with the president who went to Paris. He said Wilson could not talk plainly, mumbled more than he articulated, was helpless, and looked awful. "The stories in the papers from day to day may have been true in their way but never was deception so universally practiced in the White House as it was in those statements being given out from time to time." In his feeble way the president went along with the deception. Propped up prior to the cabinet meetings, he sat there "as one in a trance" with the cabinet members doing all the talking. He would have agreed to anything they said. "Enduring the meeting" was the paramount thought in his mind, "if there were any thoughts."[22]

As months passed and the president showed minor improvement—he was a cripple for the rest of his life, mentally as well as physically—he became querulous and irascible. Sometimes he admitted to Grayson how awkward things had become. Early in 1920 he said, "It would probably have been better if I had died last fall."[23] In the autumn of 1920 his brother-in-law, Stockton Axson, frequently read to him, and occasionally the president would be seized with emotion and begin sobbing inexplicably when the narrative in the book did not call for it.[24] Other occasions he could be hostile, as in descriptions of senators he disliked or of individuals like Lansing whom he ostracized, forcing the secretary's resignation in an abrupt, cruel letter.

But there was more to it than that—indeed an unbelievable petulance on the part of the president. Wilson had refused to see the former British foreign secretary, Sir Edward Grey, who came over as ambassador for a short time. The British government hoped Grey with his considerable prestige could persuade the president to get together with the Senate over the League of Nations and arrange passage of the

Treaty of Versailles (which contained the League's Covenant in its first twenty-six articles). The president refused to see him because among Grey's assistants in the embassy was a major in the British army named Charles K. C. Stuart whom Wilson believed had insulted Mrs. Wilson by making critical remarks. Stuart was an accomplished humorist who played the piano a bit and made comments with or without accompaniment. Gossip said he had related the following question and answer: What did Mrs. Galt do when the president proposed to her? She fell out of bed.

Had Wilson enjoyed decent health he might have laughed at the remark; instead, he was furious. Without proof that Stuart said such a thing, Grey refused to send him home. If the president had related what Stuart said, the entire country would have laughed. The president's condition was an appalling comedown from the great issues that the nation had faced before and during the war and was facing while attempting to organize the peace. Wilson had taken positions in his speeches, some of which were among the most thrilling in American history, that had lifted issues to their heights. Now he was reduced to this.[25]

Upon Grey's arrival back in England, having not seen the president, the rejected ambassador gave a statement to a reporter advising that reservations to the Covenant championed by Senator Henry Cabot Lodge of Massachusetts were unimportant, and that the other signatories of the Treaty of Versailles could easily accept them. Incensed, Wilson wanted to break relations with Great Britain, only to discover there was no ambassador to send home. He demanded that Lansing put a detective on the French ambassador, Jules Jusserand, whom he suspected of being in collusion with Grey. Lansing's refusal probably had a good deal to do with the secretary's cavalier dismissal. The nominal cause was his holding of cabinet meetings, about which Wilson had known from the beginning.

All this said nothing about domestic policy, or better the lack thereof. The last years and months of the Wilson administration were marked by continuation of the wartime inflation that took prices to 102 percent of 1914, followed by a disastrous recession; by a round of ferocious national strikes that wore itself out in arguments between labor and industrial leaders and then lost its points in the recession; and by a "red scare" that treated striking laborers, blacks, and many independently minded Americans shamefully. Everything was followed by a mindless national argument over the virtues of Prohibition.

The cover-up and its result, a paralysis of both foreign and domestic policy, brought the Wilson era to an inglorious end with a massive popular vote in November 1920 for the Republican candidate for the presidency, Senator Harding of Ohio.

3.

The death of President Harding in 1923 involved another cover-up, but it was a simple cover-up in its way and involved only the refusal of the several physicians attending Harding in San Francisco—there were four of them other than Dr. Sawyer—to blame the president's personal physician for hastening the president's death. This saved Sawyer much embarrassment.[26]

Fortunately, with Harding's sudden departure little was lost in national leadership. The nation received as its head a wispy Vermont sage, Calvin Coolidge, who was at least the equal of Harding as an administrator. Moreover, no large foreign or domestic issues were at stake. Few foreign problems beckoned because for the United States the world was a peaceful place. In domestic matters the country had climbed out, however awkwardly, of the recession, and industry was moving ahead. Exports were increasing, although they could not easily reach the level of the war and immediate postwar period. For most Americans the era was a modest, hard-working time with life a little better if not greatly better than before the war. The national mood, incidentally, was in no sense that of Frederick Lewis Allen's *Only Yesterday*, a time of profligate spending, a carnival of sports, theater, and parties, as he depicted the economy and society and inanity of New York City.

As is well known, Harding had obtained the presidency not because of any large talent on his part but because of good fortune. The nation's twenty-ninth president, successor to Wilson, was bright but lazy. He never worked at anything because he did not have to. He could speak to any subject and make his thoughts sound impressive, recalling the periods of the orator resounding to the heavens. One time he had been speaking at a now forgotten occasion in a village in his native Ohio and was received at a private house. During a visit to the privy—there behind the half moon—he met Harry M. Daugherty, an Ohio politician, who was impressed with his new-found friend and vowed to make him president of the United States. At the Republican convention in 1920 the two principal contenders for the nomination, Major General Leonard Wood and Governor Frank O. Lowden of Illinois, fought each other to a standstill and, albeit not in a smoke-filled room, the leaders of the party turned to the amiable Harding, allowing Daugherty to do what he had promised.

During the convention luck also smiled on Coolidge. A year earlier at the end of the Boston police strike of 1919 he had said, "There is no right to strike against the public safety by anybody, anywhere, any time." Delegates remembered that, and when the Senate clique after nominating Harding sought to give the vice-presidential nomination to another senator, a leather-lunged orator from Oregon stood on a chair and yelled for Coolidge and stampeded the convention.

Harding, like Wilson, was not a well man. In retrospect his symptoms were clearly those of an individual whose heart was wearing out. Everything pointed in the same direction. For years he had suffered from high blood pressure. In 1916 he nonchalantly wrote his physician, Dr. Sawyer, in his home town of Marion, Ohio, that while in Columbus, Ohio, he had called on his, Harding's, brother, also a physician, and his blood pressure tested 160 systolic. It should have been 140 or less. His brother thought this greater than it ought to be, "but I think that is about normal for me, so I shall not give it any considerable worry."[27] When he came into the White House his systolic pressure had risen to 180. The president also was suffering from cardiac asthma, his heart so weak that it was unable to pump blood out of his lungs. One day his valet, Arthur Brooks, told the secret service agent, Colonel Edmund W. Starling, that "something is going to happen to our boss." Starling asked what was the matter. "He can't sleep at night," was Brooks's answer. "He can't lie down. He has to be propped up with pillows and he sits up that way all night. If he lies down he can't get his breath."[28] Blood was puddling in his lungs, causing them to waterlog and making breathing difficult. If he was in a sitting position, the fluid could drain to the abdomen. He could breathe better and sleep until he slid down in bed, whereupon all the distressing symptoms began again.

There were other signs. Harding could no longer play golf because he lacked the physical endurance. The editor of the *Emporia Gazette*, William Allen White, upon meeting the president in Kansas City, noticed that his lips were swollen and blue, his eyes puffed, and his hands seemed stiff. These were also signs of his problem, especially the blue lips. In cardiac asthma the lips turn blue from lack of oxygen in the blood. In 1922 a cardiologist, Dr. Emanuel Libman, met him at a dinner in Washington, and after watching the president's shortness of breath and other signs telephoned Eugene Meyer and said, "The president has a disease of the coronary arteries." He predicted Harding would be dead within six months.[29]

It was true that Harding faced difficulties of other sorts when he entered the White House, and these troubles could have brought on his heart condition or made it worse. He had involved himself with at least one woman other than his wife, and she had in her possession dozens of letters, which were discovered in a shoe box in a closet of her house in Marion thirty-three years after Harding's death. In addition, by the summer of 1923 the president faced public revelations of graft and other misbehavior by the group of friends later dubbed the Ohio Gang. In May 1923 Harding spoke to one of them, Jesse Smith, informing Smith he would be arrested the next morning. That night Smith shot himself in the apartment of Harding's attorney general, Daugherty. It is impossible to know what effect these matters had on the president's deteriorating health. Perhaps they had no effect. His cardiac illness was so advanced that it did not need exacerbating factors.

Harding's choice, however, of Dr. Sawyer as his White House physician assuredly was not good for his health. "Doc" Sawyer, as he was known, the small-town epitome of a family doctor, an ebullient, happy little man, had been a family friend for years, and it was natural that Harding would take him to Washington. He had treated Harding's wife for a kidney disease, and she told her husband that she would die if he did not go. Sawyer needed a considerable arrangement if he went, for he was the owner of a successful hospital, the Sawyer Sanatorium. The president hence made him an offer that he could not refuse: he became personal physician to the president, chairman of the federal hospitalization board, and brigadier general in the U.S. Army Medical Corps. Wilson had helped Grayson rise from a lieutenant in the U.S. Navy Medical Corps to rear admiral. Sawyer went up the ladder of the Army Medical Corps in a single jump.

Doc Sawyer was essentially incompetent. He was a homeopath, meaning that he treated the same with the same; homeopathy is a system of treatment that uses minute quantities of remedies that in massive doses produce effects similar to those of the disease being treated. In its day it was popular, but its day had passed even by the 1920s. Sawyer was accustomed to prescribing medicines by color. To Mrs. Harding he gave little yellow tablets and flat white tablets, also some green medicine, the latter apparently in a bottle. To the president he once prescribed "a dose of soda water at least three times a day" together with two pink pills.[30] During Harding's presidency he was so obtuse professionally that he never realized his patient was suffering from heart failure; old-fashioned fellow that he was, at the time of Harding's death in the Palace Hotel in San Francisco he insisted querulously that the cause of death was a stroke—just like that of President Wilson, only a little more so. "Cerebral hemorrhage," he said to Colonel Starling (a bit mistakenly, for Wilson suffered from a cerebral thrombosis).[31] Or as he later put the problem, "What happened to President Wilson partially, had happened to President Harding completely."

In the early summer of 1923 the president decided to visit Alaska, a decision that cost him his life and for which Sawyer was completely unprepared. As one mishap occurred after another, Sawyer discovered explanations for his patient's increasing illness that showed inventiveness if not medical wisdom. On the way back from Alaska he allowed Harding to do far too much for a man with heart failure. The presidential party stopped in Vancouver and Seattle where the president rode in automobile parades. Harding afterward said that in Seattle he felt it almost impossible to hold his hat and wave his arms when greeting crowds on the street.[32] He attended a picnic for boys, stood bareheaded in the hot sun for two hours during a reception, and then found himself standing in the local stadium in the appalling heat before a crowd of sixty thousand. Halfway through he slurred his speech, confused the word "Alaska" with "Nebraska," and clutched with both hands at the lectern, hardly able to stand. He dropped the sheets of his address, which Secretary of Commerce Herbert Hoover, who had written the speech (save for what Hoover called Harding's "usual three-dollar words and sonorous phrases"), managed to pick up and sort.[33] The president barely made it through the speech. He was in the final stages of heart failure, and when he stood up his heart was too weak to pump blood to his brain. That evening he addressed the local press club at its postponed luncheon but sat down afterward in a state of collapse. A decision was made to cancel a stop in Portland and go straight to San Francisco, and when reporters wanted to know the reason, Sawyer said it was because Harding was suffering from severe indigestion. The president had complained of violent cramps. He had eaten crab meat, and Sawyer said it was bad crab meat, perhaps from a spoiled can, although no one else took ill from it.

No evidence of the president's problem deterred Sawyer in the next and crucial days. As the train moved south toward San Francisco, an accompanying Navy physician, Lieutenant Commander Joel T. Boone, told Hoover that Sawyer was misdiagnosing the president and that he was very seriously ill. Hoover took Boone to see Secretary of the Interior Hubert Work, who had been a doctor in his younger days, and Work went to see Harding, tapped around his chest, and discovered from heart sounds that the organ was much enlarged. Even to Work, who was not in practice, the fact that Harding needed digitalis was clear. (Digitalis, or foxglove, was the well-known medicinal way to strengthen the heart muscle.) But when the party arrived in San Francisco on Sunday morning, July 29, Sawyer allowed the president to dress himself and walk from the train to a waiting automobile, an unwise action for a man who probably just had suffered a heart attack.

Dr. Ray Lyman Wilbur, a heart specialist, president of Stanford University and of the American Medical Association, former dean of the Stanford Medical School, together with one of the best internists in the Bay Area, Dr. Charles M. Cooper, met the train, and with the president secure within the Palace Hotel everything promised to be better. Yet this could not be. After the doctors put the patient to bed, they examined him. Harding was in a good mood. Jokingly he told them, "Go ahead, fellows, I have nothing to conceal either inside or outside."[34] When they tapped around his chest he said, "Lay on Macduff." Mrs. Harding felt his feet to see if they were warm. One of the physicians asked, "Are the President's feet warm?" and he answered quickly, "This is no time to get cold feet."[35] Still, the diagnosis was distressing. Wilbur in a private memorandum dictated immediately after Harding's death related that "Dr. Cooper and I . . . did not see how it was possible to reestablish normal heart action."

> Dr. Sawyer gave a history of unsatisfactory return of strength following influenza in the spring, with increased blood pressure, attacks of dyspnea [difficult or labored respiration] at night, and also of indigestion particularly at night with pain and distress, relieved at times by pressure upon the upper abdomen. There was also the history of pain in the chest, radiating down the arms, particularly the left arm. . . . The heart rate was about 120 and 130 with extra systoles from time to time. The blood pressure was about 150, the heart was enlarged both to right and left, the lungs were clear, the respiration increased and inclined to be shallow and irregular, particularly with the least repose. There was a marked tenderness over the gall bladder region, which was most evident on a deep breath.[36]

The attending physicians sought to hide the president's condition, heart failure resulting in bronchopneumonia, and the first bulletin reported the digestive disturbance was "now localized in the gall bladder." The president's speaking engagements had "temporarily strained his cardiovascular system." The former statement was non-sense (the soreness was probably an enlarged liver from congestive heart failure), the latter a nice medical understatement so typical of the era.

One might have thought that the doctors disguised Harding's illness because they feared he would read the bulletins in the news-papers. By Wednesday, August 1, his lungs had cleared remarkably well. "I am not so much worried about them," the shrewd patient said, "but what about this dilatation of my heart?" Wilbur reported the president's relief after he had been assured that his condition would improve after the administration of digitalis. As the doctor wrote, "Evidently he was conscious of the fact that he had overstrained his heart."[37]

By this time Sawyer was showing considerable optimism. To the press he explained that there was no organic trouble with the gall bladder. As for the patient in general, he remarked to the *New York Times*, which accepted anything he said (as it had done thirty years before at the time of Cleveland's operation): "I think I may say he is out of danger, barring complications. We can never tell what sideshows may develop. By that I mean that unexpected complications may turn up, such as indigestion or nervousness, which are always probable in such a case as this."[38] The *Times* noted that the president had eaten two boiled eggs that day and again was suffering from indigestion, a com-ment that Sawyer may have produced off-the-record.

On Thursday evening, August 2, while Mrs. Harding was read-ing to the president an article by Samuel G. Blythe in the *Saturday Evening Post*, "A Calm Review of a Calm Man," the patient spoke his last words. "That's good," he told her. "Go on, read some more." Suddenly he began to sweat, his face twitched, he stiffened, shud-dered, relaxed, his mouth opened, and he slumped forward, his head lolling.

The question arose as to the cause of Harding's death. Actually, the cause was Dr. Sawyer who allowed his charge, the president of the United States, suffering from high blood pressure and, by 1923, heart failure, to carry on daily activities as if nothing were wrong. The four other attending physicians knew of Sawyer's incompetence and cov-ered it up.

Fortunately for Sawyer, the four other physicians agreed with him that the immediate cause of the president's death was a stroke. The certifying physician was Wilbur, who signed the death certificate to that effect. Wilbur and Cooper were the nonadministration doctors among the five physicians present, and they alone—as if to stress their agreement—signed bulletin number six, which defined a "sudden apoplectic seizure." This commonplace description was explained in bulletin number seven, signed by all the doctors: "a rupture of a blood vessel in the axis of the brain near the respiratory center."

In the decision of the doctors for a stroke, and quite apart from the fact that it helped exonerate Sawyer, lay a very interesting situation, worth setting out because of what it showed about medicine generally at the time, Harding's attending doctors in particular.[39] In 1910 a Chicago physician, James B. Herrick, who that same year identified sickle cell anemia, had as a patient a fifty-five-year-old banker who after a moderate meal suffered chest pain and acute indigestion and died fifty-two hours later. Herrick's diagnosis was the first identification of heart disease in a living patient; previously heart attacks had seemed only medical curiosities or inevitable results of aging. When the pathologist asked Herrick where to look for the cause of death, the wise physician said to look for a clot in one of the main arteries to the heart. Herrick published an article on the case two years later in the *Journal of the American Medical Association*.[40] To his consternation, fellow doctors greeted the account with indifference (it "fell like a dud," he recalled), and for a decade afterward he went around the country as a sort of missionary trying to persuade doctors there was such a thing as a heart attack, that a clot in a coronary artery could kill heart muscle and possibly the victim. Harding died only thirteen years after the Chicago banker, and he surely died of a heart attack, for he died instantly, the way heart attack victims go. Strokes take at least ten minutes. But Sawyer would have known nothing of the article and would not have believed it if he had read it—unless perhaps, in the way of homeopathy, he could have created a small heart attack to cure a larger one. Dr. Work had been out of practice for years. Boone may not have known of the article. Cooper was an internist. It is probable that Wilbur, the only heart specialist present, a medical and educational administrator, was not reading many articles.

A generation later, after World War II, when Wilbur was writing his memoirs, he was notably ill at ease in discussing the president's death, and three times in two pages remarked that no one could say with certainty whether Harding died of a stroke or a heart attack.[41] In

1955, Boone suffered a heart attack and must have known by then, if not before, that he and his fellows had erred in ascribing Harding's death to a stroke. In a private letter he wrote plaintively of the fact that only a doctor who suffered a heart attack could know what that meant, and beyond this confession related that "sometime" he would tell his correspondent what had happened at the time of Harding's death.[42] He may have been referring to the cover-up of Sawyer, the certification of a cerebral hemorrhage, or both.

Most Americans in 1923 were content to accept the decision of Harding's doctors that the president died of apoplexy, and so the issue stood for years to come. But some people turned to sensational explanations.[43] A few individuals said the president might have killed himself because of the imminent scandals, such as Teapot Dome, although he was hardly the suicide type and had been planning for reelection in 1924. The talk of crab meat and boiled eggs gave rise to claims that someone had poisoned him; perhaps Mrs. Harding had done so as a mercy killing. Others believed Mrs. Harding cooperated with Dr. Sawyer in a mercy killing. A year later Mrs. Harding visited Sawyer at the sanatorium, and the doctor unexpectedly died in circumstances similar to those of his late patient. Not long afterward Mrs. Harding herself suddenly passed from the scene.[44] An autopsy in San Francisco would have straightened everything out. Mrs. Harding, devoted to Dr. Sawyer, refused to allow one.

2

Roosevelt

As is well known, when World War II in 1944 and 1945 approached its climactic battles and in diplomacy its climactic negotiations, President Franklin D. Roosevelt entered into a final, if remarkably well-disguised, illness. And how inconvenient was his physical decline for the nation that had chosen him for a fourth term. The war was going well, but military and diplomatic questions of vast significance were arising. D-Day came on June 6, 1944, followed by a grand series of tactical decisions in which the president presumably was playing a part: the invasion of southern France; relations with General Charles de Gaulle, whose troops took part in the occupation of their homeland; the question of what armies (American or British) should get gasoline to carry the summer fighting into Germany; the body blow to the Western Allies when the Germans counterattacked in December. In the Pacific the island-hopping tactics of General Douglas MacArthur's divisions were taking American power north from Australia toward the Japanese home islands at the very time the fleets of Admiral Chester W. Nimitz were probing westward from Hawaii. A strategic decision needed to be made for the Pacific, which Roosevelt made at Hawaii shortly after D-Day occurred in Europe, and it favored MacArthur over Nimitz. It may have extended the Pacific war by giving in to MacArthur's grandiose ideas about occupation of the Philippines ("I shall return") instead of letting the navy bypass those islands and take the war directly to Japan. One thing led to others: continuation of the Japanese war beyond V-E Day in Europe made it easier for the Russians to intervene in the Far East and occupy Manchuria and part of Korea, and made almost inevitable the use of nuclear weapons on Japanese cities.

President Roosevelt's declining health raised other problems than military and diplomatic issues, two of which concerned his own health care, and the others domestic-political issues. After considerable confusion, FDR's medical diagnosis turned out to be high blood pressure. This was a difficult malady for a president of the United States. The height of the pressure, the erratic swings up and down, occurred in an era well before the time of blood pressure pills or other medication to bring the pressure down; so his personal activities were curtailed to rest and relaxation, which were impossible for a president of the United States. It was necessary to hope for the best, that a sudden high of pressure might not reach out for the well-known target areas, which are the heart, the kidneys, and the brain.

A second problem in his health care lay in the fact that for a long time he had been under the ministrations of a second-rate, really incompetent, personal physician, Vice Admiral Ross T. McIntire, surgeon general of the United States Navy. That McIntire was in the military may not have been too important, although the physician who entered upon the scene and changed the prescription and sought to save the day was a man of lesser rank. Perhaps the disparity in rank does explain why the admiral then engaged in a cover-up, an effort to deny what had happened. Perhaps connected with the cover-up was the fact that Roosevelt's medical records then disappeared from the safe of the Bethesda Naval Hospital.

Two domestic political calculations of importance also proved necessary during Roosevelt's last year, and both required consideration of the president's medical condition. Roosevelt had to decide whether he should run for a fourth term. The other point of decision was who should occupy the vice-presidential chair in the forthcoming term, presuming the president would win reelection. This was an important point, for the vice-president during any administration is, as observers put it, only a heartbeat away from the presidency. Woodrow Wilson's vice-president, Marshall, who once announced that what the country needed was a good five-cent cigar, said in a more serious moment that he had nothing to do in his high office except to preside over the Senate and inquire every morning as to the health of the president. For Roosevelt the decision concerned Vice-President Henry A. Wallace, who much desired a second term as vice-president. He scented the presidency.

Curiously, Roosevelt's successor once removed, Dwight D. Eisenhower, would face the same situation a decade later. As Roosevelt found himself involved in the climax of World War II, Eisenhower presided over the cold war at a time when the successors of Joseph V. Stalin were competing for power. Like Roosevelt, he was afflicted with cardiovascular disease. He also was attended by a ranking medical officer of the armed services, Major General Howard McC. Snyder, who like McIntire had turned to army administration and was no specialist in what ailed his commander-in-chief. Again, a man of lesser rank cared for Eisenhower's cardiological problems. Records also seem to have disappeared, and the same two domestic political calculations proved necessary. In Eisenhower's case it was whether to try for a second term, and if so, who should occupy the vice-presidential chair, presuming he was reelected. Like Wallace, Vice-President Richard M. Nixon wanted another term, for he too saw the possibility of the presidency.

The way in which history repeated itself, hardly a usual happening despite what one hears about history repeating itself, was unsettling. Perhaps a process of human nature was unfolding here, something that transcended the admonition of one of the Greek philosophers who noted that we never step in the same waters twice when crossing a stream. It is entirely possible that some future president of the United States, in declining health, might encounter the same problems so visible in the terms of Roosevelt and Eisenhower.

1.

Roosevelt's health went down dramatically after he returned from the Teheran Conference of November and December 1943, and the question became what to do about it, both medically and politically.[1] During the trip abroad he had heavily taxed his strength. For a while he looked much as he always had, one of the most photogenic of American presidents, what with the patrician face, the interesting, lively eyes, and mobile mouth. Dressed carelessly but carefully, he was a man to watch. Then his face thinned and his frame became shrunken, but he was still handsome and unforgettable to anyone who saw him. But he was clearly doing too much. Before the important conference with Winston Churchill and Stalin, he had stopped in Egypt where in the shadow of the Great Pyramid of Cheops, at the Mena House, he received Generalissimo Chiang Kai-shek of China and his wife. Thence to Teheran. By the end of the Big Three conference he was exhausted. After arrival back in Washington he was not his usual self. He failed to bounce back, as had happened before when he had come down with small ailments. Days passed into weeks, and then months, and he still was not up to par. He seemed to be suffering from influenza, complicated by bronchitis. Jonathan Daniels, son of FDR's old chief in the navy department during World War I, Josephus Daniels, later wrote, "Roosevelt was sick after he came home from Teheran that December and, though those who watched closest to him may differ, he seemed to me, as one of his assistants, to be never quite well again. There were people around him seeking political decisions which sometimes, in Time's weariness, he seemed to wish to avoid or postpone."[2]

As in the case of all presidential illnesses, visitors to the oval office and observers from less close at hand noticed signs of trouble. In August 1944, after a luncheon with the president on the lawn back of the White House, Senator Harry S. Truman came away shocked that the president's hands shook so much. (Roosevelt had tried to pour cream into his coffee and spilled most of it into the saucer.) Later, on his return from the Yalta Conference in February 1945, the state department liaison officer with the White House, Charles E. Bohlen, accompanying the president aboard the heavy cruiser *Quincy,* also noticed the shaking hands. Bohlen thought the president was coming apart and was tempted to ask the president's personal chief of staff, Admiral William D. Leahy, what was the matter, but hesitated to do so, as he did not know Leahy that well.[3]

Other signs bothered people. Roosevelt tended to let his mouth sag open, and it looked almost as if he had suffered a small stroke and could not control his facial muscles. His weight was dropping. His neck became too small for his shirt collars, and the president who was known as a penny-pincher refused to purchase new shirts. His weight loss also became visible in his face, which looked haggard.

The Democratic leader of the Bronx, Edward J. Flynn, staying overnight in the White House, noticed not only the debility and the haggard appearance, but something he had not seen before: irritability. "This condition in my opinion grew steadily worse as spring passed on to summer." He wrote in his memoirs that in conversation with the president at that time the question of a fourth term came up, and "I urged him not to consider it." In talking the problem over with his wife, Flynn said he felt the president would never survive a fourth term.[4]

Strange stories began to make the rounds. An attack of acute indigestion that the president suffered at Teheran gave rise to a rumor that he had been poisoned. Some years after the president's death, Dr. Harry S. Goldsmith, who has written on Roosevelt's illness, stressed two other possibilities that were talked about in 1944–1945.[5] One was that FDR in his last year suffered from a malignant tumor of the digestive tract. While a surgical resident at Memorial Sloan-Kettering Cancer Center in New York City, Goldsmith had heard Dr. George T. Pack say in a lecture that he, Pack, had learned from Dr. Frank H. Lahey of Boston that Roosevelt had been gravely ill. In 1944, according to Lahey who told Pack, Lahey had advised the president not to run for a fourth term. A second theory Dr. Goldsmith advanced as his own was that Roosevelt succumbed from a melanoma, the definitive pigmented lesion that developed above his left eye, visible in photographs by the year 1932. Over the years the lesion continued to enlarge, albeit in association with Roosevelt's apparently robust health. In his article, Dr. Goldsmith published photographs from a book by Stefan Lorant that showed the lesion clearly spreading with its fingers reaching down into the president's eyebrow.

But president watchers were far off the mark. The president's cardiologist, Dr. Howard G. Bruenn, had seen the tremors in Roosevelt's hands, and they did not disturb him for he had seen Roosevelt eat without difficulty many times. And generally individuals the president's age have tremors. The fact that the president sometimes let his mouth sag open was of no consequence. He relaxed that way, and when engaging in conversation his mouth was firmly closed unless he spoke. The subsequent weight loss from the diet was good for Roosevelt, who was overweight when Bruenn first saw him. His weight might not have seemed excessive, for it was around 185 pounds. But considering that his legs and hips had atrophied from lack of use, following the infantile paralysis in 1921, almost all his weight was in his chest and shoulders.

The irritability noted by Flynn may have been just the day—everyone gets irritable. Nor was there anything to the poisoning theory at Teheran. Roosevelt in the spring of 1944 went to South Carolina where he spent weeks on the estate of Bernard M. Baruch, Hobcaw Barony. There on April 28 he suffered severe abdominal pains. Dr. Bruenn guessed it was a small gall bladder attack and treated him with codeine administered by hypodermic injection. The distress continued a few days and subsided, although there was another attack on May 1, lasting two days. On return to Washington, Bruenn arranged X rays of his gall bladder, which showed a good functional response but revealed a group of cholesterol stones. Accordingly, the doctor placed him on a low-fat regimen.

The cancer theory, given currency by Dr. Pack's talk about what he said he had heard from Dr. Lahey, has never come to anything. Immediately after the lecture at Memorial Sloan-Kettering, Dr. Goldsmith asked Dr. Pack for the source of his talk, and Pack said he had taken notes on Dr. Lahey's remarks and was planning to make the notes available in due time. Half a dozen years later Pack died, and

Goldsmith arranged to see his journals, only to discover they had been lost or misplaced. Only one full and one half-completed journal were available, and neither mentioned President Roosevelt. The *New York Times* in 1985–1986 published a story saying that Lahey had written a memorandum about Roosevelt's final illness and given it to the longtime business manager of the Lahey Clinic and the surgeon's executor, Mrs. Linda M. Strand, with the injunction that if his interpretation of Roosevelt's death ever came into public controversy, she was free to publish his memorandum. Mrs. Strand gave it to a Boston law firm for safekeeping. When she asked for it, they refused to give it back. Goldsmith sued in superior court, and Mrs. Strand then substituted her name for his. The clinic entered the suit, objecting to publication as destroying the necessary confidentiality of the doctor-patient relationship. The judge ruled there was not enough criticism of Lahey to allow return of the memorandum to Mrs. Strand. She appealed to the Massachusetts Supreme Court, which released the account to the executor, then ninety years old. She chose not to publish it. She died in 1988, and two years later Dr. Goldsmith telephoned a representative of the Lahey Clinic's law firm and said that he had a copy of the Lahey memorandum and would publish it in due time.[6]

As for Dr. Goldsmith's theory of a melanoma, Bruenn has revealed in a recent interview that the lesion disappeared from photographs after the Teheran Conference because a Dr. Winchell of the Mayo Clinic, operating at Bethesda Naval Hospital, excised it from the president's face. It was, he said, "a very benign business." It was only in the skin and was what is described as a sebaceous cyst.[7]

One comes, then, to the blood pressure problem. Roosevelt's cardiologist, Bruenn, at last set it out in a definitive article that appeared in 1970 at the behest of the president's daughter, Anna.[8] Sensitive to the stories about her father and anxious that the truth emerge, she arranged for Bruenn to publish this account. She read his article before it appeared, and it revealed that the president's blood pressure had been going up year after year. In 1935 the pressure was 136/78, in 1937 it was 162/98, in 1940 it had gone to 178/88, and in 1941 it reached 188/105, "and the diastolic was going up, too." In his judgment the president should not have run for a third term with such readings.[9] By 1944, just after Teheran, the president's blood pressure reached crucial heights.

Oddly, the president's personal physician, Dr. McIntire, had not adduced anything special from his patient's high blood pressure. Mc-

Intire seems not to have taken readings very often, which was the custom in those days.[10] When McIntire took readings, he probably noticed they were only a little higher, and the difference did not alarm him. When the president thought that he had picked up a little flu and bronchitis, McIntire believed it. After all, the patient is the first resort for any physician seeking to diagnose physical ills.

Early in 1944, however, Anna insisted that McIntire do something, undertake some sort of consultation, to improve her father's health. At that time she and her husband, John Boettiger, a former newspaperman, were living in the White House. After receiving a commission in the army, Boettiger was acting as a presidential assistant. Anna was the closest to her father of all the Roosevelt children. He adored this sensitive and pretty young woman; her presence always raised his spirits. She was far more influential with him than her mother who, estranged from her husband, was not often in the mansion. (She lived in an apartment in New York or the cottage, "Val-Kill," on the grounds of the Hyde Park estate.) The result was a physical examination of the president at Bethesda Naval Hospital on March 27, 1944. Among other preparations McIntire telephoned the principal cardiologist at the hospital, Bruenn, and asked him to see the president. Bruenn of course said he would be happy to do so.

Roosevelt could not have done better than to pass from the incompetent hands of Admiral McIntire into those of Commander Bruenn. McIntire had spent many years in the navy, and the years in the service had taken their toll on his professional alertness. He had been the president's personal physician since 1933, receiving the job because Admiral Grayson had recommended him as a discreet member of the navy's medical corps and because FDR had long suffered from a nasal drip, and McIntire was an eye-ear-nose-throat man. His specialty encouraged him to believe that Roosevelt's trouble was in his own area of expertise. The admiral cared for Roosevelt's sinuses by irrigating them and dosing him with nose drops and sprays. The nose drops could have raised the president's blood pressure. McIntire had many other duties in the navy besides seeing the president. As surgeon general since 1938 he had the entire governance of the naval medical establishment. It had spread around the world during World War II and had grown to huge proportions with 175,000 doctors, nurses, and professionals, 52 hospitals, and 278 mobile units. The paperwork alone must have been overwhelming.

Bruenn was very much a specialist in cardiac cases. Before the war he had been a resident and a member of the faculty at Columbia Presbyterian in New York City, one of the nation's leading hospitals. As a faculty member, he kept up on the literature and spent his time dealing only with his specialty, never the generality of cases that bogs down the average physician in an incessant surveying of the medical universe. At the time of Pearl Harbor he had sought to enlist, only to be told that if he waited a short time, until he reached the age of thirty-nine, he could enter the navy as a lieutenant commander instead of a lieutenant, senior grade—that is, the equivalent rank of a major rather than a captain. He waited. After his birthday he enlisted and was sent to a naval hospital in New York State where he was in charge of a ward of mixed cases. Then, to his surprise, for he had known that in the services specialists received the most odd assignments, with neurologists, say, assigned to departments of obstetrics, he suddenly was sent to Bethesda and put in charge of cardiology as head of the department with the additional task of having referral of all cardiac cases in the area. The latter duty meant that if an officer were up for promotion and the examining physician felt uncertain of what seemed a possible cardiac or vascular problem, he sent the man to Bruenn who dealt with such cases by appointment. This was how the president of the United States was referred to him.

When the president arrived for his appointment with Bruenn, the nurses and corpsmen of his department were abuzz with excitement. Roosevelt was wheeled down the hall, and there he was. Bruenn at once was struck by the good humor, the affability. In politics the doctor was a Republican, a fact the president later discovered and often teased him about. He thought Roosevelt a charmer and years later told an interviewer that FDR could have charmed birds out of trees.[11]

But medically speaking the encounter was an appalling experience. Bruenn noticed that as soon as he and his assistants had gotten the president on the examining table there he was short of breath, a bad sign. From that point onward, everything was of the worst. The president's heart was grossly enlarged. Using a fluoroscope and X rays, Bruenn could see a "considerable increase in the size of the cardiac shadow."[12] The enlargement was mostly of the left ventricle, the heart's main pumping chamber. In view of FDR's low-grade pulmonary infection and cough, the bronchitis that McIntire had diagnosed, Roosevelt was showing early signs of congestive heart failure. To be sure, the doctor could not be certain of this diagnosis. He had seen hundreds of cardiac cases and many of them were not clear-cut. Nothing short of an autopsy could have laid bare the causes of the president's condition. Still, from clinical and physical signs the problem was obvious. The chief cardiologist of Bethesda Naval Hospital diagnosed hypertension, hypertensive heart disease, cardiac failure (left ventricular), and—in this sole respect McIntire was right—acute bronchitis.

The surgeon general of the U.S. Navy had had no warning or sensation that such a dismal diagnosis ("God-awful," Bruenn later described it) was possible.[13] Bruenn's findings and their interpretation had been completely unsuspected up to this time. Bruenn prescribed digitalization, a diet to reduce Roosevelt's weight, and bed rest. McIntire flared. "You can't do that," he said. "This is the president of the United States."[14]

McIntire summoned the honorary navy medical consultants, among them Dr. James E. Paullin of Atlanta, then president of the American Medical Association, and Dr. Lahey of Boston. On March 31 a group convened of Paullin and Lahey, together with McIntire, Bruenn, Captain John Harper, who was the commandant of Bethesda, Captain Robert Duncan, executive officer, and Captain Charles Behrens, the hospital radiologist. Before this group Bruenn presented his findings and recommendations. First among the prescriptions he had recommended was digitalizing the president. It was no complete solution to the president's problem, and would do nothing for the blood pressure, but at least it promised to "rev up" his body's engine, making it work better. Digitalization was in itself no easy solution, for a cardiologist had to watch the level carefully. It was easy to overdigitalize, which would bring unpleasant results; the toxicity from oversupply could produce among other things a lack of appetite and thereby might create the very collapse it was designed to prevent.

At the meeting the honorary medical consultants were shown the X rays, electrocardiograms, and other laboratory data, and there was much discussion. Paullin and Lahey pooh-poohed Bruenn's recommendations, thinking the patient unready for them, that they were all too drastic and extensive. Bruenn stuck to his diagnosis and said that if they did not want to follow his analysis he wanted nothing more to do with the case. That same day the consultants went over to the White House and examined the patient. They agreed that Bruenn could go ahead with the digitalization.

The changes in the president's condition due to the digitalis over the next week or ten days were nothing short of spectacular. Roosevelt's lungs, which had been congested and contained a small amount of fluid, were now clear. His enlarged heart diminished in size. The coughing stopped, and he was sleeping soundly. The consultants went back to the White House a second time and easily ascertained the success of the treatment. At this juncture McIntire said to Bruenn, "If you have rapport with the president, this is now your problem."[15] In effect Bruenn became the president's personal physician with McIntire as the public spokesman for Roosevelt's health.

The convening of a board had cleared the air, bringing an end to McIntire's misdiagnoses. It is interesting, though, that even the assembling of a board including the consultants, while having the appearance of a decision, and while a decision did come out of the meeting or at least came out of the meeting together with the visit of the consultants to the White House, even the convening of a board had not really solved the problem. McIntire was no specialist, nor were Harper and Duncan. Behrens was a radiologist, somewhat removed from the point at hand. As for the consultants, Paullin was an internist. He was a good doctor, probably, but politically inclined. As Bruenn told an interviewer years later, "Anybody that becomes president of the A. M. A. has spent a long time in the hierarchy of committees and so forth. You don't get picked out of the group to become president. You have to work for it." The politics could easily have gotten in the way of continuing competence. Lahey was obviously a very able surgeon and a prominent one. The president's problem, however, was not internal medicine or surgery but cardiology. Lahey at least was honest with Bruenn at the consultation, or perhaps it was after the consequent examination, when he said, "This is out of my field."[16]

One shudders to think what might have happened if when the board met, Bruenn had not entered the equation, or if on hand with the facts and recommendations had not been stiff-necked enough to tell the board what he thought and make an issue of it—either they took his advice or he washed his hands of their activities. And Bruenn's diagnosis explained everything. The tiredness was due to cardiovascular disease and heart failure—both of which had affected the patient's lungs. The bronchitis was the least of his problems.

For McIntire, who at Anna Roosevelt's prodding had brought in Bruenn, the entire situation must have been excruciatingly painful. The fact of his incompetence loomed because it was clear that Roosevelt had not been receiving the proper treatment. Had McIntire con-

tinued with the president into the spring of 1944, the president probably would have died that summer; he was that close to the edge.

The result was a cover-up in two respects. For one, and although
McIntire immediately passed the president's care to Bruenn, he never
mentioned in public what was wrong with the president. When the
White House reporter for the International News Service, Robert G.
Nixon, who saw the president frequently and knew something was
wrong, waylaid McIntire for an explanation, all he could get was that
the president's blood pressure was up a little and it had been thought
best for him to lose some weight to keep the pressure down.[17] To the
bitter end the admiral told press people and anyone else who would
listen that the president was in good health considering his age. After
the president died a year later, and theoretically at least it was no
longer necessary to maintain any military security, if such it was, over
the state of his health, McIntire arranged for the well-known journalist
George Creel to assist him in telling about his experiences as Roosevelt's personal physician. The resultant book was just a series of plati-
tudes, no admission at all that his ministrations had brought the president close to death because of the high blood pressure. *White House
Physician*, its title quietly efficient, as one supposed its author had
been, said that Roosevelt's blood pressure was normal, his heart signs
were normal, and everything else was normal.[18]

Nor was McIntire satisfied with lying about his patient, the late
president of the United States. He almost certainly removed the president's medical records from the safe at Bethesda. The only individuals
who appear to have had access at that time to the safe from which the
records disappeared were the commanding and executive officers, Cap-
tains Harper and Duncan, and the surgeon general, Admiral McIntire. Bruenn later believed that McIntire took the records. It would
have been a sizable file, for the president had been accustomed to go
out to Bethesda since 1933. His long connection with the navy, dating
back to service in 1913–1920 as assistant secretary under Secretary
Daniels, had persuaded him to go to Bethesda rather than the equally
nearby Walter Reed General Hospital, the equivalent army installation. Everything of first order would have been there. Bruenn remembered the file intimately, as he had contributed much to it, writing
detailed accounts of his morning visits to the president in 1944 and
1945 three or four times a week. He remembered a file two inches
thick. It did not include the X rays, which would not have fitted, but it
incorporated all other accounting of treatment, including laboratory

work and cardiograph images. When Bruenn came back the last time from Warm Springs, he remembered distinctly writing a long note "and the record was then placed in the Hospital Safe at the Bethesda Naval Medical Center. I have not seen it since that time." McIntire, Bruenn remembered, had said time and time again that there was nothing organically wrong with the president. He could not imagine him ever wanting those records to see the light of day.[19]

2.

In view, such as it was, of the president's physical condition in early 1944, the two political questions mentioned at the outset of this chapter now arose. One was whether the president would decide to run again for a fourth term. The other was, in case he did, who should be the Democratic vice-presidential nominee. On the question of running again, Roosevelt apparently made up his own mind. He did not consult Dr. Bruenn. If he had, the doctor would have advised against it.[20]

In retrospect, the doctor was dumbfounded at the president's lack of curiosity about his condition. "At no time did the President ever comment on the frequency of these visits [Bruenn's White House visits] or question the reason for the electrocardiograms and the other laboratory tests that were performed from time to time; nor did he ever have any questions as to the type and variety of medications that were used."[21] The doctor was not sure Roosevelt even knew that he was a cardiologist. Roosevelt's complete lack of curiosity struck Bruenn as odd: almost all patients, he said, wanted to know their blood pressure.

What a contrast from the time, back in 1921, when the president had come down with infantile paralysis. He then had consulted doctors until the diagnosis was accurate. At the very beginning of the paralysis he had been seen by a local doctor at Campobello, who did not know the trouble. He then saw Dr. Keen, Cleveland's surgeon of years before, a pioneer in neurosurgery, who by chance was vacationing nearby. Keen gave him a wonderful misdiagnosis. He thereupon went to a third physician who got things straight.[22]

McIntire had told Bruenn to tell the president nothing, and at the time the cardiologist thought that perhaps McIntire was informing him, but he was not very sure. McIntire later said he never did. Nor did Roosevelt make any effort to discuss his medical problems with others. One day Senator Alben Barkley of Kentucky, the majority leader,

who himself had presidential ambitions, was in the president's bedroom talking, and somehow the health question came up. Barkley may
have raised it obliquely. Underneath his southern bonhomie he was a
remarkably subtle man. But the result of his inquiry, if such it was,
came to naught save a joke that Barkley may well have told to get
himself out of an awkward situation. When he came out of the president's bedroom there were sounds of presidential laughter. Jonathan
Daniels and Anna Roosevelt were waiting outside. Anna went in, and
Daniels asked Barkley what the president had been laughing about.
The senator said he had talked about the rumors of Roosevelt's illness
and how mistaken they were. He also told the president the story
about a drunken man, to whom a bartender refused a drink, and who
had undertaken to prove he was not drunk. "Why," he said, "you see
that cat there coming in the door? He has got two eyes and if I was
drunk [I] would see four." The bartender said, "Hell, man, you are
drunker than I thought. That cat isn't coming in the door, it is going
out."[23]

Incuriosity may have come from Roosevelt's sheer unwillingness
to confide in people or to express what might have been on his mind.
Henry Wallace, who in the summer of 1944 was desperately seeking
renomination to the vice-presidency, wrote in his diary about a remark
a friend had heard from Anna. She had been quoted as saying, "He
doesn't know any man and no man knows him. Even his own family
doesn't know anything about him."[24]

One of Roosevelt's biographers, Frank Freidel, believes the president knew his condition, yet Freidel can only surmise because there is
no proof. The closest the president seems to have come to an admission of his physical state was in a casual conversation with Daniels a
year or more before he died. On this occasion Daniels spoke to him
about the author, George Fort Milton, who was writing on the protocols
of the Moscow Conference of foreign ministers in 1943. Roosevelt said
to Daniels, using what the latter described as a strange phrase, "Here
is something you ought to write if I should pop off."[25]

Perhaps the president's lack of concern for his state of health
came from a feeling that he had a job to do and nothing was going to
interfere with it. Bruenn had that impression. One time Roosevelt was
watching a movie about President Wilson and what happened with
the League of Nations after Wilson's collapse. FDR said, "By God,
that's not going to happen to me!"

Perhaps it was a feeling akin to that expressed in the well-known line by the nineteenth-century poet William E. Henley: "I am the master of my fate." The INS reporter Bob Nixon did not believe it ever occurred to the president that he would die. "He had been in the White House twelve years, and I suppose he figured he would have a fifth term. It never occurred to him that anybody else would be president."[26]

The question about running again was hardly an issue, at least in the mind of the president. He would run. Like all good politicians, he held back on disclosing that fact, letting speculation arise and allowing for something of a dramatic situation. To Postmaster General Frank C. Walker, with whom he often was willing to relate matters that he would not have disclosed to others, he said quite early, actually in 1942, that he would run.[27] Typically he said it in a whimsical way. "Well," said Walker, "there's one fellow you are playing up who hasn't got a chance in the world—that's H. W. [Henry Wallace]." The president agreed, "I think you are right." "You are the only one who would have a chance," said the postmaster general. "Get thee behind me, Satan," replied FDR.

In one respect the decision was easy. The war was on and he could rely on the Lincolnian dictum that it is best not to change horses in the middle of a stream. The military situation was pressing with the campaigns in Europe and the Far East at their height: D-Day on June 6, and in the Pacific theater the imminence of a great invasion of the Philippines. All the while the U.S. Navy was engaging the imperial Japanese Navy in huge battles, and the U.S. Army Air Force was beginning its bombing of almost every sizable city and military installation—the two were not always separable—in the Japanese home islands. In such a situation, how could the president decline a fourth term?

The chieftains of the Democratic party found themselves in a quandary. They could not keep Roosevelt from running. Actually, they wanted him to run to give the party another four years in the presidency. The only trouble was that the four years were not likely to be his, but that was the president's decision. For their own parts, they had to make a decision about the vice-presidency and impose it on Roosevelt somehow or another without betraying that they were anticipating his death. Observing the signs of the president's poor health, even though the signs pointed to the wrong illnesses, the party leaders took the necessary precaution of getting a man into the vice-presidency whom they knew they could trust.[28]

For a while the president gave them little guidance. He floated the candidacy of his special counsel, his speech writer Sam Rosenman. In December 1943, Walker asked him pointblank (so the postmaster general wrote in his diary), "Who do you want for your VP candidate?"[29] He answered, "We have three candidates—Sam R., Jimmie Byrnes and Wallace." James F. Byrnes, former senator and associate justice of the Supreme Court, was then "assistant president" in charge of largely domestic issues, while the president handled foreign and military affairs. FDR continued, "Sam would be all right but I don't know whether he would be helpful politically." By that he meant that the Jewish-American vote was with the Democrats anyway, and Rosenman might not relate to midwestern and southern Democrats. Rosenman's candidacy was hardly serious. The president adjourned the issue by telling Walker that the two had to talk politics once a week from then on. Meanwhile he wanted a "tough son-of-a-bitch" on the staff of the national committee who "could write short stories indicting Dewey, Bricker, Landon, Hoover one after another with skill and ease."

In this state of confusion some Democrats moved for clarification, part of which was to get rid of Byrnes and Wallace. The other part was to advance the candidacy of Senator Truman, who was not himself running. In the matter of Byrnes and Wallace they discovered that they had some presidential help. Roosevelt already had installed Byrnes in the White House, but here was the deft working of the presidential left hand, for Byrnes's appointment as virtual assistant president was a way to get a lot of work out of him and yet make him anathema as a vice-presidential candidate. Roosevelt did not like Byrnes, though he admired his ability to get things done, and was quite up to doing him in, politically speaking. And what better way than to get him into a position in domestic affairs where he would have to come down hard on labor unions during the war when labor was in a vice between manufacturers and the public, both of which wanted low labor costs? By mid-1944, Byrnes had aroused the hearty dislike of labor. He also possessed some natural political disqualifications, such as the fact that he came from South Carolina, meaning his racial attitudes were not acceptable to the increasingly vocal part of the electorate composed of black Americans, and the fact that he had been born a Roman Catholic but had gone over to the Episcopal church, his wife's faith.

As for Wallace, party leaders hated him and certainly did not want him as Roosevelt's successor; they thought him a visionary. It was known among some of them that the vice-president had corresponded with a woman psychic in New York in dozens of letters. The two visionaries discussed various matters using aliases and coded references to describe their names and theories. A child probably could have broken their code. According to Roosevelt's press secretary, Stephen T. Early, this correspondence threatened to get out of control in 1940 at the time of the national convention, for it had passed into the hands of a Pittsburgh newspaper publisher who arranged to deliver it to the delegates. The delegates did not like Wallace and would have enjoyed it, but the president already had designated Wallace as his running mate. In a panic, the party leaders sent for the New York lawyer Morris Ernst, whom they put on a plane for Chicago where he arrived shortly before the train bearing the publisher (or his emissary) carrying the documents. Ernst threatened libel and other dire penalties, and the documents passed out of sight but not before presumably people along the way had made copies.[30] There was danger that they might reappear in 1944. In addition to the impending scandal, there was the fact that Wallace never had run for a public office in his life until he ran for the vice-presidency in 1940. Moreover, during the next four years he antagonized almost every member of the U.S. Senate by paying no attention to them, singly or collectively. To inquirers he explained that he was interested in issues, not people. All the while he undertook a series of international missions and accompanied them with speeches. Whether he said that every Hottentot should have a quart of milk was beside the point, for his traveling gave currency to the supposed remark. When President Roosevelt saw Wallace shortly before the convention, he mentioned the point about milk for the Hottentots. It had stuck in Roosevelt's mind.

In the Wallace case the president helped the party leaders along by engineering a trip for Wallace that was so typical of Roosevelt that there can be no doubt of his intention. He arranged for Wallace to go on a mission to China and the Soviet Union. He told the perhaps annoyed vice-president, who could hardly do other than what the president wished, that he hoped Wallace would pay special attention to Siberia. Whether he laughed after the vice-president left his office is unknown. He perhaps told his next visitor that he had sent "Henry" to Siberia. The result was that Wallace was out of the country during the crucial weeks before the 1944 convention when he and his followers should have been organizing in every way to seize the vice-presidential nomination during the convention's first balloting.

As was his wont, Roosevelt told neither Byrnes nor Wallace that he had set his seal of disapproval on them. On the contrary, he told Byrnes that he was his chosen candidate for vice-president and told Wallace that if he, Roosevelt, were a delegate to the convention, he would vote for Wallace. Both repaired to Chicago in hope of the nomination. Meanwhile the party leaders, dedicated to choosing a sensible man as Roosevelt's successor, had done some work on their own. The party treasurer, Edwin W. Pauley, got together with the president's appointments secretary, Major General Edwin M. (Pa) Watson, and the two arranged for anti-Wallace individuals to receive appointments to see the president. They then went to work on the party's leaders, so that when a group assembled in the president's study after dinner on the evening of July 11, for the express purpose of designating a vice-presidential nominee, everyone there except the president knew that the finger of destiny was to point to Senator Truman.

Everything went according to plan during the party leaders' meeting with Roosevelt except that at one juncture the president, who did not know Truman well at all, decided it might be interesting to find out how old he was. He asked his son-in-law, Boettiger, who had joined the group after dinner, to go out and find a congressional directory and get Truman's birth date. Boettiger came back bearing the book, and by that time the conversation had turned elsewhere. Pauley took the book and hid it in his lap, and the president forgot his own question. Everyone there save Roosevelt knew that Truman was born in 1884, meaning he was only two years younger than the president. The ravages of Roosevelt's vascular disease had made him an incomparably more fragile individual than the vigorous Truman.

Unsure that the president would keep his word on the choice of Truman for the vice-presidency, the leaders after leaving the meeting sent back an envoy, the chairman of the national committee, Robert E. Hannegan, to get the decision in writing. Hannegan, at the behest of Postmaster General Walker, used the excuse that he had forgotten his jacket. To Hannegan's horror, and that of the others when they realized what Roosevelt had done, the president added a name to the note he wrote out: Supreme Court Justice William O. Douglas. But then at the convention this inclusion did not prove important because Douglas knew absolutely nothing about his candidacy for the vice-presidency and the leaders of course did not tell him, with the result that his supporters had no opportunity to organize the Chicago delegates. Perhaps the president had planned it that way and introduced the confusion to let the leaders know that he still was the boss.

Even after the convention opened the president's near indifference over the choice of his successor was capable of causing a dangerous situation: Wallace had taken the president's nominal support as a signal to do everything he, Wallace, could do to achieve the great prize. As a result, his supporters packed the convention galleries, counterfeited tickets to the floor, paid the convention organist to play the Wallace song, "Iowa, Iowa, that's where the tall corn grows," and all but stampeded the convention into taking Wallace by acclamation. How much the then vice-president knew of these arrangements is an open question, but he may have felt that the president's dallying with his candidacy, and Roosevelt's outright dishonesty in asserting that if he were a candidate to the convention he would vote for Wallace, deserved repayment in kind. Besides, Wallace might pull off a real upset. In the Republican convention of 1940, Wendell L. Willkie had done just that. But the tough leaders of the Democratic Party were not about to allow a rebellion by the Wallace-ites. One of Pauley's emissaries told the organist to change his tune, or he would cut the organ's cable with a fire axe. Mayor Edward J. Kelly of Chicago declared the packed convention hall a fire hazard, which put off the balloting until the next day when the leaders could issue new tickets. Thereafter, they controlled the proceedings. The delegates consumed the first ballot by voting for favorite sons, subtracting from Wallace's total, giving the vice-president's supporters a feeling of imminent victory. Then on the second ballot, when delegates had gotten the word, delegation after delegation changed their votes to Truman for vice-president. Or was it Truman for president?

Not long after Truman's nomination at Chicago, an episode occurred that almost lifted the lid on Roosevelt's serious illness. When he had passed through Chicago on the train he was en route to the Pacific coast, and thence boarded a cruiser for Hawaii, to consult with General MacArthur and Admiral Nimitz. The president returned by way of Alaska where he inspected military installations. He returned to the West Coast by destroyer and at Bremerton gave a speech on the destroyer's bridge to a large audience seated or standing on the dock. He made the speech standing, and because of the weight loss his braces did not fit, and that alone was an ordeal. But during the speech, for fifteen minutes, he suffered an attack of angina, and it was all he could do to make it through until the speech's end. He managed to get through the text, gripping the podium with both hands, almost obviously in distress. Fortunately, his audience was far enough away that hardly anyone saw what was happening. Afterward when he went below deck he told Bruenn he had suffered sharp chest pains, and the doctor immediately stripped him down, took his blood pressure and EKG, and discovered an attack of angina, not a cardiac infarction. There was no damage to the heart. Bruenn then realized that because the president engaged in almost no exercise, which would have revealed the angina, because he was lifted into and out of his chair in the oval office, lifted into and out of bed, and wheeled everywhere, he had not shown the telltale sign of arterial vascular disease.[31]

About the same time that summer of 1944, talk among doctors at Bethesda threatened to get out of hand. The president's press secretary, Early, began to read stories about Roosevelt's health that were too close to the truth, and with help from Assistant Secretary of State Breckinridge Long, put the FBI on the case. Agents discovered that the doctors had seen photographs of Bruenn standing close to the president and were adding two and two. The agents informed one of the doctors that loose talk in wartime was dangerous.[32]

Perhaps in response to these near revelations of the president's desperate physical condition, it was arranged that autumn for FDR to tour the boroughs of New York City. By chance, the weather was nasty with incessant rain. The president triumphantly stayed the course, his automobile passing through the streets to the cheers of hundreds of thousands. At a point or two, he was taken inside a building and stripped down, dried, rubbed, and outfitted with new clothing. The deception worked.

The rest soon was history. Roosevelt celebrated his fourth inaugural on a winter day in January with the proceedings held out in back of the White House before eight thousand attendants, who stood in snow and slush. Dr. Bruenn brought his wife to the ceremony so that she might meet the president, who, it turned out, did not stand in the reception line inside the mansion. At the luncheon inside, the two hundred and fifty invited guests did have the opportunity to observe the president close at hand. "He looks exactly as my husband did when he went into his decline," said Mrs. Woodrow Wilson. "Don't say that to another soul," cautioned Secretary of Labor Frances Perkins. "He has a great and terrible job to do, and he's got to do it even if it kills him."[33] Shortly after the inauguration the president left for the Yalta Conference, a most tiring trip to the Soviet Union. He managed to make the journey, but it was anxious work for the three individuals there who knew how ill he was. As his daughter Anna wrote her husband,

> Just between you and me, we are having to watch OM [the old man] very carefully from the physical standpoint. He gets all wound up, seems to thoroughly enjoy it all, but wants too many people around, and then won't go to bed early enough. The result is that he doesn't sleep well. Ross [McIntire] and Bruenn are both worried because of the old "ticker" trouble—which, of course, no one knows about but those two and me. I am working closely with Ross and Bruenn, and am using all the ingenuity and tact I can muster to try to separate the wheat from the chaff—to keep the unnecessary people out of OM's room and to steer the necessary ones in at the best times. This involves trying my best to keep abreast as much as possible of what is actually taking place at the Conf[erence] so that I will know who should and who should not see OM. I have found out thru Bruenn (who won't let me tell Ross that I know) that this "ticker" situation is far more serious than I ever knew. And the biggest difficulty in handling the situation here is that we can, of course, tell no one of the "ticker" trouble. It's truly worrisome—and there's not a heluva lot anyone can do about it. (Better tear off and destroy this paragraph.)[34]

Two months after the Yalta Conference, on Thursday afternoon, April 12, 1945, with Admiral McIntire in his office in the White House, and Dr. Bruenn in the swimming pool more than two miles from the presidential cottage at Warm Springs, everything seemed quiet, another day in the president's vacation at a place that had given him much pleasure and relief from his affliction of infantile paralysis. When his correspondence secretary, William D. Hassett, saw the president early that afternoon he did not look at all good. He was up and fully dressed, seated at the card table near the fireplace in the big leather chair he favored with his back to the windows that looked out over the pine trees. He went through the mail. Elizabeth Shoumatoff, the artist, arrived and set up; she had been doing his portrait and to Hassett's annoyance constantly interfering with the paperwork, telling him to turn this way and that.

Hassett left, and not long afterward, as he wrote, in the quiet beauty of the Georgia spring "came the day of the Lord."[35] The first need was for Bruenn; a secret service man came down to the pool and told him the president had collapsed. The doctor was surprised but not greatly so, for he had known something like this might happen. When he got to Roosevelt's side he found him already in bed and helped get him into his pajamas. He saw at once what was the trouble. Roosevelt's neck was rigid, his right pupil widely dilated. It was a massive cerebral hemorrhage. A blood vessel had broken, pouring blood into large sections of the brain, creating such damage that the president, had he survived, would have been a piteous human wreck, a shell of a man. Bruenn called McIntire in Washington, who called Paullin in Atlanta. Paullin raced to Warm Springs. When he arrived he found Bruenn working frantically, giving the president artificial respiration, as his breathing had stopped. His pulse was barely perceptible. His heart sounds then stopped. Paullin administered a hypodermic of adrenalin, directly to the heart. Within minutes Dr. Bruenn was pronouncing the president dead.

The *Oneida*, where Cleveland's operation took place.

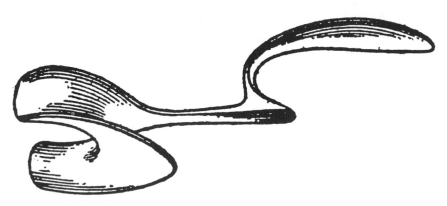

The cheek retractor bought in Paris from Luer in 1866 by W. W. Keen. With it the operation was done wholly within the mouth, thus avoiding any external scar. (From W. W. Keen, *The Surgical Operations on President Cleveland in 1893*, p. 39.)

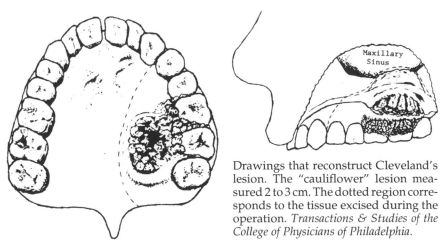

Maxillary Sinus

Drawings that reconstruct Cleveland's lesion. The "cauliflower" lesion measured 2 to 3 cm. The dotted region corresponds to the tissue excised during the operation. *Transactions & Studies of the College of Physicians of Philadelphia.*

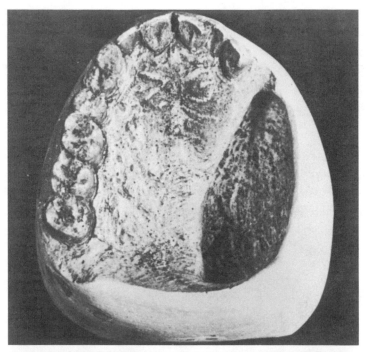

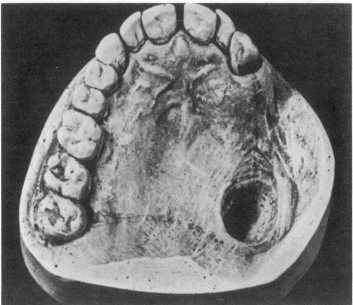

Cleveland's dental casts. Comparison of the cast on the top (1897) with the cast on the bottom (1893) illustrates notable healing and shrinkage of the palatal defect. *Transactions & Studies of the College of Physicians of Philadelphia.*

Harding in Vancouver, en route to Seattle, shortly before his death. Courtesy Ohio Historical Society.

Vice-President Thomas R. Marshall, who should have been president of the United States, poses for his portrait. After Wilson suffered the stroke in October 1919, Marshall never saw him until the inauguration of Harding in March 1921. Courtesy Library of Congress.

Woodrow Wilson at his last cabinet meeting, March 3, 1921. Courtesy Library of Congress.

The Bremerton speech on the deck of USS *Cummings*. FDR suffered an angina attack and barely made it through. Courtesy UPI.

3
Eisenhower

D wight D. Eisenhower, president of the United States from 1953 until 1961, was the sort of person who easily could have suffered from cardiovascular disease. And it is an interesting fact that his cardiologist from just before the beginning of his first term in 1953 until his death in 1969, Dr. Thomas W. Mattingly, believes that Eisenhower had two heart attacks in 1949 and again in 1953 before he encountered the major heart attack in the midst of his presidency in 1955. What this new evidence means is that Eisenhower probably should not have run for the presidency in 1952. It is true that a decade later the American people found themselves with a president who had had a major heart attack—Lyndon B. Johnson, who succeeded John F. Kennedy in 1963. By that time medical science had made it possible to control blood pressure through medication, but in the 1940s and 1950s this was still not possible. As in Roosevelt's time, the only course a physician could take to prevent a surging blood pressure, with all that might mean for the heart, kidneys, and brain, was to put the patient on a low-sodium diet, hold down his or her weight to avoid overworking the vascular system, place him or her on bed rest, and avoid—this was the other side of bed rest—anything that would excite the patient and bring highs of pressure together with the very heavy risks that would ensue.

And so for the Eisenhower era, as for the last part of Roosevelt's administration, the American people again had a president whose health at best was fragile and at worst had deteriorated to a danger point. This for a time when domestic affairs were fairly well in order and inflation was barely perceptible, less than 10 percent in eight years, and when the nation's standard of living was rising: in the years from 1950 to 1965 the country doubled the wealth it had accumulated from the founding of Jamestown in 1607 until 1950. Foreign affairs, however, were not in order. True, the Korean War came to an end in the summer of 1953, but thereafter each year usually saw some international downturn. The year 1954 marked the defeat of ten thousand French and French colonial troops at Dien Bien Phu, the first post-1945 major Western defeat in a colonial war, presaging American defeat in Vietnam nearly fifteen years later. In 1955 peace seemed confirmed by the Geneva Conference, the first summit meeting of world leaders since the Yalta and Potsdam conferences a decade before: Eisenhower, the Russian premier of the moment, Nikolai Bulganin, Prime Minister Anthony Eden of Britain, and French Premier Edgar Faure. But next year brought a crisis at Suez in which the Egyptian leader Gamal Abdel Nasser nationalized the Suez Canal and inspired an Anglo-French attack and occupation with the Israelis seizing everything up to the eastern side of the great ditch, all in a vain effort to turn the clock back. In 1957 the United States tried to cool the Middle East with money provided under the Eisenhower Doctrine, a thinly veiled formula for bribing local countries to keep the peace. Only the Lebanese government, whose president desired an unconstitutional second term, took the money, resulting in the Lebanon crisis of 1958 and the temporary occupation of that country by American troops to protect it from revolution. The year 1958 also brought a crisis over possession of islands close to Communist Chinese ports, islands held by troops of the Chinese Nationalist government on Taiwan. In 1958–1959 the Russians threatened to turn Berlin over to the unrecognized (by the West) East German government. In 1960 it was the downing of an American U–2 spy plane deep within the Soviet Union over Sverdlovsk, the Soviet Pittsburgh. All the while Soviet leaders sought to scare world public opinion by boasting about their country's nuclear power—bombs and ballistic missiles—even though the Soviet Union possessed only a few intercontinental missiles. In 1957 the Soviets sent up a satellite in a crude attempt to prove their power.

1.

As Dr. Mattingly later described Eisenhower in a detailed medical history, which is the basis for many of the pages that follow, he was likely to get into physical trouble because of his family's tendency to develop circulatory problems and because of the family's emphasis on achievement. The entire Eisenhower family had a history of hypertensive cardiovascular disease, cerebrovascular disease, and coronary disease. Both of Eisenhower's parents lived into their eighties but suffered from high blood pressure and its associated ills and died from it. Beyond question the six Eisenhower brothers, including the general president, were of the same physical bent. Fading family photographs taken in the 1920s, with the father and mother and the sons all sitting on the porch of the Abilene, Kansas, house, show a group of individuals for whom hard work and little play had long since been a way of life.

Along with the work came the tension that could lead to trouble from blood pressure and coronary disease.

In these factors of Eisenhower's makeup, the intense work ethic may have been more important than the physical inheritance. According to the Friedman and Rosenman behavior classification, Mattingly writes, Eisenhower was a Type A personality. Such an individual is careless about health, immoderate in regard to working hours, driven by the need to go at top speed day after day. He is hyperactive to stress, unable to take things as they come. As a youth Eisenhower showed none of the driving ambition and the tension that later became so obvious. Perhaps it was there, but no one recorded it. After graduation from high school in 1908 and three years of working for his father in the Belle Springs Creamery, he went to West Point in 1911, from which he graduated in 1915. At the Military Academy, however, he acquired two habits that physicians later described as causes for concern. One was the way he ate his food—he ate in a great hurry, wolfing it. At first he did it for a reason, and later out of habit. When he arrived at the Point he was a rather tall youth, 5'11", but his weight was 152, impossible for the football team. He took up a crash regimen of eating everything in sight in the dining hall and ran his weight up twenty pounds, making him eligible for the team. He played until his junior year when an injury during a game with Bucknell sent him to the bench and threatened his future military career. Injuring the cartilage in his left knee, he seemingly would not have enough stamina for service with troops. Perhaps equally important in the eyes of the martinets at West Point, he would not be able to ride a horse, then a requirement for all cadets.

The second sign of his Type A personality at West Point was smoking. It is difficult to believe that Eisenhower smoked in Abilene, as his parents would have considered it a habit sanctioned by the devil and a waste of money. Far away at the Academy, however, he was not under their rule but doubtless under the rule of his fellow cadets who must have smoked. In Eisenhower's case it quickly went beyond that, and by the time of World War II his consumption of cigarettes had become immoderate until in 1949, under Dr. Snyder's orders and, as Ike liked to relate, his own, he suddenly quit. By this time he had become a chain smoker, consuming four packs and more a day.

The present narrative is no place to relate Eisenhower's career after he left West Point.[1] Suffice it to say that he moved up rapidly in rank during World War I and by November 1918 was a lieutenant colonel in charge of a large tank cantonment (without any tanks) at Gettysburg, only to revert to captain and then back to major, which rank he held for sixteen years. In the early 1930s he served in Washington in the office of the chief of staff, General MacArthur. In 1935 he went out to the Philippines with MacArthur, whom President Roosevelt had designated to train the troops of the Philippine Commonwealth.

All the while the appearance of the older man whom the nation knew so intimately as a general and president was easy to see in the youth and man of early middle age. The wide forehead topped by sandy hair became the forehead topped by rapidly increasing baldness. The Eisenhower eyes did not simply peer at a visitor, they snapped. The face revealed an easy affability, but behind it was a tension that sometimes came out in irritation or anger and in any event showed a personality desirous of making every minute count. Through the years the face of the youth of Abilene showed the changes of aging, but the purposefulness was always there. In the laughter and occasional high jinks was the feeling that life was a contest in which those who worked to the limit of their physical abilities would win.

It must have been in the thirties, under MacArthur, both in Washington and the Philippines, that Eisenhower's health began to come under a strain for several reasons, most of them related to MacArthur. Although he engaged in no program of physical exercise, he kept fairly well to his football weight at West Point of 172 pounds. But the frustrations of working with his imperious superior were constantly present. In 1932 the general insisted on wearing full uniform and forced Eisenhower to do the same when expelling the so-called Bonus Army, the world war veterans who had camped out near the capitol building in Washington. A photograph was taken of MacArthur and Eisenhower watching the melee as the regular troops sent the bonus veterans on their way with cavalry charges and tear gas. Eisenhower was chagrined to have to perform such duty and wore an expression on his face that Dr. Mattingly was to see many times later, a telltale sign of intense irritability. And in the Philippines it was a series of frustrations working with a totally inadequate budget in training the raw Filipino recruits; the trials of this work wore constantly on his nerves. Then there were the shouting matches with his chief. It was one argument after another, including an occasion when MacArthur instructed Eisenhower to arrange a big parade of Commonwealth troops in Manila, and insisted upon it, though it would have severely depleted the funds available for training; then MacArthur tried to lie his way out of what he had said, and the issue came to shouting.

After his return to the mainland in 1939 a series of duties followed, and in 1941, as is well known, Eisenhower showed up well during Louisiana maneuvers and having already become a colonel was raised to brigadier general. Thence, a few days after Pearl Harbor, to Munitions Building duty in Washington under the approving eye of the chief of staff, General George C. Marshall, promotion to major general that next spring, and assignment to England as commander for the future invasion of the Continent. The Mediterranean campaign intervened in 1942–1943, and then back to England to prepare for D-Day.

The pace from 1941 to 1945 was frantic and given Eisenhower's assignments during the 1930s, the years with MacArthur, most of which he disliked, it could easily have been too much in terms of his health. He seems to have been all right physically, although he was not in the best of shape. The constant strain manifested itself as stomach upsets and sometimes influenza. He was not sleeping well, highly nervous, and smoking four packs a day. The only downright physical disability he suffered was a badly wrenched knee, this on September 3, 1944, when while flying with a pilot in a small observation plane he was forced to land on a beach. He tried to help the pilot push the plane away from the water, and this time—West Point football had affected his left knee—he twisted his right knee. Matters became worse when he had to walk for a mile to a road before being picked up.

There were no problems with his cardiovascular system during the war except for an episode of high blood pressure in 1943. People who saw the general talked of blowups, which he usually controlled when confronted by the prime subjects of his animus, such as General Bernard L. Montgomery. It is difficult to draw much from the blowups, which might be considered, and some of them he doubtless staged as, theatrical necessities of being a general. He made no mention of chest pain in any examination prior to 1945. On one occasion in 1943 while conducting the Mediterranean campaign from Algiers, he returned to headquarters from Sicily where matters were complicated militarily; he was attempting to get the Badoglio government in Italy to surrender, which involved endless consultations with military and civil officials in London and Washington, and his staff assistant, Commander Harry C. Butcher, reported Eisenhower's visit to a dispensary to take a physical examination for promotion to colonel in the regular army. The doctors found his blood pressure too high and prescribed bed rest. During the war, with its attendant confusions, the army maintained a two-tier rank system, one for temporary officers AUS (army of the United States), the other for RA (regular army), in which a regular army officer might hold a higher AUS rank. Eisenhower was a general AUS and a lieutenant colonel RA. Fortunately, when he took the physical exam a second time his blood pressure did not reveal any elevation. (As for his promotion, it turned out that because of General Marshall's intervention he was promoted to major general RA.)[2]

The only other possible sign of cardiovascular disease during the war was the rather odd prescription of testosterone given him by Major General Alfred Kenner, supposedly because of mild arterial hypertension. Eisenhower so told a urological consultant, Colonel Lloyd G. Lewis, in 1946 and said he felt it helped. Such could hardly have been the case; it could have made any hypertension worse. In 1946, he was still taking it and was promptly taken off it.[3]

The next four years, 1945–1949, constituted another frustrating period in Eisenhower's life, worth retelling because outsiders, looking upon his remarkable progress in rank from lieutenant colonel in 1939 to five-star general in 1945, tended to believe everything had been onward and upward. In terms of incessant frustration, the war years with all their troubles are easy to understand, even if rapid promotion accompanied them. What often is overlooked in Eisenhower's medical history is that the next years when matters might have seemed much easier, his duties almost tailor-made for relaxation after the arduous wartime assignments, were equally difficult.

At first everything was all right. The general came back to the United States in triumph after the end of the European conflict and toured New York and Washington and Abilene, holding up his arms in a V sign and grinning his boyish smile. Back for a while in Germany, he was hospitalized there for treatment of bronchitis. At that time an EKG showed his cardiovascular system normal with no persistent hypertension or any clinical features of hypertension or coronary heart disease.

Then he returned to the United States to become army chief of staff, a job that he did not like. The office might have gone to his army group commander, General Omar N. Bradley, but President Harry S. Truman already had commandeered Bradley to head the Veterans Administration, then a key job for it required its head to supervise the benefits of the newly released veterans of World War II. Truman promised Eisenhower that he would bring in Bradley as chief of staff as soon as he could—that the assignment would be only temporary. Instead it lasted nearly three years until the summer of 1948. Eisenhower's first task naturally was to arrange demobilization of the millions of men drafted or enlisted who were no longer needed, and demobilization was intensely difficult and required constant testimony before Congress. Then, too, it was dispiriting to see the collapse of the huge force that had ensured victory over Germany and Japan.

A second problem during this era was Mrs. Eisenhower, who was not in a good mood. The exact reason for her displeasure was a chauffeur-receptionist in her husband's wartime headquarters, at first a member of the British transport corps, then a lieutenant in the U.S. Army. The Kay Summersby story has since become a staple of historical and public gossip. At worst Eisenhower had committed an indiscretion by engaging an attractive British subject as his driver; Kay Summersby was too pretty to drive a general's car. The same held for her duties as a receptionist in headquarters. There is not a scintilla of proof that anything happened beyond a few bridge games. But Mrs. Eisenhower thought it more than that, having been supplied gossip, one supposes, by her Washington bridge group, and she had applied to her absent husband for information in August 1945. Lieutenant Summersby was of Irish extraction, and the general's wife wrote that she supposed him "highly interested in Ireland." At this point he made a grave error. For whatever reason he chose not to face the music with his wife of almost thirty years and wrote Mamie a piece of fluff about how he once had spent twenty-four hours in Ireland, getting there one evening, carrying out a schedule that would have killed a horse, leaving under weather conditions that compelled a bad landing in England where he was weathered in for eighty-six hours. "But I certainly didn't stay in Ireland a second longer than I expected and only ⅓ as long as the dignitaries desired."[4] Thereafter he was in trouble.

When he returned to the United States in November 1945 to become chief of staff, Mamie did not want to move out of her small apartment at the Wardman Park Hotel into the luxurious Quarters Number One at Fort Myer, home to chiefs of staff. The army's chief of staff seems to have enlisted Dr. Snyder's assistance (not long before, he had treated Mamie for pneumonia) in getting her out of the Wardman Park. A consultant physician recommended phenobarbital. Mamie hated phenobarbital. Snyder, an old army doctor, was equal to such an emergency. He labeled a compound with a flavored extract of cascara, "Fluid Extract Rhamnns Purshianna 54.0, Elixir Phenylethylmalonylurea qs ad 240.0," which is another way of saying "Elixir of Phenobarbital." But that did not work. From Snyder's draft medical history of Eisenhower, which describes this incident, the archivists of the Eisenhower Library have excised six pages. It was necessary almost to transport her physically to Quarters Number One. Mrs. Eisenhower was off the reservation until the summer of 1948 when a book appeared by the peripatetic Kay, by that time in New York City, relating that she had been nothing more than a driver and receptionist and bridge partner.[5] At that late date, after thirty months of irritability, Mamie Eisenhower relented.

After the bad duty in the Pentagon and the reproaches of an angry wife, the possibility opened of a pleasant retirement—nominally a relief from duty because Eisenhower as a five-star general could technically not retire—beginning in the summer of 1948 as president of Columbia University with a large house in the city where the Eisenhowers could associate with a group of people quite different from army and political brass. As Eisenhower undertook the presidency of Columbia, succeeding the ailing Nicholas Murray Butler who had held the university's presidency for nearly fifty years, he must have looked forward to the presidential office high up in Low Memorial Library. It was accessible by a small elevator where his military aide Major Robert L. Schulz (his active duty status permitted several officers and enlisted men as assistants) would screen applicants for his time. He could represent the university to the public and seek endowment funds, leaving academic details to academicians.

But then came a third disturbance to the general's equanimity, and this was the cloud of politics, which appeared on the horizon in the first postwar years no larger than a man's hand. In the springtime and early summer of 1948, just when he was beginning at Columbia, came a frantic attempt to gain his permission to run him as a candidate. Oddly, the attempt was made by Democrats. The Republican party was securely in the hands of Governor Thomas E. Dewey, who was not about to miss the chance of the presidency during a year in which all the omens were for Republican victory.

In 1944 Dewey had given Roosevelt a run for his money, and years later the chairman of the Republican national committee, Herbert Brownell, attorney general during the Eisenhower administration, would remark that the Republicans could have won if they would have used the issue of Roosevelt's health. A council of war was held on this subject, with Brownell in favor, but the candidate, Dewey, flatly refused; he thought it would be unpatriotic in the midst of the war.[6] Four years later Dewey saw no trouble with the election and easily edged out any Eisenhower boom, which had hardly gathered around the GOP for in those days Eisenhower's party affiliation was unknown. On the Democratic side, however, the desire to get Truman off the ticket was widespread. Truman himself was thoroughly aware of it and not very sure he could defeat any landslide at the convention once it started. His emissaries at first obtained a fairly mild "no" from the general. At near the end of Truman's patience, just before the Philadelphia convention, he asked for and obtained a "General Sherman." Interestingly, Chester Bowles, who among other Democrats talked with Eisenhower late that uncertain spring, found the general hoping that both parties might nominate him by acclamation. Bowles pronounced him politically innocent, but the matter was closer than Bowles thought, the general's innocence hardly proved.[7]

Suffice it to say that during the Democratic maneuvering of the spring and early summer of 1948, Eisenhower again was highstrung, tense, and uncertain about his future. Yet a nomination passed him by, even though during the Philadelphia Democratic convention a sound truck stood opposite the hall blaring Eisenhower propaganda. After all this, and convention time passed, and Truman's "whistlestop" campaign brought the biggest upset in the history of presidential elections, he received an assignment from the president that was at least as awkward for his cardiovascular system as had been the office of chief of staff, the irritabilities of his wife, and the frustration over the presidential election. This was his appointment by Truman as acting chairman of the joint chiefs of staff. The chiefs were fighting over the military budget, and the president needed someone to control them.

When Truman chose Eisenhower as acting chairman of the joint chiefs he, the president, thought he had solved a problem. Eisenhower believed the president was trying to solve another problem, the general's candidacy for the 1952 presidential election. As president of Columbia, Eisenhower was not an open candidate. To all visitors he said that politics were not for him. But he was doing nothing to quiet his supporters, and his every action seemed calculated to prepare him for the election. Then Truman gave him a hot potato, the task of going down to Washington once or twice a week and presiding over the chiefs. Eisenhower may be forgiven for believing that the president did this on purpose, to give him a job that he could not possibly handle, showing the American public that whatever the general's wartime triumphs they did not extend to the postwar era. Years later, after Truman and Eisenhower both had left the presidency, the retired Republican president could not get this appointment out of his mind, and told Dr. Mattingly repeatedly that Truman did this to him.[8]

With an intense feeling of disgust that he was being "had," Eisenhower set out to work with the chiefs, and it was not long before he found that these relatively young men, secondary to him in command during World War II, were defying him. Bradley was thoroughly cooperative; there was no trouble with him. But the air force chief of staff and the chief of naval operations and all their supporters were, each in his certitude, totally uncooperative. They made agreements only to break them or go public with disagreements. Everything went wrong. The administration wobbled, willing to provide half a billion more, but that was not enough in a total military budget of $11 billion that Truman intended to lower the next year. In Washington on March 14, 1949, Eisenhower wrote to General Henry H. Arnold, "I am so weary of this inter-service struggle for position, prestige and power that this morning I practically 'blew my top.' " He added, interestingly, "I would hate to have my doctor take my blood pressure at the moment." On March 19 he wrote in his diary, "The situation grows intolerable."[9]

By this time Eisenhower's personal physician was Snyder, who had been looking after him since the general's return from Europe in November 1945. He had come back to find that Snyder had been seeing Mamie and thereupon made him his personal doctor.

Snyder had had a long career in the army medical corps. Born in Cheyenne in 1881, he attended the University of Wyoming from 1899 to 1901 and graduated from Philadelphia's Jefferson Medical College in 1905—where he doubtless studied with Dr. Keen. He seems to have liked the military life. Medical practice in civilian life then was frequently unremunerative—physicians' incomes were not much better than those of other professional people. The army offered regular employment and the hope of advancement. After becoming a contract physician at Fort Douglas, Utah, he joined up in 1908. As the years passed, Snyder advanced, until the vast expansion of the medical corps during World War II gave opportunity of high rank, brigadier and major general. He was ready for retirement in 1945, but Eisenhower who had met him in Europe made him his personal physician and kept him on active duty. He served the Eisenhowers throughout the years that the general was chief of staff, 1945–1948. After Eisenhower assumed the presidency of Columbia, he asked Snyder to retire from the army and serve as senior adviser to the university's Conservation of Human Resources Project and as his personal physician. Snyder moved to New York.

Snyder was intensely political in his outlook. He sensed the possibility that, if not in 1949, then in 1953, he might return to active duty as personal physician to the president of the United States. When in 1949 he was urging Eisenhower to quit smoking he argued, among other reasons, that it would be good politics.

> I used many arguments, among them telling him the story of how Willkie lost his voice when in the midst of his campaign because his throat played out on him; that the nose and throat specialist who treated him said that smoking so many cigarettes had a great deal to do with it. I cited the fact that he might become very dependent upon his voice in the midst of a campaign for a public office.[10]

2.

Two serious episodes in the next years, the more important one in early 1949 and a second attack in April 1953, seemed medical fulfillments of the combination of Eisenhower's family background and upbringing and the nearly two decades of tension that marked his life during the 1930s and 1940s. In retrospect, looking at all the signs, and a very considerable body of medical evidence, it does appear as if Eisenhower suffered two heart attacks before he underwent his major attack in 1955.

It almost goes without saying that Snyder understood very well what those attacks could have meant for his charge's political career. Had word of the first become public, Eisenhower could not have secured the Republican nomination in 1952. If the second had become known, people would have linked it with the attack of 1955 and beheld a series, and he would not have been able to convince them, as he did, that he was able to serve a second term.

Snyder's problem, or so he felt it to be, was to prevent Eisenhower from self-destructing physically. The doctor had reason to fear for his patient's cardiovascular system. In describing the years just after the war when there were strained relations with Mrs. Eisenhower, he later wrote that

> the possibility of serious damage to General Eisenhower's health was evidenced to me on these occasions by the twisted cord-like temporal arteries standing out on the sides of his head. There was

little I could do about it. My forty years in the practice of medicine taught me that I should not get into the middle of it. This, however, did not relieve my anxiety. I feared that at some time the General might suffer a cerebral accident.[11]

During an episode on January 21, 1947, he acutely feared the possibility of a stroke. On that date Eisenhower asked him to come to his office where shortly after 8:00 A.M. he found the general in straits, sitting at his desk supporting his head on his folded hands. He said he felt perfectly well when leaving home, but that when he got out of his car he felt wobbly and had trouble getting into the elevator, and once inside had to support himself against the wall. The elevator opened directly into his office so that without too much difficulty he was able to navigate to his desk. As Snyder recalled,

> I thought immediately that he might have had a vasospasm in a branch of the middle cerebral artery. I didn't feel it wise to quiz him as to whether or not there had been any upsetting incident immediately before he left the house because, had I referred to it, it might have exaggerated the reaction if such a situation had been the cause. I immediately assisted him to the elevator and to his car, and we set forth for Walter Reed.[12]

On arrival at the hospital after this affair everything seemed all right. Colonel Charles R. Mueller, the chief of medicine, examined him, and reported a blood pressure of 150/100. He diagnosed Ménière's syndrome, a hemorrhage into the semicircular canals of the internal ear, in Eisenhower's case perhaps only fluid, and after rapid clearing of the symptoms the general went home the following day by which time his blood pressure was normal.

A few days later Eisenhower and Snyder were in New York, and Snyder arranged to have him seen in consultation by Dr. David B. Barr, physician-in-chief at New York Hospital and professor of medicine at Cornell University. At that time Eisenhower's blood pressure was normal, 130/80. Barr did a very complete cardiovascular examination, including fluoroscopy of the heart and EKGs, and considered the general to possess a normal cardiovascular system. He thought the chief manifestation of the episode was severe dizziness and associated difficulty in standing and walking, but no true vertigo, ringing (tinnitus), or hearing loss. He said nothing about Ménière's syndrome. He considered the possibility of cerebral transient ischemia (deficiency of blood, local anemia) and evaluated circulation in the carotid arteries for presence of occlusive lesions. He checked for bradycardia (slow action of the heart). He found nothing.

Years afterward Eisenhower's cardiologist, Dr. Mattingly, concluded that it was difficult to know what to draw out of this apparent episode of hypertension. The same held for times when Eisenhower was riled up, occasions that frightened Snyder. For them Snyder seems not to have dared to take blood pressure readings. "It was well," he wrote, "to keep out of his way when he was angered."[13] Without such readings it was impossible to establish what happened. In November 1947, the general went to Walter Reed for a medical survey that included an evaluation by Colonel James S. Taylor, chief of cardiology. Taylor considered him to have a labile (up-and-down) blood pressure but no evidence of long-standing hypertension, hypertensive heart disease, or cerebrovascular disease. He did find the average pressure of several determinations to be 156/92, mild hypertension by later standards. After Eisenhower's death an autopsy revealed a small adrenal tumor, which could have caused the hypertension. The pathologist considered it too small to be functioning and did not check it out.

One turns to the probable heart attack of 1949, a serious incident when it happened on March 21, with the general staying at the Statler Hotel in Washington. He was there in his role as acting chairman of the joint chiefs of staff. As he described the attack in a small volume of reminiscences entitled *At Ease*, published in 1967,

> On the evening of March 21, 1949, I stretched out in my Washington hotel room, and knew that I was sick. General Howard Snyder, my physician, treated me as though I were at the end of the precipice and teetering a bit. For days, my head was not off the pillow. The doctors transferred me to Key West, Florida, and I remained on the sick list, forbidden solid food and cigarettes. During most of that time, I was so ill that I missed neither.[14]

How to interpret this affair that Eisenhower described as a "collapse"? It seems almost certain it was a heart attack. To the present day, however, no final proof has appeared, and perhaps none ever will, for a combination of circumstances conspired to keep the affair quiet.

Eisenhower himself was unwilling to describe the attack in any detail other than what he set out in *At Ease*. This account astonished Mattingly, who never heard of it before 1967. When the general president had given his cardiologist a history of his illnesses, preliminary to examination at Walter Reed in 1952, he never mentioned it. In 1967, Eisenhower presented Mattingly with a copy of *At Ease*, and after reading his description of the 1949 illness Mattingly talked with him. He could get nothing out of him, other than a recitation of the problems with the joint chiefs and with Truman who, as mentioned, Eisenhower believed had tried to get him into a losing battle with the chiefs. Mattingly made several attempts to get him to talk but could only get a repeated response that he had a "collapse from which it took time to recover." There was no mention of the signs of gastroenteritis: abdominal pain, abdominal gaseous distention, vomiting, difficulty in moving bowels. Nor did he give symptoms suggestive of a heart attack or of coronary disease or treatment for the same. The cardiologist pushed him as far as he could, and then "I realized that he was not anxious to discuss the subject further as he kept going back to the Pentagon and the Truman situation. I realized that he was indirectly telling me I was on a touchy subject, so I terminated my prodding, hoping to be more successful on the next try."[15]

Nor was Mattingly able to get anything out of Snyder, who never told him about the episode. By the time *At Ease* appeared, Snyder's health had failed. He had been Eisenhower's personal physician during the years after he normally would have retired, hence was in his seventies when he was on active duty at request of the president of the United States. When he retired for the final time, in 1961, he received an office near Walter Reed so he could work on a proposed medical history of Eisenhower and also follow the latter's hospitalizations after retirement from the presidency. But the next year, 1962, Snyder developed a tumor of the lung, and the year afterward suffered the first of a series of strokes that affected him physically and mentally. In the latter 1960s he was, as Mattingly put it, in a "vegetative state." He died in 1970, one year after his famous patient.

The year of Eisenhower's death, 1969, with prodding from the surgeon general, Mattingly considered undertaking a cardiovascular history of Eisenhower and believed he might find something in Snyder's papers on Eisenhower's earlier and suspiciously unclear illness. Then in 1983 when he finally had access to Snyder's papers, he found that the materials Snyder had collected and arranged to be deposited in the Dwight D. Eisenhower Library in Abilene were hardly helpful. Snyder's papers suggested that he had engaged in a cover-up of the illness of 1949. He had begun, Mattingly suspected, with a letter of

April 13, 1949, to Dr. Herbert A. Black of Pueblo, Colorado, an old friend of Mrs. Eisenhower's family, the Douds, a letter he found in Snyder's papers explaining that what had occurred was a "simple, though very acute, gastroenteritis, induced by indulgence in a Mexican supper of chili con carne and tamales."[16] The letter went into great detail in setting out normal cardiovascular findings. It mentioned no suspicious cardiac symptoms. Why Snyder wrote such a detailed letter, saving a copy ostentatiously for his files, was odd. Mattingly suspected it was a "plant" to emphasize for posterity that the general's problem was not cardiac. But, then, beginning in 1956 a plant was no longer necessary. That year Eisenhower was diagnosed as suffering from Crohn's disease, a malady in which rough food lodging in the terminal part of the small intestine where it joins the large intestine gradually scars the ileum, twisting it, creating the likelihood of an obstruction that requires surgery. Shortly after the diagnosis Eisenhower had a severe obstruction and underwent an operation to rid him of the problem; therefore, Snyder had a perfect diagnosis. In his draft medical history for the 1949 illness, he then added more evidence that he was not about to let anyone know anything if it stood in the way of a political career for his illustrious patient. "Nothing leaked out to the press or to anyone who might reveal a confidence about the probability of an intestinal obstruction being responsible for the abdominal attack the General had suffered," he wrote. "I feared that if the General got into politics, someone would surely pin upon him the label that he was a chronic invalid and couldn't stand the strain of office."[17]

Mattingly also began to question the completeness of the papers that Snyder left, which included letters, the draft history, a diary begun in November 1955, and copies of medical records. Here he found a disturbing situation. There were two sets of records. The president's physician had kept his own records from 1945 onward, and they were disappointingly sparse, indeed, surprisingly so. It was quite possible that he winnowed them, taking out, say, any EKGs that displayed alarming heights, removing evidences of his treating Eisenhower for heart attacks rather than, as he claimed, gastroenteritis. In attempting the medical history Snyder, too, had borrowed records from various sources dealing with the years from 1945 until the 1955 major attack and made copies of pertinent items. He had returned the originals to the office of the surgeon general, after which they disappeared. There was absolutely no way that Mattingly could check out the papers deposited in the library after Snyder's death in 1970. In the instance of Snyder's own records, there could have been a culling of anything that might have brought embarrassment. As for the borrowed records from the medical records depot in St. Louis, lent to Snyder in 1956, the originals were gone. Snyder's office stated that they were returned to the depot through the office of the surgeon general before 1961.

During the period of 1980–1987, Mattingly moved slowly in developing his cardiological history. He retired from the army in 1958 but continued as a civilian consultant to the army, the White House, and the department of state until his final retirement in early 1980. But as he thought about the Snyder situation, he recalled uneasily his own relations with his predecessor Taylor at Walter Reed. He had been an assistant to Taylor in 1950–1951; Taylor retired in the latter year. Taylor was, as Mattingly later drew him, "a very quiet gentleman, extremely well-qualified in his specialty, very modest and never boastful." On retirement he turned over copies of his records of the VIP military patients he had been following. Those records included Eisenhower, and in his file was a 1947 complete evaluation but nothing for the year 1949. In passing the records to Mattingly Taylor said, "You will probably be seeing him some day." Nothing more. Mattingly felt certain that if Snyder had asked or suggested to Taylor that a record of any 1949 consultation be kept out of the files, Taylor would have obliged. In that regard, the possibility of such a consultation, General Bradley related in his autobiography that Eisenhower had gone to Walter Reed just before going down to Key West after his gastrointestinal attack of March 1949. Taylor hence might have kept any account of it out of the file. Mattingly and Taylor liked each other and continued their association after his retirement until his death. He frequently asked how Eisenhower was doing, especially after the heart attack in 1955. In describing this odd situation Mattingly added, "I always had a feeling that he wished to tell me something."[18]

The project of a cardiological history languished until 1982 when Mattingly attended the annual meeting of the Association of Medical Consultants to the Armed Forces and there renewed his acquaintance with Colonel Charles L. Leedham, who had been chief of medicine at Oliver General Hospital in Augusta before it closed in 1950. What he heard from Leedham shocked him. Leedham had known of Mattingly's association with Eisenhower but had never made any comments or engaged in any discussion of Eisenhower's illness. But then, at the medical meeting, thirteen years after the death of Eisenhower, twelve after Snyder died, "he made a very boastful statement to me and to others in the gathering": at the time he was at Oliver General he treated Eisenhower for a heart attack sometime during 1947–1950. Mattingly told him that he, Mattingly, was seeking information on heart attacks prior to 1955. Leedham instantly "clammed up."[19]

It proved impossible to get anything out of Leedham, who claimed he kept no notes, records, or a diary and did not even remember the time of year or exact year when Eisenhower was a patient. Mattingly asked if Snyder was involved in the hospitalization and care, and he said that Snyder and Eisenhower's aide, Schulz, were in almost constant attendance. Snyder participated in the evaluations, and Schulz essentially guarded the door. He said the hospitalization was a very "hush-hush affair." He offered as evidence of his participation in Eisenhower's care his possession of a large inscribed photograph of the general. In subsequent months Mattingly made efforts to obtain more information, both by phone and letter, "but he just continued to provide excuses, chiefly that of not remembering after the long period of 33 years since the event."

The situation was tantalizing. There can be no question but that Eisenhower was at Oliver General. In Snyder's papers were copies of laboratory studies at Oliver General requested by Leedham on April 19–26, 1949. After Eisenhower had gone down to Key West he had stayed about three weeks and then went up to Augusta where he spent a month playing golf and putting himself, so Snyder would have said, Eisenhower too, and this was what the newspaper press learned, in shape. The lab studies requested by Leedham, in the Snyder papers, had no hospital register number on them. There was no copy of an EKG or record of a cardiology consultation. In the latter respect Mattingly noted that Leedham, an internist, considered himself also a cardiologist and doubtless would not have asked his chief of cardiology to perform an evaluation or provide treatment on his VIP patient.

The conversation with Leedham galvanized Mattingly to begin anew the project he had been toying with, the cardiological history, and to turn it into a full-scale medical history. He was now retired from private practice and so the free time was available. As he thought about what Leedham said, he could only conclude that years before Snyder had sworn Leedham to secrecy. He believed Leedham violated that secrecy by the remarks at the meeting in 1982, and thereafter backed away from them. Leedham, in poor health, died in 1985. Oliver General Hospital had closed in 1950, and its records should have been deposited in the medical records depot, but they were not included in records made available from the depot in 1984.

For the 1949 attack circumstances all pointed in the direction of a heart attack, and there was one piece of evidence that corroborated that diagnosis. Mattingly, now engaged in the full-scale history, found it in 1983 among the papers of Snyder in the Eisenhower Library. Presumably Snyder as he covered up everything that might have revealed the heart attack had failed to eliminate this evidence. Snyder was going downhill physically and probably could not quite control the paper record that surrounded his famous patient. He had gotten out, presumably, most of the records that revealed a heart attack, but he kept an EKG dated April 5, 1949, made at the U.S. Naval Hospital at Key West. There were no copies of EKGs before or after. Actually none seemed to have survived between the years 1943 and 1947 (1947 being the year when Eisenhower was at Walter Reed under Taylor's care). None seemingly was made during Eisenhower's assignment to NATO as supreme commander in 1950–1952. The first, thereafter, were for 1952, made at Walter Reed in June and Fitzsimons General Hospital in Denver in August when the Eisenhowers were visiting Mamie Eisenhower's mother, Mrs. Doud. Still, the EKG for April 1949 survived.

The EKG made at Key West was very interesting. Its date meant that it was made two weeks after the onset of the illness of March 21. Unlike the EKGs of 1947 and 1952, the Key West recording was abnormal. It was interpreted as normal at the time—the probable reason, Mattingly thought, for its retention in the Snyder papers. But his interpretation and that of other reviewing cardiologists was that it had abnormalities. In the technical language it had "abnormalities in the ST segments and T waves in the right precordial leads compatible with a resolving anteroseptal damage such as may result from an intramural anteroseptal infarction of two weeks' duration. Similar ST-T waves could possibly result from a localized pericarditis, but this would be extremely unlikely." This single EKG made two weeks after onset, and without later EKGs at Oliver General, made an absolute electrocardiographic diagnosis impossible. But as Mattingly concluded, "The single tracing, however, does fall into the category of an abnormal electrocardiogram suspicious of myocardial damage and, therefore, would be included as a risk factor in a male of 59 years of age."[20]

The evidence of another heart attack in April 1953, after Eisenhower was in the presidency, was of an episode exactly similar to that of March 1949 except that the latter attack was much less difficult, only a slight affair, not in any sense requiring nearly two months of recovery that followed upon the attack of 1949. In this instance Eisenhower did not go to bed immediately but continued his daily activities, somehow getting through the attack without a collapse, public or private.

The trouble came on April 16, 1953, in the midst of an important speech to the American Society of Newspaper Editors. The president's press secretary, James C. Hagerty, prompted by Snyder, told the press that the cause was "a slight attack of food poisoning."[21] Mattingly in review firmly believes it was another heart attack, if only a small one. In his memoir, *The White House Years*, Eisenhower described what happened:

> The night before its scheduled delivery I endured an attack, one that several years later was diagnosed as the same kind that occasioned a serious operation for [Crohn's disease]. . . . The doctor provided medicines and sedatives, but when the time came for the luncheon at which my talk was to be made, the pain was such as to cause heavy perspiration on my face and head, and at the same time, chills of a very disturbing kind. The result was that I could concentrate on the text only by supreme effort; at times I became so dizzy that I feared I would faint. Immediately after lunch I had a short period for rest, but unfortunately the day's schedule called for two additional engagements. The first was the President's traditional presence in Washington at the opening game of the American League. Since my promise had been given weeks ahead, I felt it would be putting too important an interpretation on what I thought was a temporary illness if I should cancel the engagement. After leaving the ball game I had another appearance to make, this one in Salisbury, North Carolina, celebrating on that day the two-hundredth anniversary of Rowan County. I spoke for about ten minutes, and the press reported that I seemed to be enjoying myself. Finally, that evening in Augusta, I went to bed and with the continuous care of my very knowledgeable doctor, General Snyder, was able to get back on my feet within another thirty-six hours.[22]

In the years after this attack neither Snyder nor Eisenhower connected the episode with the heart attack of 1955. In evaluations later in 1953, 1954, and 1955, to Mattingly and to Dr. Edwin M. Goyette, cardiologist at Fitzsimons in Denver, neither man gave them any history of this second earlier illness and denied the presence of any previous cardiac attacks or symptoms. In the memoirs Eisenhower again stressed his feeling of a state of collapse or impending collapse. There was neither vomiting nor abdominal distention. Such description was more common in a heart attack rather than a gastrointestinal attack. But he kept to Snyder's diagnoses of gastrointestinal problems—"that the attack was like the episode of intestinal obstruction associated with the chronic [Crohn's disease] ileitis requiring surgery in 1956."[23] The conclusion must be, as Mattingly has made it in his medical history, that there is "abundant evidence" that the illnesses of 1949 and 1953 were heart attacks.

4
Crisis

The major heart attack that President Eisenhower suffered in September 1955 caused Dr. Mattingly no end of concern. In part he worried over his patient because he liked Ike and did not want to see him hurt. He was alarmed when he heard the news. His wife, Fran, interrupted him while he was working at his desk at home to say that the commanding general of Walter Reed, Major General Leonard D. Heaton, was on the phone, and that from the sound of his voice something terrible must have happened. When Heaton came on, the message was clear enough. "Tom," he said, "the president is in F.G.H. [Fitzsimons General Hospital] with a heart attack. They want you to .come to Denver immediately." General Snyder, Heaton said, desired him to bring the president's records from the Walter Reed cardiac clinic. Heaton said he would have a car sent around to take him to the Military Air Transport Service terminal at National Airport.[1]

Beyond his sadness over Eisenhower's attack, Mattingly was concerned because of something that happened that night on the plane out to Denver. On board, in addition to the crew, were only two other people, Press Secretary Hagerty and Merriman Smith, White House correspondent of United Press International. Smith sat down with Mattingly and without the slightest tact said that Eisenhower had earlier heart attacks and why had Mattingly covered them up? He was quite insistent and soon became obnoxious, shoving himself forward perhaps in an effort to "get a rise out of" the doctor. After a while of this, Mattingly excused himself, said he had to get some rest, and went to the back of the plane to sit by himself.

Smith, he knew, was not the nicest person around, yet what he said was disquieting. The reporter considered himself the dean of the Washington press corps. During the Roosevelt administration he had arrogated to himself the right to say, "Thank you, Mr. President," at the end of press conferences. That was the signal for everyone to rush for the telephones. He was a schemer and a bit of a manipulator. During the Truman administration he quickly calculated in 1948 that Truman would lose, Dewey would win, and without further ado attached himself to Dewey, only to have to slink back to Truman after the voters proved him wrong. Thus, in his conversation with Mattingly, Smith was probably pushing his point, as was his wont.[2] But after going to the back of the plane Mattingly did not rest, as he told Smith he was going to do; he carefully reviewed Eisenhower's medical records. They included all records of known illnesses since 1947. They did not contain any history of diagnoses of or treatment for prior heart attacks, only a history of a labile hypertension.

1.

Upon arrival in Denver, Mattingly soon discovered that the president's personal physician, Dr. Snyder, had not been handling Eisenhower in the way he should have. Snyder simply was not the right person at the right place and time.

Consider at the outset the location of Denver, a mile above sea level, and then the Byers Peak Ranch where the president had gone with a congenial group of cronies, owned in part by an old Doud family friend, the Denver financier Aksel Nielsen. The ranch was 2,500 feet beyond the height of Denver. Both locales would require some adjusting to because of the altitude, so if Eisenhower exercised too quickly, say by playing golf, he could strain his heart. To be sure, Denver's chance location as the home of Mrs. Doud, a place to which the Eisenhowers had been going for years, made it hardly possible for Snyder to have forbidden them access; he could never have done such a thing. Moreover, the president perhaps found it reassuring to be in Denver near Fitzsimons, a general hospital he had used for many years. He actually arranged to have his appendix taken out there in 1923—a move that showed his concern over the stomach upsets he had suffered, in those days doubtless signs of the Crohn's disease he would have finally defined and eliminated in 1956. Still, it was up to Snyder to calculate his charge's preferences in terms of what they might do to Eisenhower's health.

The doctor reported the president without symptoms on the several-day stay at the Byers Peak Ranch but left no record of having taken his blood pressure during that period. Nor were there records that he had done so during the seven previous weeks since the president's arrival from Washington. Mattingly had recommended blood pressure checks because during Ike's 1954 summer vacation in Denver the Fitzsimons cardiologist, Colonel Goyette, had observed heightened blood pressure. Mattingly thought the altitude might have been a factor. Eisenhower had gone to Walter Reed where Mattingly had seen him just before leaving for the vacation, and at that time his signs were normal. The cardiologist was unsure of the Denver area, and he had apprised Snyder.

When Mattingly later discovered what Eisenhower had been doing on the day preceding the president's illness in the middle of the night, he found the description similarly disconcerting. The president had been playing golf beginning that morning of September 23 at the course at Cherry Hills. He had hardly begun when word came that Secretary of State John Foster Dulles was calling on the telephone from Washington. Eisenhower went to the clubhouse to discover that Dulles could not wait, was en route to an engagement, and would call again in an hour. At the appointed hour the president found the lines in trouble. A third time he went back and talked with Dulles. The party then decided to stay through the noon hour because the game had been interrupted by the phone calls, and for lunch everyone had "a huge hamburger . . . generously garnished with slices of Bermuda onion and accompanied by a pot of coffee."[3] Back on the course he was called off a fourth time, only to discover that someone along the line thought Dulles wanted to get through again, and Dulles did not. By this time the president was riled up, almost angry, not so much at Dulles as simply at all the nonsense about going to the phone.

For an individual subject to bouts of intense anger when the arteries on the side of his head could stand out, the telephone jaunts were not at all beneficial to his health. Eisenhower himself afterward believed that the ruining of his golf game plus the huge hamburger caused his subsequent symptoms, which unbeknownst to him revealed all the preliminaries, and perhaps more than that, of a heart attack. That day he played twenty-seven holes—nine of them in the afternoon. An uneasiness developed in his stomach that he mistook for indigestion. On the twenty-sixth hole he told the golf professional, Ralph (Rip) Arnold, with whom he was playing, "Boy, those raw onions are sure backing up on me." That evening he and George Allen and their wives ate dinner at the Doud house, and afterward the two men were in the basement knocking billiard balls about and contemplated a drink but decided against it because they were tired and expected to go to bed early.[4]

The attack came in the middle of the night and is best described in a little bedside memorandum made the next morning by Snyder. When Mattingly years later reviewed Snyder's medical history of Eisenhower's 1955 heart attack as deposited in the library, he and Lieutenant Colonel Olive F. G. Marsh found this memo. It was undoubtedly Snyder's as they both recognized his handwriting. It is entitled, "Memorandum made at bedside between 7 A.M. and 11 A.M."[5]

> Sept. 24 '55—
> 2:54 A.M. Mrs. Eisenhower called. Said Pres. had pain in his chest about 2:45 A.M. She had given milk of magnesia. No relief, pain getting worse. (Mrs. E. told me later that about 2:30 A.M. she had gone to the bathroom, passing the door to his bedroom on her return. She heard him muttering in his sleep, she stopped at his bedside and asked him if he was having a nightmare—"Ike" replied "No, dear, but thank you" and smiled. About ten minutes later, she had returned to bed, he came to her bedside and said "I've got a pain in my lower chest." It was for that reason and because "Ike" had spoken of having indigestion the prior afternoon that she gave him the milk of magnesia, which frequently before had relieved such symptoms.)
>
> 3:11 A.M. I arrived at the house (by chauffeur's watch). As soon as I arrived, listened to the President's heart and took blood pressure, I realized it was a heart injury. BP 160/120, pulse 90. The President was restless and alarmed. I broke a vaporole of amyl nitrite and gave it to him to sniff while I prepared and injected a 2 cc. ampule of papaverine hydrochloride (1 grain). I then prepared and injected immediately ¼ grain morphine sulphate. The patient was still restless although his pulse had steadied and blood pressure was coming down. About 20 min. later I gave him by intramuscular injection an ampule of heparin—10,000 units. The Pres. was still restless. I therefore gave him a second injection of ¼ gr. morphine sulphate—about 45 minutes after arrival. I had kept sphygmomanometer [blood pressure cuff] on arm. Blood pressure had dropped to 130/80—pulse 68.
>
> I asked Mamie about 4:35 A.M. to slip into bed with the President to see if this would not quiet him and assist in warming his body. He had developed a cold sweat in the meantime. Moaney [Sgt. John Moaney, orderly] had brought a couple of hot water bottles early and we used warm 195 proof alcohol to dry his skin. The President had desired to go to the toilet about 4:30 A.M. Mrs. D. and Moaney did not know where they could quickly find the bed pan. The Pres. said he did not want to use it. I therefore supported him to the bathroom. He had a b.m. and expelled a good deal of gas. He felt more comfortable and shortly after Mamie got into bed he was quiet.

At 12:15 P.M. Snyder called the commanding general at Fitzsimons, Major General Martin E. Griffin, and asked for a cardiogram.

The hospital doctors were there in a hurry and in forty-five minutes the Fitzsimons cardiologist, Colonel Byron E. Pollock, had taken an EKG and suggested that the damage was more than nine hours old. This observation together with the patient's description of indigestion during the preceding afternoon raised the question whether the myocardial damage began at that time or in the early morning hours of September 24.

While this private drama was being played out in the Doud house, with most of the residents of Denver sound asleep and unaware of the president's condition, Dr. Snyder covered up the heart attack. Ann Whitman, private secretary to the president, was in Denver and kept a diary. The following is her account of what she learned from the president's private physician:

> The next morning [September 24] General Snyder called me at about six-forty-five to say the president would not be in early—he might be in at ten o'clock or so. If Murray [Assistant Press Secretary Murray Snyder] had to say anything, General Snyder said to call it a "digestive upset." I thought it was one of the periodic upsets he had had and was not in the slightest worried. Around eleven or so Bob Clark called International News Service and said that because of Murray's reluctance to say it was not serious, the wires were blowing it up into some serious illness. Could I call General Snyder and if it was not serious, ask him to tell Murray so. This was accomplished in approximately forty-five minutes. General Snyder, for reasons of his own—the president was still asleep—said his digestive upset was not serious and this was carried on the wires. This I accepted at face value—of course it was not serious, it would not be serious.[6]

Snyder's explanation was a downright lie, as objectionable as the covering up of Cleveland's cancer operation, Wilson's stroke, Dr. Sawyer's incompetence, and Roosevelt's heart failure.

As days passed, Snyder composed a sort of form letter that he sent with minor changes to the president's brothers and close friends and his own medical and army friends and family members. It sought to bridge the gap between credibility and incredibility:

> It was difficult for me to assume the responsibility of refraining from making public immediately the diagnosis of coronary thrombosis. I postponed public announcement because I wished the President to benefit from the rest and quiet induced by the seda-

tion incident to combating the initial manifestations. This decision also spared him, his wife, and mother-in-law emotional upset attendant upon too precipitate announcement of such serious import. The end result was that all who were intimately concerned were much better able to accept this information, delivered by suggestion during the intermediate hours of rest which were afforded the President. This action, I believe, limited the heart damage to a minimum and enabled us to make an unhurried transference from home to hospital.[7]

The Snyder letter sounded reasonable upon quick reading, even upon slow reading. But in essence it was not. Its explanations made little sense. That the Eisenhower family and the president felt better because Snyder gradually let them understand the seriousness of that attack—that it was in fact a heart attack—is easy to understand. But it was beside the point, which was the need for a public explanation. The letter was a labored statement of why Snyder felt better. He delayed announcement of the heart attack as long as he could while he gathered his thoughts and, one must suspect, hoped against hope that he might not even have to admit that Eisenhower had suffered a heart attack—his august patient might recover fairly quickly, snap back, as in 1949 and 1953.

The more basic need was not for the care and feeling of the Eisenhower family, nor of the patient, nor the doctor, but for information given promptly to the American people, who had chosen a president in belief he was in good health and could handle the job. For this reason it would have been far better if news of the attack had gone on the wires as soon as Dr. Snyder discovered it—that is, shortly after 3:00 A.M. Instead, news went out half a day later.

But to return to the scene at the Doud house that Saturday, September 24, 1955. At 2:00 P.M. General Snyder telephoned, according to Agent James Rowley of the secret service, and asked for the president's chauffeur, Deeter B. Flohr, to bring the presidential car to the Doud residence and place it at the side steps of the porch. A half hour later General Snyder, having had the president dressed, helped him down the narrow stairs of the Doud house onto the porch and with the assistance of Rowley and Moaney into the waiting car. Rowley and Snyder went in the car with Eisenhower to Fitzsimons. Using a circuitous route and stopping at the rear of the hospital, they and the attendants moved the president to a wheel chair and took him by elevator to the hospital's eighth floor.

In this extraordinary manner, with a combination of actions and omissions that raised serious questions about his professional capacity, Dr. Snyder managed the first twenty-four hours of Eisenhower's major heart attack. Looked at altogether, it was a tissue of errors. When the phone call went out to Snyder from Mrs. Eisenhower, early in the morning of the twenty-fourth, the physician admittedly got to the Doud house in record time, rushing over in a few minutes, as well he should have. His prescriptions in subsequent minutes and hours seem to have been approximately proper, but with several notable exceptions. He happened on a scene in which his patient already had been moving about, an alarming proposition in itself. The president had gone into his wife's bedroom to apprise her that he was not feeling well. Then, having gone back to bed, and after Snyder's appearance, Eisenhower needed to go to the toilet, but there was no bedpan; so Snyder supported him to the bathroom and back to bed, an appalling thing to do for a patient in heart attack.

Second, Snyder did nothing in terms of calling the specialists at nearby Fitzsimons, who could have been at Lafayette Street within minutes, bringing whatever was necessary, including a cardiologist for a desperately ill man with cardiac problems. The people at Fitzsimons learned nothing about the attack until 12:15 P.M. on the twenty-fourth, not too long before the president was on his way to the hospital.

Third, it was unconscionable for Snyder to allow the president to walk down the stairs of the house onto the porch and then upon arrival at the hospital, getting him out of the car and into the wheel chair. Could he not have been carried down the stairs on a stretcher or a chair?

Fourth, allowing Eisenhower to sit in the back seat of an automobile with his affected heart shoved up against his lungs and stomach was equally unbelievable treatment. A stretcher would have been more appropriate. The hospital had ambulances at beck and call, and one could have taken him on the nine-mile trip. It would have been logical to call the hospital.

Years later, when the time came to write the medical history, Mattingly discovered a final disquieting fact about Snyder's treatment that brought him back to the conversation he, the cardiologist, had had with the reporter Smith on the plane going out to Denver in September 1955. He learned from Snyder of the equipment he had brought with him early that dire morning when he rushed by automobile to the

Doud house. In his car, along with the usual items physicians in general practice carry in their medical bags, Snyder brought along several medicines useful in cases of heart attacks. He also carried with him a tank of oxygen (which, incidentally, Snyder did not use and surely should have, given Denver's altitude). Could it be that he knew almost what to expect—that he had been down that road at least twice before in 1949 and 1953?

2.

In the next days Dr. Snyder's lapses gradually disappeared from public view, despite the enormous public interest in the president's illness and hospitalization and, as it became apparent, the beginning of his recovery. At the outset the New York stock exchange suffered its worst fall in history, a loss of $14 billion on Monday, September 26, the first day of trading since the heart attack of the preceding Saturday. News of Eisenhower's illness stunned his countrymen. Even administration figures, inured to the ups and downs of political life, were shocked. The steel executive Clarence B. Randall, in charge of the administration's foreign economic policy, told his wife that it was the end of the Eisenhower administration, that the president surely would not be a candidate for a second term

> and I am positive that such is the fact. He surely will not run and, if he did, I doubt if he would be elected. It wouldn't be right for him or for the country for him to head into those responsibilities after having had his first coronary. In fact, as I dictate this, I hold the opinion that if after the critical period of about ten days, which usually follows a coronary, the President upon talking with his doctors is told that he must have three months of convalescence, he will resign.[8]

But then, almost as quickly as the attack itself had come upon the president, the American people turned their attention to the progress of the therapy at Fitzsimons, the small events of each day, the care that modern medicine could lavish on a patient, particularly on a patient who was president of the United States. Indeed, they almost took pleasure in the treatment of their president, knowing, or so they believed, that he was getting the best that medical miracles could bestow upon a man who had become not merely the leader of the nation but the personification of its hopes; a hero during World War II who had carried victory from the battlefield into politics and was taking the United States into the empyrean of national and international achievement. Listening to the spokesmen for the administration and the physicians surrounding the famous patient, watching all this on the screens of their television sets, listening to radios at home and in their automobiles, viewers and auditors heard about Eisenhower's progress and followed it and began to forget the disturbing reportage of what had happened at the Doud house.

The resources of Fitzsimons lay at the president's disposal, and they were formidable. The entire eighth floor was devoted to his care. How the hospital possessed a VIP floor of this sort is difficult to know, except that someone years before had discerned a possibility that a famous patient would need not only seclusion but space, and so the hospital had a floor that contained a room for the president and an adjoining room with a bathroom for an aide. On the other side of the president's room was a small room with a bed for a nurse. To the left of this center of operations, on the other side of the double stairs, was a room for the wife of the patient, and behind it a smaller room for the attending physician. Behind, across a hall, was a larger room for another physician. In the middle of the complex stood three elevator shafts. On their far side was a dining room. Behind lay an auditorium, presumably where reporters or medical personnel might assemble, seeking to discuss the condition of the patient. And then on either side of the complex, east and west, were sun decks where a patient might be wheeled to observe the Denver skyline, the mountains in the distance, and soak up the sun and air.

Alerted by a call from General Snyder, the hospital staff were ready when the president's car came around to the back entrance. The physician in charge was Colonel Pollock, the staff cardiologist, a member of the American Board of Cardiology. Noncardiac problems were the province of Colonel George M. Powell, chief of the department of medicine. Powell's assistant was Lieutenant Colonel John A. Sheedy, who like Powell was a member of the American Board of Internal Medicine, that is, was board certified. Board certification required several years of practice in the special field and a very stiff examination by board members. In the 1950s, and for some years thereafter, only a few applicants for certification passed the tests; it was a large honor to have such certification. Years later in the 1980s, a more lenient arrangement came in, whereby four-fifths of applicants at each examination for certification passed.

Taking every precaution, the staff at Fitzsimons talked matters over with the surgeon general of the army, Major General Silas B. Hays, in Washington, and everyone agreed that if only for the purpose of satisfying the public where there might be concern about the quality of U.S. Army medicine, it would be advisable to bring in a civilian consultant. The choice was the best-known cardiologist in the country, Dr. Paul Dudley White of Boston; his reputation was indeed international.

Dr. Snyder with the concurrence of General Griffin asked General Hays to send for Mattingly from Walter Reed and to ask Dr. White to come from Boston. Mattingly, as mentioned, had come out on the evening of September 24. White arrived from Boston at noon on Sunday, September 25. Mattingly soon discovered why he had been invited to Denver apart from the need to obtain the president's records from the cardiac clinic at Walter Reed. Snyder said the president had asked for him.

On Sunday morning, Mattingly shaved, bathed, changed uniforms, and attended an early mass at the post chapel where he prayed for guidance in the making of decisions—and he soon found himself in the midst of several. For one thing, shortly after mass he found Snyder seeking him out. The general wished to speak with him privately. Mattingly was surprised at his appearance but thought it was due to a lack of sleep, which was in part true. But Snyder immediately presented him with copies of the local newspapers. He said the press was being highly critical of his care prior to the president's admission, particularly of his failure to seek help and for the delay in providing the correct diagnosis. Mattingly found him hardly the calm, confident, almost stoic person he had come to know. Indeed, the general was in tears, saying he had done everything he could, prior to the president's arrival at the hospital, to improve the chances of recovery. The press, he said, was not trying to understand.

Mattingly believed it was not the proper time to ask why Snyder had taken the actions he did. Later he wondered about his judgment because he had passed up the chance to strike while the iron was hot. He hastily looked over the press accounts Snyder had given him and did his best to assure him that criticism would cease as soon as reporters realized the president was making progress. White was due in a few hours and would necessarily have to hold a press conference as spokesman for the attending physicians. He promised Snyder he would personally discuss the situation with White. He believed White could direct press attention to current care and make the reporters forget anything that happened prior to hospitalization. He encouraged Snyder to rest and sleep before White appeared and offered to get medication to help the general sleep, but Snyder refused.

Mattingly then met White at the airport and was delighted to see him. He had worked with him as a student at Massachusetts General in 1949–1950 and later had solicited White's assistance in the care of military personnel at Walter Reed. The public, medical profession, and especially the press received White's appointment enthusiastically. Some years later, on the occasion of a joint celebration of White by friends and acquaintances, Mattingly related in detail what his presence in Denver meant. It was a moving appraisal in which he remarked,

> The tremendous job which Dr. White performed at that time and for a period thereafter was to treat the disturbed and panicky nation and world that became sick and anxious with the news of a heart attack in a very popular President and world leader. The art of medicine, the perfect bedside physician, the inspiring confidence and human touch which I had repeatedly observed him to apply to the individual patient and family were expertly applied in his reports to the nation and the world. No other physician in America would have gained their complete confidence in these early days of the President's illness and later convinced the nation that a President, recovering from a heart attack, could return to the stressful job of the Presidency. As ever, a teacher and a great humanist, he made use of this opportunity to explain to the public factual information about heart disease, particularly coronary disease, and to sponsor a campaign against invalidism in those unfortunate enough to have a heart attack. Every surviving victim of coronary disease today is indebted to him for this help.[9]

During the ride to the hospital, Mattingly gave the Boston cardiologist a quick rundown of the situation. He also told him of the press reports critical of Snyder, of Snyder's predicament, and the general's appeal. White, a bit of a statesman and perhaps amused by Snyder's concern, said only, "We shall discuss it later."[10]

Upon arrival at the hospital White went immediately to the president's room where he found him in a large oxygen tent, drowsy under sedation, but free of symptoms. They had never met before, but Eisenhower smiled in greeting. He felt his pulse, took blood pressure, and listened to heart and lungs, this in about twelve minutes. He told him he was doing well. He had seen, he later wrote, a "perfectly typical" coronary attack (thrombosis) with damaged heart muscle (infarction, later to become a scar) about the size of a large olive in the anterior wall of the left ventricle.[11] He agreed with the regime and offered no additional therapeutic suggestions. He said the patient's condition should be graded a three out of a possible five, and therefore an illness of moderate severity (this was a slight upgrading to what the Fitzsimons group had concluded; their reading had been of a "mild" attack). He met with Mrs. Eisenhower and the president's son John, and later with Vice-President Nixon, the presidential chief of staff Governor Sherman Adams, and Press Secretary Hagerty.

That afternoon Mattingly took his first tour as physician on duty. He had asked that Pollock remain as the president's cardiologist responsible for such care, and said he would assist and advise as desired, and would make all his recommendations to Pollock. This met with general approval. He likewise offered to take a duty as physician in the presidential suite at such times as he was present in Denver. This offer was accepted quickly, as it meant four physicians to share the twenty-four-hour coverage: himself, Pollock, Powell, and Sheedy. He became in effect a member of the staff at Fitzsimons, and General Griffin treated him as such, together with members of Griffin's staff. During the duty he encountered no problems and had an opportunity to visit with Mrs. Eisenhower, who had settled into the bedroom on the other side of the stairs from her husband.

At 9:00 P.M. White returned to the hospital, examined the patient again, and read more of the information in the president's chart. The arrangement was for him and Mattingly to room together at the officers' club, and they walked the short distance over there. White said he had gone to the Doud residence to see the layout, especially the narrow stairs. When they reached the club entrance, White noticed the golf course across the street and decided that they should go for a walk. Mattingly was not much in favor, having had only a nap in the last forty-eight hours. But the two walked in the moonlight for perhaps an hour, discussing first the Snyder situation, then some of the problems facing them as their patient recovered.

The Snyder problem was not easy to analyze. They did not know Snyder's thinking or reasons for his initial announcement of an "intestinal upset," his contradictory treatment of the president for a heart attack, his delay in seeking assistance and hospitalization, the reasons for his taking Eisenhower down the narrow stairs and walking him out to the car, and his choice of transportation to the hospital by car rather than ambulance. As the press and public did not understand these actions, neither did they. White or Mattingly, probably White with Mattingly momentarily in assent, then seems to have concluded that with the president safely in the hospital, one might say, by hook or crook, and doing satisfactorily without any evidence that the management prior to hospitalization had harmed him, why make an issue of it?

The next problem was the press conference scheduled for the following morning. How to present things? The president had instructed Hagerty to "tell them everything." In one way his instruction made perfect sense. It was similar to the response of Cleveland in 1884 when he was running for the first time for the presidency and a question arose of what a Buffalo newspaper described as "a terrible tale," his liaison with Mrs. Halpin. Cleveland's answer was, "Tell the truth." Circumstances were different, the Cleveland issue hardly life-threatening, yet in both cases such procedure was the best possible. Truth contains its own logic, which any circumstances likely to arise, some unforeseen, will corroborate. But in another way that Hagerty may well have thought of, and perhaps Eisenhower, telling everything also provided a way out. Truth does not always mean all the truth, nor does telling prevent the possibility of getting off the subject. White chose the latter course. As the two men exchanged views, turning around what they, in this instance White as spokesman for the others, might do, White related, perhaps with a twinkle, "I shall give the press and the nation a course on myocardial infarction. They will get so interested, the press will not raise the question of management before hospitalization, especially if in the morning he continues to be doing satisfactorily."[12] With that they returned to the officers' club where Mattingly "died" for the next hours until just before 7:00 A.M.

Fortunately, everything worked out well the next morning, Monday, September 26. After breakfast at the club, White and Mattingly walked to the hospital and found a way to enter from the rear and to take an elevator at the level below the main entrance, avoiding reporters and a throng of onlookers gathered outside. By this time Pollock had obtained another EKG and made other studies. Powell had recorded the night's activities. Everything looked good. White made recommendations for the rest of the day and told the staff he planned to return to Boston after the forthcoming press conference. Pollock would contact him at least once daily after the return and thus keep the consultation going. Hagerty, General Snyder, and the Fitzsimons staff then met with White and Mattingly; they drafted an outline of the president's status, and the arrangement was for everyone to attend the press conference, except for the duty physician. Hagerty would conduct the conference with White making a statement and fielding questions.

The Boston cardiologist's management of the press conference was masterly. In the administration building at Lowry Air Force Base, Hagerty introduced White, who then began his statement by announcing he was returning to Boston in part because the president's condition was satisfactory, partly because the care was so excellent, medically and otherwise. He went on to say that he thought the press would find it of interest if he spoke briefly of "what the condition is that the President has," and proceeded to describe exactly what a heart attack was—coronary thrombosis—and how physicians would manage it.

Mattingly had told White about the experience with Merriman Smith, so White described how he had gone over the patient's medical history from records at Fitzsimons and Walter Reed and found no evidence of an earlier heart attack. Smith did not say a word, although he was present in the audience. No one mentioned Dr. Snyder's earlier activities at the Doud house or in getting the patient to the hospital.

In connection with the president's own requirement to tell everything, Hagerty read to the reporters the morning progress report that included the phrase, "He had a good bowel movement." White broke in with "Now I put that in—this is an encouraging point." As much as the course on myocardial infarction, this statement may have thrown reporters off the track. Years later White wrote of it proudly in his autobiography. He said that not only were tens of thousands of cardiac patients interested in his discussion of heart attacks, but he also knew thousands of doctors would be listening and that in this normal physiological event so early in the president's illness they would see a favorable prognostic sign. After the conference one of the British reporters said to him, "Dr. White you certainly are very frank. Just suppose that our Queen were ill." Afterward he received in his fan mail two or three letters to the effect that the writers were pleased to learn of Eisenhower's good progress, but they wished he had not mentioned the presidential bowels. Eisenhower later wrote of "acute embarrassment" when he read the bulletin. (On reflection he concluded, "Well in any event it's too late to object now; forget it.") The reference led one exasperated observer to describe Dr. White as the Boswell of the bowels.[13]

After the conference White, usually unexcitable, was elated, more so than Mattingly had ever seen him. To his roommate at the officers' club he announced, pleased as punch: "Tom, it worked."[14] And it had worked: The national and international concern, including the American stock market and international markets, calmed down, and General Snyder thanked Mattingly for talking to White. He never mentioned again the events of the early hours of the heart attack.

3.

As the president rested at Fitzsimons and his physicians studied his case, people everywhere took heart in the extraordinary attention he was getting, both in the newspapers and over radio and television and in the general hospital where the staff treated him, where Mattingly from Walter Reed was in attendance, and where Dr. White arrived from Boston. It was to all appearances a testimony to American medicine, now concentrating on the president himself. All of the great popular affection that had marked Eisenhower's triumphs during World War II and swept him into office during the election of 1952 seemed to gather around the suite in Fitzsimons in which the president spent his days and nights. The suite had two sun decks, and before long corpsmen brought the patient in a wheelchair out to take the afternoon sun. The photographs of him went out over the wire services and it was cheering—encouraging in the extreme.[15]

What the public did not know was that differences over his care had arisen, differences between his regular cardiologist, Mattingly, and—on the other side—the Fitzsimons cardiologist Pollock and the hospital's radiologist Colonel Allan B. Ramsay, together with Dr. White. For one thing, Mattingly was not keen for the program of early physical activity that the other doctors endorsed and approved. Mattingly was aware of the criticism that had been made of Snyder's activities in getting Eisenhower to the hospital during the period of the attack. He believed that the patient had already been subjected to too much exercise beginning with what perhaps was the initial myocardial insult commencing on the golf course the afternoon of September 23, the major damage early the next morning, then the trip to Mamie's room, later to the bathroom, and walking down steps from the second floor and to the car, and out of the car after arrival at the hospital. All this was to be followed by a program of early chair sitting, to begin on the fourth day in the hospital.

The other doctors favored it, and the patient liked it very much. When on September 28 Mattingly together with the president's son John went in to see the patient before returning to Washington, they found him enthusiastic about being permitted to sit in a chair. Mattingly said jokingly, "I suppose you will be walking by the time I return." Then he made his point, suggesting caution. "Mr. President," he said, "if you had a broken leg, you would accept a period of rest to permit healing. The same is necessary with an injury to the heart muscle. My motto is *festina lente*—hurry up slowly."[16]

Mattingly went back to Washington and remained two days, returning September 30, and that night took floor duty, midnight to eight, finding the president sitting up for an hour or more several times a day and enjoying it. Early the next morning, Generals Snyder and Griffin came in to check on the condition of the president. Snyder was back to his old self, "confident and jovial."[17]

Then there were a few signs that everything was not quite right with Eisenhower's heart. The patient himself had no symptoms, but there was the return of a pericardial friction rub (the pericardium is the capsule or conical sac of membrane that encloses the heart) and some changes in the EKG, and Pollock considered the problem a pericardial reaction with a return of active pericarditis. This became evident on October 1. Next day, just to play safe, and after Pollock talked on the telephone with White, the two of them decided to discontinue the daily chair sitting until the clinical picture became more definite. Mrs. Eisenhower and John immediately became upset. The decision to discontinue the chair sitting greatly bothered the Eisenhowers. The White House staff picked up on the anxiety in spite of a report to Washington by Pollock and Snyder that no serious problem had developed—only a little caution in the program of activity. The surgeon general learned that the White House was concerned about the president's progress and urged a return visit by White.

All this was made worse by the president's experiencing a transient chest pain while being transferred from chair to bed. It had no relation to the discontinuance of the chair sitting. No matter how diplomatic and careful Pollock was in explaining the discontinuance, everyone was in a dither. Pollock was in daily touch with White, and on October 8, after White returned to Denver, they decided to resume the daily activity program, but on a slower progressive schedule.

Meanwhile, Mattingly had taken another position at variance with the opinions of his colleagues. He had given a slightly different interpretation to an EKG of September 28 than "just a recurrent pericarditis." He had been on the trip to Washington at the time of the EKG but on return put a note on the chart about a possible extension of the original area of infarction or a new infarction beginning that date or shortly thereafter. This had concerned White, who asked Pollock to send copies of EKGs since September 28. He wanted to have a consultation with Dr. Eugene Lepeschkin of the University of Vermont Medical School, whom he considered a world authority on EKGs. It was after receiving the views of Lepeschkin, and his own arrival on the scene, that he and Pollock agreed to resume the activity program.

The day that White came back, Mattingly made a thorough evaluation of the president's clinical status as he saw it and entered it in the record, not as any challenge to White and Lepeschkin, whom he of course respected, but because that was the way he saw the clinical situation. He feared that White and Pollock might continue to push the activity program.

Arriving in the company of John Eisenhower and Vice-President Nixon, White evaluated the record and findings, examined the president, and carefully read Mattingly's note. He proceeded to discuss the possibilities, Lepeschkin's opinion, and entered no note in the clinical record. To the attending physicians he expressed the opinion that the president's case was probably just a matter of slow resolution and healing and agreed that the group should proceed cautiously.

Later, alone with Mattingly in their room at the officers' club, they had another discussion. At the beginning of treatment, indeed, during his first trip, White had been uneasy about what he was looking at. He had written in his medical notebook, "I don't like the heart sounds or rather fast pulse . . . but there are favorable points otherwise. The next few days are critical."[18] Now, in the privacy of the room, he made another confession.

> He admitted that an extension of the area of infarction was most probable and that this was the basis of the slow healing. He considered it best for the President's future and all concerned to simply announce to the press the next day that it was just a process of slow healing. He wisely decided that it would only upset the nation and the world (and the stock market again) to mention the probability of an extension of the original infarction or a new infarction as the cause of the slow healing.[19]

The next day White used his bedside manner effectively again, first in talking with Mrs. Eisenhower, John, and the vice-president, managing to dispel the gloom of preceding days, then with the press.

For the next days the Denver front was "all quiet and happy" with the president doing well and pleased with White's visit and his own increasing activities, especially his resumption, if gradually, of presidential responsibilities. At this juncture Mattingly left again, this time to attend an American Heart Association meeting in California. Snyder knew of his prior commitment to participate in it and urged him to go. He did, although he was concerned that the press would try to seek him out. He desired to stay away from the limelight with White continuing as spokesman from Boston and daily reports from Pollock in Denver. Fortunately, the reporters pushed him into only a single interview.

Upon return everything was fine, and he thereupon went back to Washington for a week, flying out once more to Denver on October 21 in the company of Governor Adams by way of Boston to pick up White. The two physicians talked on the way out, a leisurely night flight that arrived in Denver at about 7:00 A.M.[20] One of the subjects of conversation was a medical-political matter. Mattingly's chief at Walter Reed, General Heaton, desired the president to return to Walter Reed as soon as possible. The president had said, however, that he desired to stay at Fitzsimons until he could walk out of the hospital, walk on and off the plane, and not have to transfer to Walter Reed. Mattingly had not told Heaton of this decision, which he knew would hardly please his superior. He wanted word of it to come from Snyder.

Upon arrival, White and Mattingly evaluated the president's physical condition, cardiac status, and all the reports, as well as a follow-up evaluation of the EKGs by Lepeschkin. White continued to hedge—this was Mattingly's word—on the meaning of the serial EKGs, holding to an earlier interpretation that they were due to "pericardial reaction and slow healing of the original infarction."[21] As earlier, he failed to enter a note in the clinical record. Mattingly again recorded his own evaluation, which remained in the minority.

Next day White failed to handle the press conference as well as before. Reporters raised questions about a second term, and White was not too quick in answering them. Afterward White and Mattingly were talking with Snyder about the scientific session of the American Heart Association meeting in New Orleans, which White planned to attend. Mattingly had a paper that one of his associates was going to present. Snyder saw no reason why he could not give the paper, and the president's aide, Schulz, said the presidential plane was returning to Washington to take back White House staff members and could go by way of New Orleans and drop off the two physicians. That then was the arrangement. White enjoyed the special attention and praise he always received from members of the association.

After the Heart Association meeting, the Walter Reed cardiologist returned to Washington on a commercial flight and remained there until a final Denver trip November 8, as Snyder desired him to accompany the president on the return to Washington, scheduled for November 11. White planned to go back to Denver on November 6 for his final evaluation and hold a press conference next day. Thereafter he was to leave for Albuquerque, which he eventually did, but returned to Denver and went back on the president's plane on November 11 along with Mattingly and the presidential party.

During these last days, Mattingly held to his opinion that Eisenhower's condition had worsened. On November 9, he went through the clinical events and progress since he last had seen the president. He was not pleased with the interpretations of the X rays and fluoroscopic examination of the heart and asked to repeat the fluoroscopic examination with the radiologist, Ramsay. They repeated it the next day, and Mattingly was convinced that what he was looking at was not just a myocardial scar and/or adherent pericardium, as previously reported by Ramsay, but an aneurysm of the left ventricle.

The Walter Reed cardiologist was basing his position on a diagnosis he had made and substantiated many times. From fluoroscopic examination and in review of the EKGs, he agreed with the general tenor of the reports by the Fitzsimons radiologist. But he did not agree with his interpretation. The reasoning was cunningly close to the truth. Like many general radiologists of that time, Ramsay had little experience in cardiac fluoroscopy and cardiovascular radiology. Mattingly felt certain that Eisenhower had an aneurysm of the left ventricle. Ramsay disagreed. The radiologist, Mattingly wrote years later, had a sort of classical idea of a ventricular aneurysm as large and bulging, and especially presenting paradoxical motion if compared to the surrounding healthy muscular ventricle. Instead, Mattingly believed they were looking at a thick-walled aneurysm where the fibrous heart wall restrained the paradoxical motion.

In some sense it was cardiology opposing radiology: the former clinical, the latter the interpretation of photographs without seeing the patient. If the wall did not bulge and move paradoxically in the photographs there could be no aneurysm. Mattingly had noticed how radiologists refused to give way on what, despite their pictures, was largely theory. Residents in radiology had come to the cardiology clinic at Walter Reed for help in this regard. The clinic, as Mattingly ran it, actually performed most of its own fluoroscopic studies and sent few patients to radiology.

It was a subtle confrontation. As mentioned, during the evaluations in early October when Mattingly considered the setback of that time as probably the result of a second infarction or an extension of the original infarction, Pollock had considered it probably a postpericardial reaction, and White considered it a problem of slow healing of the original infarct. The bedside X ray showed cardiac enlargement, and Mattingly suggested that when the president was ambulatory he should have a second evaluation of the heart size by X ray and a fluoroscope and EKG study to determine if an aneurysm had developed.

When Mattingly arrived on November 8 Ramsay had performed the special X ray, and the fluoroscopic studies and findings included an increase in heart size and a small bulging of the left ventricle, which did not contract normally but showed no opposite pulsation to the remainder of the ventricular contraction. The radiologist interpreted this as a healed myocardial scar, not an aneurysm. When Mattingly reviewed this X ray and fluoroscopic finding, he requested another fluoroscopic study and said he would like to view the fluoroscopic findings with the radiologist. Through his many years in cardiology beginning in 1934–1935 he had performed fluoroscopic examinations either with a radiologist or in the fluoroscopic unit in his own clinic in cardiology at Walter Reed after he returned there from Massachusetts General in 1950. Likewise during a period in 1933–1934 when he was a fellow in pathology in one of the Washington hospitals he had observed and studied aneurysms of the heart in many patients and had continued to study aneurysms at autopsies that occurred in patients subsequent to that date. He therefore had a long experience in the special study of aneurysm formation following myocardial infarctions.[22]

Dr. White himself, a great cardiologist, never showed much interest in cardiac fluoroscopy. Mattingly was aware of this blind spot in White's diagnoses, as he had studied with him. The issue was hardly theoretical when it arose not long after treatment began at Fitzsimons. Mattingly in his open and honest way had put down on the chart that he thought there was further damage than the olive-sized break that everyone agreed upon. White himself was not making comments on the chart, leaving them to Pollock and Mattingly and in the case of medicine, Powell and Sheedy. He made notes in his medical notebook for typing up by his secretary. He did not enter these notes in the medical record either at the time or after his return to Boston.[23] White's views, however, were well known, namely, that there was no further damage, and the others, save Mattingly, agreed. The latter could not be very sure of himself until the patient toward the end of hospitalization underwent fluoroscopy.

Once again Mattingly's was a minority report. White returned from New Mexico and recorded a final summary for the president's entire hospitalization. This was his first entry in the medical record. He denied the presence of an aneurysm. Pollock did the same in his narrative summary. Each gave other explanations for the abnormalities observable in fluoroscopy. Both, however, agreed to long-term anticoagulants after discharge. The last recommendation delighted Mattingly, for he felt it necessary because of increased complications from thromboembolism with a ventricular aneurysm.

November 11 proved the great day for leaving Denver. When Mattingly went up on the eighth floor early that morning he found the president having completed breakfast and all dressed in a white shirt, bow tie, dark brown trousers, and "beaming his best big grin."[24] Everyone soon was taking pictures of the president posing with the Fitzsimons staff and Snyder. The Eisenhowers made their good-byes to the staff, including everyone down to the corpsmen. Hagerty and Schulz scurried frantically around trying to get their party free and down the elevators. A crowd stood outside in almost funereal fashion, waiting for the president to walk out the door. When he went out he burst forth with his big grin, and the crowd cheered, and the waiting automobiles moved off for Lowry Air Force Base. Across the gate from the hospital someone had stretched a banner reading "Good Health and Good Luck."

Cheering crowds stood outside the entrance to Lowry as the cavalcade passed into the base. The cars wound their way into the field. Then, in front of the plane, the president stepped out, bade good-bye to Mrs. Doud, and proudly walked up the steps to the plane with all the confidence of a casual passenger.

5
Second Term

J ust before Eisenhower left Denver, the cardiologists advised, and Eisenhower accepted, an arrangement whereby he would move back toward his presidential duties slowly and carefully. They all felt that it would be unwise for him to return to the White House to assume duties even involving a limited number of hours a day, for he would find himself confined to the walls of the executive mansion and thus the turmoil of the day would surround him. During the remainder of the autumn before the onset of winter, he would reside at the Gettysburg farm where he could participate in outdoor physical activities and gradually increase presidential activities with his chief of staff, Adams, as intermediary with the White House staff. He could also travel the short distance to Camp David to hold cabinet and other meetings and conferences. As winter came on he would return to the White House for Christmas and then go south to Key West where the weather would allow increasing outdoor physical activities. Afterward, he would return to the White House or Gettysburg as desired where he again could increase his participation in his duties. During this period the cardiologists could observe him periodically through visits and outpatient studies at Walter Reed and make their final evaluation and recommendations.

By mid-February 1956, the doctors had to decide whether their patient might safely run for a second term. In making this decision they would have to consider the body of statistics available for patients suffering serious heart attacks. The statistical studies were discouraging. Dr. White and Dr. Edward F. Bland had demonstrated in 1941 that after the first month the five-year survival of patients was 50 percent. More recent reports, one from the Michael Reese Hospital in Chicago in 1954 and another from Vanderbilt University Medical School in Nashville the next year, verified the survival rate of the White and Bland study. Moreover, if Eisenhower had suffered a left ventricular aneurysm, as Mattingly suspected, the prognosis was a good deal worse. This meant he was susceptible to complications such as heart failure, arrythmias, and embolisms from intracardiac thrombi. Mattingly's own patients had had lower death rates than those reported in the medical literature, but the literature itself was almost frightening. In a large study of 102 cases of ventricular aneurysm complicating myocardial infarctions reported in 1954, 88 percent of the patients died in five years.[1]

There is no evidence that the president knew how poor the statistical odds were. His brother Milton knew about them and thought it a good idea to keep them from him. Dr. Snyder readily agreed.[2]

1.

In due time, the doctors would make their decision on the second term; that seemed clear enough. Presumably within the group White's views would dominate. White would be in the driver's seat with Mattingly sitting beside him, and Pollock at Fitzsimons would be consulted from time to time. They would make the decision. The president's personal physician, Snyder, would sit in the back seat and do what White and Mattingly said. White would make occasional trips from Boston to supervise the patient's recovery. Mattingly would be the physician in situ, seeing the president frequently for checkups and reporting the situation to White.

But at the outset, in November and December 1955, the danger was that the hierarchy of medical decision-making as arranged at Denver might not hold. White's diplomatic talents were sometimes formidable and at other times remarkably slight. White had been at the center of cardiology for many years and was accustomed to getting attention for whatever he wanted. He was a forceful, straightforward fellow, and such qualities had taken him far in his chosen field. They were not always useful in nonmedical situations, particularly around such a highly charged arrangement as the White House, and for such a tempered president as Eisenhower. White at the outset began to push his authority so hard that there was danger in the air: If by some untoward act he irritated the president, he might find himself dismissed. If Eisenhower dismissed him, authority would pass to Snyder. Technically, upon the president's leaving Fitzsimons it already had passed to Snyder as the president's personal physician. There was danger it might turn into real authority.

White did several things that threatened his relations with Eisenhower. For one thing, he became a bit familiar. He did it in an avuncular way and did not mean to be impertinent, but the result was the same. When the president left Denver, White was on the plane. It had not been planned that he would be on the plane, for he had gone to New Mexico; the presumption was that he would fly back to Boston from there. Instead he went the great circle route, via Denver, for the obvious reason of flying with the president. Aboard the plane he also failed to keep his distance; Mattingly saw him get up from his seat and go over and sit down with the Eisenhowers. Upon arrival in the capital he delayed his departure for Boston and told Mrs. Eisenhower and Milton that he would like to go over the president's care with them and the president before he left. He received an invitation to remain for dinner and the evening movie.

Familiarity was not one of the qualities Eisenhower admired in people who surrounded him. For all of the president's democratic qualities, his smile, the laughter, and good humor, familiarity was anathema. Eisenhower had spent many years in the military and knew what rank meant. Probably his long service as a major had brought special recognition, particularly when dealing with another rank-conscious military man, MacArthur. He knew who was boss and liked to feel the tension. The worst thing anyone could do in his presence was to be familiar. Mattingly ruefully remembered the White House visit of a WAC sergeant, a superb technician but otherwise "somewhat uncouth and unpredictable," who made a serious faux pas. On approaching the president's bed to take an EKG, she patted Ike on his bald head and greeted him with the remark, "How's my president today?" From the president's facial expression the cardiologist knew the remark did not go over well, and Mattingly never asked the WAC to make the trip to the White House again.[3]

Another thing White did was to interfere with—mess up, Eisenhower might have said—the chain of command. Upon return to Boston he sent a letter to the president outlining the oral instructions of the previous evening and sent copies to Snyder and Mattingly by registered mail. A series of letters followed, to the president and the two physicians, with instructions for day-to-day care and outlining plans for a visit to Washington, with more instructions as to studies that he wished made prior to the visit. He thus made a serious error with the militarily inclined Eisenhower, who liked everything to go through channels, which meant first Snyder, then the president. There was no comparison between the medical talents of White and those of Snyder, and White probably thought it was as simple as that. He could not have been more wrong. Eisenhower told Snyder that he, Major General Snyder, was still his personal physician and adviser, and he expected his consultants to make recommendations and offer advice through him.

Then, too, White basked in the approbation of the press, and this caused trouble. Eisenhower began to think that White was becoming a publicity seeker, and to some extent it was true. Mattingly noticed it, and he was White's good friend. The publicity that surrounded White was altogether understandable. He deserved it, and perhaps everyone likes a bit of the limelight. Furthermore, White had done Eisenhower a great favor by coming out to Denver and certifying that he was doing all right. He shortly would do him another great favor. But in November and December 1955, Eisenhower's tolerance of White's prominence began to wear thin. If there was any publicity to spread around, Eisenhower may have wanted the light closer to his activities. After all he was president, not some doctor. "I really need you tomorrow morning," the president wrote George Allen, "because I am thinking of doing some cardiogram work myself. I must not let Dr. White get all the headlines."[4] Too, the publicity that came to White was because of the president's ill health, and this was another reason for resenting it. The president began to tire of doctors' press conferences and on one occasion, upon hearing that Snyder was giving a press conference, he snapped to Heaton, "What the hell are you having a press conference for? Can't you just tell them I am still living?"[5]

White also misbehaved in terms of the sheer busyness of the president once Eisenhower got back into circulation. White wrote too many letters, and they were too long and fussily overladen with penned-in corrections. It was a bit much.

But if White caused trouble, far more worrisome was the continuing presence of Snyder as the president's longtime friend and personal physician. The Walter Reed cardiologist knew how politically minded Snyder was and how inexperienced in cardiology and in rehabilitation of a cardiac patient. It was difficult to predict what the general might do next. It was possible that whatever care the cardiologists proposed for the president, Snyder, who was constantly on the scene, would rearrange it.

Snyder was an odd mixture of shrewdness—intelligence, attractiveness, camaraderie—and ignorance, and the mixture medically was volatile. The former qualities he had demonstrated by making his way up in the army over the many years. He was a good conversationalist and just the man to have around for a card game. Like all old army officers, he had learned how to stow the liquor away and could do whatever drinking was necessary. Eisenhower was drawn to him, even though the president could exasperate the doctor sometimes by paying little or no attention to him. A couple of years later he paid attention to him in an almost pitiful way. When he was visiting England and went out to the residence of Prime Minister Harold Macmillan, at Chequers, the two world leaders together with the British foreign secretary, Selwyn Lloyd, and the American ambassador, John Hay (Jock) Whitney, decided to knock some golf balls around, and Eisenhower told Snyder to get off about a 100 or a 150 yards and serve as a target. Major General Snyder did as he was told. Snyder, without being too rueful about it, for his commander in chief had told him what to do, recorded it in his diary.

Then there was what Mattingly was sure was Snyder's cardiological ignorance. Snyder himself did not see things that way. Years later when he was into his eighties, he recorded in his draft medical history of Eisenhower that he was not too worried when he went to see his commander in chief in the middle of the night on September 24, 1955. He was equal to the occasion. Perhaps this thought indicates a little braggadocio due to old age, but he probably also felt that way.

> Although my principal requirement for many years of very active practice had been general surgery, I had had considerable experience in cardiac infarction and had treated for years many digitalized patients. These patients had been men of real stature in America. These treatments had been reinforced by consultation with eminent cardiologists in major cities. I did not because of these experiences feel unprepared to deal with a grave cardiac emergency.[6]

Nor was this the limit of his cardiovascular knowledge, for when he had gone out to 750 Lafayette Street that night he also was ready for a stroke. He had had experience with stroke patients and "felt reasonably qualified to deal with that."[7]

Mattingly braced himself for trouble and it soon was at hand. The first scare came on November 13, just two days after his return from Denver: before Mattingly departed from his quarters at Walter Reed en route to the White House he looked at the headline of the front page of the newspaper and was startled. The headline said, "The President Is Back to Golf." A front-page photograph showed the president swinging a golf club! He asked himself whether Snyder had "gone nuts."

What had happened? Fortunately, upon arrival at the White House he met John Eisenhower who immediately apologized for the photo, and when he saw the president there was another apology. John related how he and his son, David, had gone for a short walk with the president on the grounds in back of the mansion, and David had taken along a golf club. The president demonstrated to David how to hold the club and raised it to a swinging position. A photographer with a telescopic lens was watching from the Ellipse and got a prize picture.[8]

Snyder was to take Eisenhower to Key West after Christmas, and Mattingly wondered if he could recognize early signs of heart failure or was capable of managing any arrhythmia or complication that might develop in monitoring the president's cardiac status during increased physical activity. Reporters would be everywhere, and Snyder would want to show how well the president was recovering, which probably meant having him play golf. Mattingly evaluated the president at the White House prior to departure on December 28 and displayed some anxiety about the trip. Snyder said he, as personal physician, would like to have him, the cardiologist, go to Key West but feared that his presence or that of another cardiologist would "give the wrong message to the press that the president's cardiac status was such that it required a cardiologist in attendance."[9] Several days after the presidential party left Washington, Snyder telephoned about an irregularity of the pulse that had developed with the increased physical activity. It apparently was premature contractions, experienced intermittently since the president left the hospital. More important was Snyder's report of an increase in the overall heart rate and easy fatigability, and Mattingly feared Eisenhower might suffer heart failure before Snyder knew what was going on. Simple medications for suppression of the premature beat, and a slowed pace in physical activity, solved the problem.

To Mattingly's relief, the White and Snyder flaps gradually died down. There were no changes in the arrangement of medical authority. It had been a close call, indeed two close calls, what with White and Snyder doing what seemed right in their own eyes.

2.

As might have been expected, White in his forthright way tried to dominate the medical decision on the second term. On December 17 he came to Gettysburg where he was joined by Mattingly and Snyder. It was the first time he had seen Eisenhower since the return from

Denver. The three doctors held a press conference afterward for which White's notes included two statements: "The progress to date has been excellent and encouraging but he has not yet been subjected to his full load of work. Four or five weeks of exposure to that should suffice for a medical estimate as to the ability of his heart to stand it." And again:

> The future rests in the "lap of the gods," as it more or less does with all of us in this room. With average luck and common sense care the President can live for years and be fully active, as have many others among my patients who have recovered similarly at this stage of their convalescence, but since none of them has been president of the USA I cannot speak with experience on that point. We can only advise the President medically—he must make his own decision.[10]

The session seemed to have gone off all right, and Mattingly and Snyder went back to Washington. Whereupon White again invited himself to a meal with the president, this time with two purposes, one of which he accomplished in the afternoon when, as he wrote the two army physicians, he and Eisenhower "walked quite a long distance around the farm, not rapidly, but over much rough ground through the cornfields and up and down several gentle slopes. We went at a pace that was just suited to the ground but we didn't stop to rest. I think it took us half an hour and there was quite a cold wind." As he observed the president, "He was not short of breath in the least nor did he complain of any discomfort, leg weariness, or fatigue." He wrote his fellow doctors that this was an "excellent functional test."[11]

It was at lunch that White tried to accomplish his second purpose. Years afterward in his autobiographical memoir he spoke of "my vain effort to persuade the President not to run for re-election in 1956—a story which was extremely confidential at the time and for many years afterwards." He described how he and the president sat out on the veranda enjoying light picnic fare and then turned to a philosophical discussion about the decision Eisenhower soon would make. "I contended," White recalled, "that since I knew from previous conversations that his major aim in life was to promote world peace, he should not run for re-election." The Boston physician told the president that his heart would stand the strain but that the inevitable political maneuvering could endanger his peacemaking role. White thought Eisenhower should take on an even higher role than president of the United States: he should become a world ambassador for peace.

Here was a fascinating moment in the lives of Eisenhower and White. The president, full of years and honors, about the same age as his consulting cardiologist (Eisenhower was sixty-five, White sixty-nine), was having lunch with a man he had not invited and whose advice he had not asked (years later Eisenhower told Mattingly such was the case), but necessarily spending his time this way because White "almost had a veto power over Dad's political career," so John Eisenhower said afterward. "There's no doubt that without White's endorsement, Dad could never have run a second time."[12] If White so much as intimated to the newspaper press that he, the most famous cardiologist in the country, probably the world, had advised the president not to run, it would have raised the gravest questions. The president would have had to retire. White, on his part, had seen a chance to get Eisenhower out of the presidency and also accomplish what he, the doctor, thought highly desirable—a campaign, perhaps even a crusade, for world peace.

During the heart attack and his weeks of recovery Eisenhower had not lost an iota of his mental sharpness, and he took the measure of his situation with White. "He answered," White wrote years later, "that as an ex-president he might have little influence. . . . He would have more as president."[13]

Pushing his point, White wrote Eisenhower the next day, "I think that you would be very smart to announce your decision before the doctors confer about you again in February." He was reminding the president how awkward it was to find his fate bound up in doctors' conferences, and how much easier it would be to become a world ambassador and push the doctors aside. In this letter White volunteered his personal assistance. He noted his own position among cardiologists, nationally and internationally, and his post as clinical professor of medicine, emeritus, at Harvard. When Mattingly years later saw these almost embarrassing statements, he ventured that White thought the president and he, together, might achieve the Nobel Peace Prize. White had been put up earlier and had not had enough clout to get it.[14]

But White had miscalculated. If he had known the ways of politicians, especially such a refined one as Eisenhower, he would have realized that the soft answer he received at the Gettysburg lunch was soft because of his own, White's, momentary hold over the president. Eisenhower was playing for time. He knew of the indecision of his doctors about the state of his health, an indecision born of differences.

On December 12, just before the Gettysburg consultation of December 17, White had told him in a letter: "Confidentially, I believe that my own attitude is midway between the slightly divergent views of General Snyder and Tom Mattingly. The General's attitude is, I believe, a little more liberal than mine and Tom's a little more conservative."[15] In dealing with White, the president surely was going to see if the doctors' differences might distance them from his decision. Somehow he seems to have conveyed this idea to White, who wrote Snyder the day after the Gettysburg meeting that "he does not want to be dependent on our advice for his decision unless it should be, of course, distinctly unfavorable." A few days later White received more enlightenment. On December 22, Mattingly advised him that Eisenhower was accustomed both to independence and clarity:

> I am glad that you have learned firsthand from the President that he does not desire his physicians to make decisions about his future. He will make his own decisions. He has much experience in the past in making decisions on important and vital problems in both war and peace. What he likes from his staff and advisors, medical or otherwise, is accurate and usable information, regardless of whether it is optimistic or pessimistic.[16]

On January 8 the doctors—White, Mattingly, Snyder, and General Heaton of Walter Reed—held a dinner conference at Snyder's apartment trying to decide whether Eisenhower was fit to serve a second term. Fortunately for the president, who could not have expected a positive attitude, a sort of stand-off resulted. According to White's notes:

> Much debate—prolonged and from all angles concerning the hazards and wisdom re continuing in the Presidency after this term is completed. It was obvious that all believed that the President would be active no matter what he decides about the Presidency and that the hazards to him might not be very different, but he is concerned deeply about the possibility of recurrent illness or death while in office after this term is finished. . . . Dr. Snyder stated that he was giving the President all information he thought necessary about the risk of the next five years. The President realizes this. Mattingly and P.D.W. insisted that he must make it clear that the risk is great. Dr. Mattingly thinks it is even—P.D.W. inclined to think it is less than even but also agreed that no adequate statistics are available even though they may be referred to

and quoted ad nauseam. Dr. Mattingly's experience has obviously been far more unfavorable than that of P.D.W. . . . The impressions of some are unfavorable, of others favorable.[17]

Eisenhower must have found out that the meeting was inconclusive. It seems impossible that he failed to discover who said what at the meeting. Snyder was too close to the president to have kept the result from him. Snyder, too, had resented his secondary role in the president's health care after the cardiologists took over and would not have minded siding with the president, if only for that reason.

Then on Friday, January 13, the president held a meeting of his own, in which he assembled in the White House a group of his most intimate advisers and asked them if he should run. With a single exception, his brother Milton, every person present advised him to run. Milton had appointed himself rapporteur of the group, and lined up two people to oppose his brother's renomination, but in the congeniality of the occasion these two men failed to do their duty. Milton then made the case against a second term and found his brother not altogether receptive. After the meeting Milton talked to his brother and added a few points and then put them all together in a two-page memorandum, the most important paragraph of which was the following:

> Finally, may I point out the obvious, more personal, perhaps more selfish view: if you decline to run, you will clearly go down in history as one of our greatest military and political leaders, with no major domestic or international difficulty to mar your record. If you go on, you might enhance your standing, contribute mightily to peace and to sound principles at home; or you might face serious economic setbacks at home and upheavals abroad. You might jeopardize your health and your ability to carry the burdens of office.

Upon receiving the memo the president drew a long line beside this paragraph and scribbled beside it in ink, "Of no great moment; even though history might condemn a failure it cannot weigh the demand of conscience." In this regard, perhaps, conscience had two parts. At the meeting the general belief was that if the president retired and Vice-President Nixon ran for the presidency, the Democrats would run Adlai Stevenson again, and Nixon would lose. No other Republican presidential candidate loomed, other than Eisenhower.[18] The other part of Eisenhower's reasoning probably was that he had not yet secured his program, nationally and internationally, and that the GOP was not yet a trustworthy implement for either purpose—the party's conservatives were constantly threatening to get out of line.

The day after the White House meeting, January 14, Eisenhower sent a letter to White turning down a world ambassadorship for peace. He did it deftly, of course—he was not about to write a harsh or sarcastic letter. He wrote that he had tried to test out the idea of a world ambassador, telling his friends about the notion, and "it is astonishing how universally they have rejected the idea that an individual no matter how well known in the world, could be reasonably effective in the promotion of peace based on understanding, unless operating from an official position of great power."[19] In other words, he needed, if he did not himself want, the presidency.

Sometime after the dinner in Snyder's apartment, quite probably before the soft but conclusive answer of January 14, the president also must have begun moving in earnest against White, for he needed to disabuse the cardiologist of the notion that he, White, had a hold over the president. He began telling Snyder and Mattingly that White had been undercutting them, that White had not only been negotiating but had been going directly against what he, White, had claimed to be their serious medical role of determining whether the president should run again.

As perhaps Eisenhower expected, although that is difficult to know, Mattingly in a remarkable letter to White dated January 28 brought everything out in the open. He wrote it by hand, and there is but a single copy, in the White papers, though a draft is in the medical history in the Eisenhower Library.[20] During the dinner session at Snyder's apartment Mattingly seems to have said at some point that his friend White was a Dr. Jekyll and Mr. Hyde. During the meeting he did not explain the remark but did so in the letter. He was not referring to statistics, he said, but to the conflicting attitudes that White was presenting. At press conferences White had gone out of his way to present the president's recovery and health as excellent. He made light of the fatigue the president's other doctors had mentioned. "The Republican Party has accepted your attitude as a flat endorsement from you that the President's health is no longer a question, and from a health standpoint he is capable of running again. In fact, various members of the Cabinet and Jim Hagerty have taken such for granted from your confident attitude." But, on the other hand, the president had told the two army physicians that White had personally advised him "during your invited dinner and luncheon visits and in several personal letters" that he should not run again. Eisenhower also had remarked the difference in White's attitude to the press and that in personal conversation and letters. "Wouldn't it have been better as a consultant," Mattingly asked, "to have given the President such advice in the presence of General Snyder and myself?" White spoke of working as a team but sent advice and instruction directly and ignored the team. As late as January 23 he had written, "I hope that he will not decide one way or another before he knows of our own present careful appraisal of the hazard." All this was confusing and caused Mattingly, he wrote, to have anxiety as to what White's next recommendations and advice might be, or what he might say in a press conference. White's good friend, and such he was, ended on a note of friendship: "your professional judgment and your wonderful patient relationship" for which he had such respect.

White in reply wrote a handwritten letter abjectly apologizing for getting out in front. "I do believe that we can still act as a team," he explained, a little weakly, "and now that I have made this confession to you . . . you might tell General Snyder . . . my motives have been of the best (actually probably too idealistic for this rough and tumble world) and I hope that you and General Snyder (and the President too) will accept my explanation and apology for any confusion."[21]

3.

By this time the doctors' press conference of February 14 was fast approaching; the president's physicians would present their decision on whether Eisenhower was fit for a second term. It was not too difficult to guess what the doctors as a group would say—they would be favorable. But the exact nature of their enthusiasm was anyone's guess, depending upon who said what.

The process of decision had been going on for weeks among a group that included not merely the cardiologists from Walter Reed and Fitzsimons but the radiologists. The latter weighed in first. On December 10, Eisenhower was hospitalized overnight at Walter Reed for a cardiac evaluation by Mattingly. At this time the fluoroscopic examination of the heart was repeated with Colonel Elmer A. Lodmell, head of radiology. Mattingly was again convinced that the fluoroscopic findings indicated an aneurysm of the left ventricle. Lodmell did not agree and considered it just a healed scar from the old infarction that caused the poor contractility of an area of the ventricle. He believed, as had Ramsay from Fitzsimons, that because it did not show paradoxical pulsations it did not represent a true aneurysm. Shortly after the examination Lodmell attended a radiology meeting in Chicago, at which Ramsay was present. The two radiologists compared their findings and were essentially in agreement. Lodmell on return to Walter Reed indicated that he and Ramsay believed Mattingly's interpretation of an aneurysm might be correct, but they were not convinced from their own criteria that such an aneurysm was present. They acknowledged that if they reported an aneurysm it would probably be detrimental to the continuation of Eisenhower's presidency.[22]

The cardiologists then gave their opinions. The Fitzsimons cardiologist, Pollock, denied the presence of an aneurysm. White was favorable, although having said publicly there was no aneurysm, but admitted privately a widening of the infarction or a new infarction. Mattingly later discovered that a month after Eisenhower's heart attack White had written Dr. E. Cowles Andrus, cardiologist at Johns Hopkins Hospital and president of the American Heart Association, and the physician who White had sounded out for filling in as civilian consultant during a trip he planned out of the United States, that an extension of the infarction or a new infarction had developed, and that the infarction was more extensive than previously announced.[23] White's consultant on EKGs, Dr. Lepeschkin of the University of Vermont, had made an initial interpretation of the EKG changes that was ambiguous about further myocardial damage. White, as Mattingly sensed his position, was unenthusiastic about a second term but did not come out and say so. His advocacy of the world ambassadorship was a way of getting Eisenhower gracefully out of office; then there was all his equivocating back and forth.

Snyder of course favored a second term.

The count was two radiologists and two cardiologists and Snyder against Mattingly, who found himself making a last stand in favor of a conservative decision. On December 10, after he had seen the president at Walter Reed, he conferred with Snyder and Heaton. Snyder expressed himself irritably over Mattingly's continued belief in a left ventricular aneurysm. Mattingly snapped back, telling the two generals he did not want to attend the press conference they had scheduled and that they were free to use such portions of his evaluation and consultation as they desired, including omission of any reference to his interpretation of the radiological findings as showing an aneurysm. They insisted he attend because the press would expect a cardiologist to be present to answer questions. He finally agreed, saying he would simply concur in Snyder's report. He suggested that they not ask him to future press conferences and remarked that "if they did not have confidence in my diagnosis and opinions that they should have another consultant." By the time he reached his Walter Reed office that Saturday evening a note had arrived from Snyder, asking forgiveness for his hot temper and reaffirming confidence in Mattingly's professional judgment. Mattingly immediately forwarded a handwritten confidential report explaining why he considered it important to offer his best advice, considering his responsibility to the president. Earlier that afternoon he had promised Snyder he would not perform or participate in any subsequent fluoroscopic examinations of the president but simply include the radiologist's report in his evaluation, thus avoiding conflicting opinions. He did not participate in another fluoroscopic examination for nearly ten years, until the president had another heart attack in 1965, and Snyder by that time was no longer Eisenhower's personal physician.[24]

There was little more he could do. On January 4 while Snyder was in Florida with the president, he wrote him a formal letter reiterating his belief that the president should not run, that a second term would offer "definite hazards to the President's health and life."[25]

Everything then came down to February 14. That morning White and the others first saw the president, and then held a press conference presided over by Hagerty. Snyder began by reading a 450-word medical bulletin, which among other things said there were no symptoms indicating either weakness of the heart muscle or insufficient coronary reserve. The president's blood-clotting rate was "about the middle and upper third of the normal range." A reporter asked how long Eisenhower could serve as president. "We believe," Snyder said, "that he can serve four to five years or longer in a very active position of great responsibility."

At this point White entered the discussion. It must have been a moment of agony. Eisenhower's principal doctor, at least so far as the public was concerned, had been almost literally racking his brain for weeks prior to this occasion, wondering what he should say. In box 35 of his papers at the Countway Library of Medicine of the Harvard Medical School is an entire folder (number 17) devoted to the problem of what to say. In his neat, tidy manner White kept his draft statements in careful order. The task was to find a form of words that would combine his desire that Eisenhower run again with the dismal statistics of cardiovascular patients.

The drafts were numerous, and each time it was not so much the preliminary material—the sentences always started off all right—but the centerpiece of the contention, namely, how long might the president reasonably continue? In an early, perhaps the earliest, draft the doctor wrote a statement that disappeared from later drafts. As he described the problem, there were two points. One was that acquaintance with the job, the presidency, made the job easier. Eisenhower's predecessor, President Truman, had said so on one occasion. That point was all right. The other was that constant use of anticoagulants reduces the risk of further attacks of coronary thrombosis and of early mortality, which mixed politics with a medical point. Worse, it raised the mortality issue. In another draft two problems remained, he wrote, the strain of the work and uncertainty about the future. He said some correspondents thought the risk worth taking, others not, and the disagreement itself constituted the choice. This, he must have thought, was too flip a statement. He saw a different choice, between optimism and pessimism, and "reviewing my own experience, and recognizing the risk ahead I find myself inclined towards the side of the optimists though for pure personal safety's sake I would be relieved if he should decide not to run." The "personal" presumably meant the president. Then he turned favorable: "If the President chooses to run, we believe that the risk is medically an acceptable one." In an apparently later draft he was still looking at the dichotomy, optimism or pessimism, and penciled in the admission of "a greater incidence of new coronary trouble in a person who has had thrombosis already than in one who has not." But, he wrote, liability to recurrence was unpredictable, and he was against dogmatic prophesies.

The perfect phrasing, the proper wording, was intensely difficult because he was dealing with nothing less than a presidential second term. In one of his drafts he remarked that hardly any two persons were alike. He turned to another idea of similar nature: the strain of the presidency was great and no precedent existed. The presidency might be an underlying risk factor—its stresses raising the risk. But then hard work had little to do with underlying coronary artery disease, what was called atherosclerosis. On another page it became a question of how much good the president might do in his high office, which would be a lot. Perhaps more good than serving as a sort of superpresident. He returned to the risk and believed that both Eisenhower and the country, the latter in a vicarious way, could share in the risk.

Statistics? On a card he scribbled statistics from his 1941 study with Bland and said it was true that a majority of coronary cases eventually died heart deaths. But in the U.S. more than half of deaths, generally, were cardiac deaths. Too, deaths after initial infarctions sometimes were a long time later. He returned to the notion that hardly any two persons were alike; statistics had limited value. There might or might not ("perhaps an even chance," he inserted in brackets) be further coronary trouble within the next five ("to ten" he wrote in brackets) years.

Slowly, in these surprisingly uncertain and almost train-of-consciousness drafts, he drifted toward the opinion he would offer. He began by taking the middle course in a threefold choice. He would be neither an optimist nor a pessimist but a middle-of-the-roader. Puzzlement entered. His next phrase was "by stating," a wordy admission he was unsure of himself. The following phrase was "that there may or may not be," and that was no decision either. Then he came to the crucial phrase, "perhaps an even chance." He went on—of "further coronary trouble within the next five to ten years." In his draft he bracketed "perhaps an even chance." When the press conference came he omitted it.

February 14, 1956, Paul Dudley White chose the next president of the United States. Before the rows of intensely listening, furiously writing reporters he spoke the necessary words. "Now as to the future, after weighing carefully all available evidence, including our own experience, and fully aware of the hazards and uncertainties that lie ahead, we believe that medically the chances are that the President should be able to carry on an active life satisfactorily for another five to ten years."

Mattingly was aghast—White had made a wild guess. He had gone farther than Snyder, and, to be sure, White's words were what reporters at the conference immediately picked up. White's photograph, not Snyder's, got on the front page of the *New York Times.* According to James Reston's analysis of the conference, "Dr. Paul Dudley White did not exactly push President Eisenhower into another campaign for the Presidency today, but he certainly opened the door and invited him in."[26]

The remark about "another five to ten years" gave no attention to statistics. White had thought out what he said; it was no off-the-cuff comment. Reston saw him reading from a small library card. Still, the statistics of heart attacks as compiled by White and his colleague Bland, verified in 1954 and 1955, stood directly against such a projection. If Eisenhower had a left ventricular aneurysm, he was much worse off. Technically, White did not say ten years, only that "the President should be able to carry on an active life satisfactorily for another five to ten years." But even this was a gross distortion of the statistics, and he might as well have said flatly that the president would last ten years. The only explanation possible is that White's confidence, always buoyant, his missionary zeal to show sufferers from heart attacks that they could carry on, his enjoyment of the limelight, perhaps some sense that he had a veto power over the career of an incumbent president of the United States, his embarrassment at attempting to persuade the president to be a world ambassador for peace, and his Republican instincts (he was a registered Republican and told the press conference he would vote for Eisenhower if the president ran): all this led him astray. It was a great moment in his life, but not a responsible one. A colleague at the Harvard Medical School, Dr. David D. Rutstein, professor of preventive medicine, vice-president of the American Heart Association, published an article in the *Atlantic* the following August, entitled "Doctors and Politics," recounting his consternation over White's behavior. The article was an open rebuke. Rutstein began by citing the White-Bland statistics, also the later studies of general heart attacks. Had he known of Mattingly's diagnosis of a left ventricular aneurysm, there is no telling what he might have written.[27]

But after White's statement during the medical press conference, it was too late to change anything. No article of months later could be of avail. On the morning after the conference, a front-page headline of the *Washington Post* extended across eight columns: "Eisenhower Can Run, Doctors Decide: 5–10 Years in Public Life Seen Ahead." The doctors' announcement came after the New York Stock Exchange had closed. On the West Coast, however, volume spurted with Du Pont gaining four points over its New York close, Bethlehem Steel two and three-quarters, U.S. Steel two, and General Motors one and one-half. Many other leading issues rose between one and two points.

The president must have sighed with relief. The next day he wrote his consultant cardiologist:

> I want to send you at least a brief note to express my gratitude to you for coming to Washington yesterday. It is seemingly quite

useless for me to attempt to tell you how much your professional opinion means to me, and what a great service you have done to the American people in giving them your honest estimate of my condition. And, of course, as always it was a great pleasure to see you.

Thank you, too, for my "Valentine." I hope all the hearts in the postman's pouch pass their cardiograph tests with flying colors!

With warm personal regard.[28]

Eisenhower left Washington for a two-week vacation at the Thomasville, Georgia, plantation of his secretary of the treasury, George M. Humphrey, to consider the question of seeking reelection.

The president found himself with not merely a medical release, so to speak, but an enthusiastic one, and that in itself was exhilarating, as he had told Dr. White in his note. His own decision had to rest on the medical release; it could have no other basis. Beyond that he had all the urgings of his friends at the meeting of January 13. He himself wanted a second term. The party had no other candidate who could win, and Eisenhower's national and international program was incomplete. Milton Eisenhower advised against a second term. The president's son John composed a long memorandum against a second term and gave it to his father, who received it noncommittally.[29]

Mamie was neutral; she readily agreed that if her husband did not have something seriously to do, something to contain his nervous energy, something like the presidency, he could easily bring himself around to another heart attack. Shortly after return to the White House, Eisenhower announced on February 29 that he would run again.

4.

After the president's announcement that he would run again, one final decision remained: his choice of a running mate.[30]

Eisenhower could have had no real complaints about Nixon's performance as vice-president. He had given him serious assignments, such as defending the administration against Adlai Stevenson's midterm criticisms in 1954, also the anticommunist criticisms of Senator Joseph R. McCarthy of Wisconsin, and he had sent him on a goodwill tour of Australia, Pakistan, and India. Nixon had done well, although in the case of the 1954 campaigning he had gone after former President Truman's secretary of state, Dean Acheson, with a good deal more zeal than Eisenhower thought wise. The president took Nixon aside after a committee meeting and told him so.[31] The vice-president seemed to be, and probably in every way one could measure was, loyal. When Hagerty called to tell him that Eisenhower had suffered a heart attack, Nixon said all the right things over the telephone—showing concern only for the president and no concern for the possibility that he, the vice-president, might become president. When White and Mattingly spoke to him out in Denver about Eisenhower's chances for recovery, and gave assurances that the chances were excellent that the president could resume his duties, Nixon for a moment perhaps dropped his guard. Mattingly watched the vice-president's face with care and thought he detected an expression of disappointment. On the day the president went back to Washington from Denver, Clarence Randall, who filled his massive diary with choice gossip, heard from a friend that Nixon was already thinking of running for president in 1956 but would not run, so the friend said, unless Eisenhower asked him. Apparently Nixon told this to Randall's friend.[32] But other than the unguarded disappointment that Mattingly thought he saw, and the rumor that Randall picked up, whatever one could make of those incidents, Nixon seems to have done nothing to persuade onlookers of undue ambition. Nothing got back to Eisenhower, who had no obvious, definable reason to believe his vice-president was unworthy of a second term.

The president seemed much attracted to his vice-president. To anyone who inquired, even his brother Milton, he declared how Nixon and he held to the same principles, saw eye-to-eye, each doing his best to make the Republican party a vital, forward-looking force in the life of the nation. He beheld his vice-president as a wonderful young man, full of the right principles, just the sort of New Republican the country needed to get it out of the old Democratic ruts. Milton did not like Nixon and undoubtedly told his brother exactly how he felt. He found Nixon delightful in private conversation, friendly and at ease, but when the vice-president thought he was being a public figure he turned to stone. Nixon, so Milton thought, showed an intense ambition that was not at all attractive. To this his brother the president seemed impervious, but the two agreed to disagree. In this family conclave, Milton's brother held to his views of "Dick" Nixon.[33]

And yet Eisenhower's views of Nixon showed a marked lack of enthusiasm. Despite all the encomiums Nixon could not offer the magic something or other. He was, in a word, uncharismatic. The presidential reasoning? The vice-president was young and could wait a while; he did not have to be in a hurry. A decade earlier he had been an even younger naval lieutenant, just out of the service, and it was a little incongruous to run a lieutenant with a general of the army. Then there may have been another reason lurking in the recesses of the presidential mind. Eisenhower was no simpleton, and it was not easy to guess his thoughts; he possessed an outlook that many men and women of power seem to have, which is that while they like all the people around them and are full of feeling about how equal they all are, even the leader among the led, they do not quite want to see much achievement among their subordinates. They husband a feeling that they, themselves, are the achievers. It is not a good situation whenever anyone gets too close, and the margins narrow. Eisenhower may well have had something of this outlook for his ambitious vice-president.

The president did not place his vice-president at the top of lists he made of possible running mates. Early in 1953 he made a list of "somewhat younger" individuals whom he admired, and in that list Nixon's name appeared ninth in a group of sixteen. His first two choices—and this was a series of judgments committed only to his diary and may have been offhand—were his brother Milton and Henry Cabot Lodge, Jr. Late in 1954 he made another list for an old Abilene friend. This time he liked, best of all, a renegade Democrat from Texas, Robert B. Anderson, at that moment deputy secretary of defense. "Another fine man is Herbert Hoover, Jr. In addition there are Dick Nixon, Cabot Lodge, Herb Brownell and Charlie Halleck. Some still believe that Harold Stassen has a political future."[34] The younger Hoover was undersecretary of state, Halleck a leader of the House, Stassen director of the Foreign Operations Administration. By early 1956 the president had three favorites: Milton, his bridge partner General Alfred M. Gruenther, and Anderson.

During the period from December 1955 until near the end of April 1956, the president refused to clarify Nixon's position. When Eisenhower on February 29 announced his own willingness to run again, Press Secretary Hagerty briefed him for the forthcoming press conference and mentioned that questions might come up on the vice-presidency. The president needed no advice from "Jim, my boy," as he often described him. He knew exactly what he would say. He would remark that the subject of Nixon's role in a possible second Eisenhower term had already received too much attention. Never before, he would say, had the vice-president announced or not announced. The convention would handle this issue after nomination of the president.

Eisenhower said he could not be sure the Republican party wanted him, that is, the president, and he would not say a word about the vice-presidency until after it chose him, Eisenhower. Hagerty said there might be a question as to whether the president had talked to Nixon. The president said of course he had.[35]

For week after week Eisenhower played this cat-and-mouse game. On March 7, Marvin L. Arrowsmith of the Associated Press tried to draw out the president and utterly failed, in part because he sought to be clever.

> "Mr. President," he said, "there have been some published reports that some of your advisers are urging you to dump Vice President Nixon from the Republican ticket this year; and, secondly, that you yourself have suggested to Mr. Nixon that he consider standing aside this time and, perhaps, take a cabinet post. Can you tell us whether there is anything to those reports?"
>
> "Well, now," answered the chief executive, "as to the first one, I will promise you this much: if anyone ever has the effrontery to come in and urge me to dump somebody that I respect as I do Vice President Nixon, there will be more commotion around my office than you have noticed yet. Second, I have not presumed to tell the Vice President what he should do with his own future."[36]

And so the time passed with Nixon in an altogether unenviable position. The possibility of his being "dumped" presented him with a great deal of trouble. On December 26, 1955, the president told the vice-president that he should consider taking a cabinet post, perhaps as secretary of defense, for such a position would prepare him for the presidential nomination in 1960. Shortly afterward, he told Secretary of State Dulles he might make Nixon secretary of commerce because the vice-president lacked the qualifications for secretary of state. In early April he told the chairman of the Republican national committee, Leonard W. Hall, that Nixon could take the secretaryship of health, education, and welfare, then a single department.

Whatever the presidential reasoning about how a cabinet post would prepare Nixon for the presidency, the vice-president wanted no part of such preparation. It was like sending a Ph.D. back to kindergarten. Why should he take a cabinet post when if he could hang onto the vice-presidency he might gain the presidency itself through the resignation or death of his chief?

The president's own difficulties with his lists of alternates to Nixon eventually brought a sort of surcease to the vice-president's troubles. The problem with Eisenhower's lists was that all the most attractive individuals he thought of, save one whom he decided against, were unavailable. It would have been politically impossible to run with Milton, however attractive and even reasonable such a course. Some years later when President John F. Kennedy brought his own brother into the cabinet as attorney general it was an exceedingly awkward arrangement, and to have made Robert F. Kennedy vice-president would have been impossible. For a while Eisenhower played with the idea of a ticket consisting of his secretary of the treasury, Humphrey, for president, and Milton for vice-president. But Humphrey was too conservative to be a presidential possibility, and anyway Eisenhower was going to run again. As for Lodge, by 1956 he had cooled on him. For other reasons he was no longer thinking—if he ever thought seriously—of Hoover, Brownell, Halleck, or Stassen. It was impossible to run with General "Al" Gruenther, for two generals on the ticket might have made both men vulnerable. There had been criticism of Eisenhower's predecessor, Truman, for appointing generals to ambassadorships and in the case of George Marshall, the secretaryship of state. So far as concerned "Bob" Anderson, Eisenhower in early April 1956 offered him the nomination and he refused it.

After the choices narrowed, actually eliminated themselves, and without knowing who some of the choices were and in the case of Anderson how far the presidential enthusiasm had gone, Nixon still found himself in a box without a presidential invitation to be on the ticket. The vice-president had to ask Eisenhower, as if it were a favor (which indeed it was), if he could run again. When Nixon on April 26 went to the oval office and told the president it would be an honor to be his running mate, he must have felt deeply humiliated. (He would have felt more so if he had realized that the president was surreptitiously taping this personal conversation.)[37] The vice-president tried to make the most of the occasion. He said he had been thinking about the president's suggestion of perhaps two weeks earlier that he ought to consider a method of indicating his availability as a candidate for renomination. (This was a fine left-handed approach.) His thinking, he said, was along these lines: "Obviously any man, and he would not be an exception, would welcome the opportunity to be a Vice Presidential candidate on this ticket—or to serve in any other capacity that the President and the Party felt was the proper spot for him." (The second part of the sentence was a fib, but he had to say it.) The vice-president, to underline his point and gain a little conversational time, said that was exactly what he would say in the event he should answer a question that to date, he said, he had avoided: "In the event the President and the Convention indicate that they would like to have you run, would you turn it down?" (The last few words posed an unbelievable choice, the query was so dumb it needed no answer.) The vice-president, solemn-faced and nervous, made a few more remarks that repeated his desire to answer the silly question. At that juncture Eisenhower, perhaps with a suppressed grin, brought the charade to an end, remarking that as long as the vice-president was content, he, the president, would be delighted to have him. He called in Hagerty, who volunteered (had he been programed?) to take the vice-president outside to meet the gentlemen and ladies of the press, who were waiting, and apprise them of his decision.

The president thus chose his running mate. In retrospect it is of interest that of the leading possibilities in May 1953, in 1954, and in early 1956—Milton Eisenhower, Lodge, Gruenther, Anderson, and Nixon—two probably would have worked, and the others were very poor choices. Milton would have made a good vice-president and so would have Gruenther. Lodge, the Boston Brahmin, was a lightweight, a bright man with a marked streak of laziness, which Eisenhower may have discovered. Anderson seemed attractive ("just about the ablest man that I know anywhere"),[38] marvelously knowledgeable about national and international financial matters, but many years later he got into trouble because he was too nimble-witted. He evaded his personal income taxes and operated an illegal bank in the West Indies, and a federal judge sent him to prison. He was also an alcoholic. As everyone knows, Nixon went on to ignominy.

Behind Eisenhower's choice of a running mate was hardly the calculation the president should have made. He had just suffered a serious heart attack. For a moment, during the first few days when he was in the oxygen tent, lifted to the bathroom and back, forbidden to get out of bed, and sedated, he surely knew that things were serious. Then had come the chair sitting, and the appearance of one aide and cabinet official after another, and trips in a wheel chair out onto the sun decks of his VIP floor. Gradually the world came back into focus, and as it did, his mind, now keenly alert, must have heard the throb of politics again, the distant drums of the forthcoming election. As if he were putting on an old and convenient coat, the president began making the political equations in his mind, equations in which no president had ever chosen a vice-presidential running mate because the latter was successor to the president. Cleveland despised his vice-president, Stevenson, and indeed they had no similarities of intellect or opinion. Wilson gave no attention to Marshall, whom he considered an Indiana nonentity capable only of making embarrassing quips. Harding had not even chosen Coolidge; the GOP convention of 1920 thrust him on the ticket. Thereafter Harding gave the Vermonter no thought. And so did Eisenhower treat Nixon. He had announced the latter as "my boy" in 1952 after the hullabaloo over the "Checkers" speech died down, and then he forgot about him. He never measured Nixon as a possible successor, measuring him only as an assistant, in which case he preferred Anderson and tried to get "Dick" into a minor cabinet post on the theory that he lacked experience to be secretary of state. After Eisenhower regained his confidence and began to regain his health, he was intelligent enough to realize that Mattingly thought his physicians may have underestimated his illness but did not pursue that point of truth to its logical end. It is impossible to escape the conviction that, as was so evident among party leaders in 1944 when Roosevelt toyed with several possible candidates for vice-president and finally accepted a man he hardly knew, Truman, so Eisenhower in 1956 displayed a similar unconcern. He really did not care much beyond the setting out of preferences—he did not consider the possibility that his second term might have ended as Roosevelt's fourth term had.

6
Two More Crises

After the president underwent his heart attack and recovered, he declared himself a candidate for reelection and chose a vice-presidential running mate, which he did in a circuitous, slightly duplicitous, way (but then no more so than the ways of most of his predecessors). Yet the president's problems were not at an end, as became apparent when in the summer of 1956, even before he had been renominated, he suffered an attack of Crohn's disease and had to have an operation. In November 1957 he suffered a small stroke.

1.

First came the Crohn's disease attack, but not before the president was diagnosed as suffering from the disease. On May 10, 1956, Eisenhower went to Walter Reed overnight for a comprehensive cardiovascular evaluation and a general medical survey. Mattingly was delighted with his part of the examination; everything was in good order, and he saw no untoward signs of what he still strongly believed had been a left ventricular aneurysm complicating the cardiac infarction of the preceding September. The radiologist, however, during a study of the gastrointestinal tract identified the presence of Crohn's disease in the terminal ileum.

The question became one of what to say. Should the doctors "tell them everything"? Snyder decided not to do so doubtless on the theory that if an obstruction was not present at the moment perhaps it would not develop in the future, and in any event the future could take care of itself. He released a statement about the entire examination, which included a commentary that the president had a "normally functioning digestive tract."[1]

As luck would have it, not quite a month later, early in the morning of Friday, June 8, the president developed an acute intestinal obstruction. He had gone to a formal dinner the evening before and had eaten moderately, but for lunch that day he had had a salad. Both he and the butler, Charles, knew that he was not supposed to eat salads because raw vegetables could bring on stomach troubles. But he ordered himself one, and the butler served it. Snyder later wrote that he, the president's doctor, just knew there was a plug of celery stuck in the president's twisted ileum (and sure enough, the operation revealed the plug of celery).

The Crohn's disease attack had several sides to it, medical and otherwise. One was Snyder's initial prescription of milk of magnesia when Mamie called him in the middle of the night. Perhaps Snyder thought it would dissolve the celery plug. Eisenhower, however, had taken milk of magnesia at the Doud house in the early morning hours of the heart attack not many months before. When it eventually became known that Snyder's patient on two serious occasions when he was really ill had taken milk of magnesia, reporters wrote stories about the president's private physician, born in Wyoming, who had spent all his adult years in the army, and whose principal solution to medical ills was milk of magnesia.

Another Snyder embarrassment was that as at the outset of the heart attack, so again this time at 8:00 A.M. on the morning of June 8, he instructed Hagerty to announce that the president had an upset stomach. At 11:45 he changed his mind because it was evident that the plug of celery was not going to come out by ordinary means and might require an operation. He called Hagerty again and changed the diagnosis to Crohn's disease—a move that was worse than prescribing milk of magnesia or referring to a stomach upset. The alert Dr. Rutstein and a group of doctor friends were sitting around in Boston and unanimously concluded that the president's doctors made no sense. In his article in the *Atlantic* he said, "It is very doubtful that any physician can make an unequivocal diagnosis of this disease in a patient whose presenting symptom is intestinal obstruction unless the physician has had previous knowledge of the existence of this disease in the patient." He mercilessly quoted the press announcement of a month before about a normally functioning digestive tract. His group agreed, he wrote, that "the history of the acute illness as released to the public up to that time was inconsistent with the diagnosis of [Crohn's disease], because [it] is a chronic disease which very rarely has obstruction as its first symptom."[2]

There is an old admonition about the truth, which everyone knows more or less, and it surely held for Snyder's cover-up of the finding in May and the misleading diagnosis of an upset stomach. This is that quite apart from the morality of telling the truth it is wise for prudential reasons. As mentioned, the truth has its own logic; no one will trip himself up by telling the truth.

The details of the Crohn's disease operation might not seem important, since everything worked out according to plan. Heaton's description in the clinical record makes no effort to inform the lay reader but is graphic enough:

> The ileum was brought into view and the terminal 25–30 centimeters presented the typical appearance of Crohn's disease; namely, the involved ileum was grayish red, thickened, indurated and contracted, and presented typical clawlike projections of mesenteric fat to the antimesenteric border. The contiguous mesentery was markedly thickened, shortened and opaque. There were no large succulent lymph nodes seen over the above mesentery. The above process was sharply and dramatically demarcated. The bowel immediately proximal to the involved segment was markedly dilated, of good pink color, and slightly edematous, and its contiguous mesentery was quite normal in length, transparency and consistency.[3]

But the plan of the operation had a possible political aspect worth mentioning. The question in General Heaton's mind—the commanding general of Walter Reed was the operating surgeon—as he contemplated operating on the president had to be which of two procedures he would use. One was simple to do and involved a quick recovery; the other not so easy with a longer recovery. The first was a bypass, which leaves the blocked portion of the ileum or bowel in place; the surgeon simply opens a hole in the side of the bowel and attaches it to a similar hole below. The other requires removal of all the diseased intestine and takes a longer period of recuperation. Heaton surely knew that for the president to come down with a second illness within months of the heart attack, and in the midst of his campaign for reelection, was terribly embarrassing, and Eisenhower needed to show he could recover quickly.

It was impossible at the time and is still impossible for anyone to describe the bypass as a political decision. General Heaton and the participating surgeons all agreed that a bypass was the only recourse. The principal consideration was that they were dealing with a patient who recently had had a heart attack. In the operating room the professor of surgery of George Washington University Medical School, Bryan Blades, was standing right behind Heaton, and Blades said to him,

> "Leonard, if you resect that bowel, I'm going to have your license taken away from you."

"Bryan," Heaton answered, "you know this is the accepted method of treatment." But no one wanted to do that. "I mean," said Heaton, "we've got to get this patient off the operating table. And we got to do it damn fast."

"I agree with you," said Blades.

A secondary reason for a bypass was that the surgeons were operating on an emergency basis. They had had no time to prepare the bowel—clean it out—for the operation. A third was the danger of a "blowout"; if they resected the diseased part of the ileum, having not prepped the bowel, food might back up against the sutures and try to push its way through with appalling results. In his own operating experience Heaton had had two blowouts.[4]

As the surgeons must have feared, in the long run the bypass proved unfortunate. The discoverer of Crohn's disease, Burrell B. Crohn (he had defined it only in 1932), had said a bypass could allow the disease to recur. Years later Eisenhower had a recurrence after he suffered a series of heart attacks. "He had a developing pain in the abdomen with resulting distention and all the signs and symptoms of a serious bowel obstruction, and we were forced to open up his abdomen and relieve the obstruction . . . and found that there was a loop of distal ileum about eighteen inches proximal to the previous ileocolostomy site adherent to the abdominal wall. And we just relieved the obstruction of that loop and got out."[5] He died shortly thereafter, admittedly of a heart attack, perhaps brought on by the strain of the operation.

There was no real public discussion in 1956 of the bypass versus a resection, for it involved medical subtleties. In other ways, though, the president's doctors did not tell reporters as much as they well might have. Hagerty presided over the press conference following the operation and warned the gentlemen of the press not to ask political questions because the doctors, he said, were not politicians. The questions inevitably appeared and the doctors answered them, if sometimes obliquely. They gave it as their considered medical opinion that nothing had happened to prevent Eisenhower from following his plans as president, candidacy included. Nor did they say that Crohn's disease is a chronic disease with recurrence varying between one-third and two-thirds of those patients operated on, depending on the stage of the disease, type of surgery, and follow-up. They did not say that most recurrences came within the first year after operation, nor did they mention that it might be difficult for a president to maintain nutrition and weight. Someone asked the doctors if the attack and operation had affected the president's life expectancy. The answer: "We certainly don't think so." They added: "We think it improves his life expectancy." The latter was a silly comment. As Rutstein relentlessly observed, "There is no question that the relief of the intestinal obstruction improved the health of the President. On the other hand, the emergence of a second chronic illness cannot by any stretch of the imagination improve the total health status of the patient."[6] Physicians throughout the country began to enter the argument, saying that Crohn's disease was a chronic disease, that recurrence near the side-tracking site was likely, that the president might have recurrent periods of disability.

The reporters were told that patients over sixty-five do not have recurrences—this in face of the fact that scientific reports in the medical literature referred to age at onset, not at operation. Wherever enough cases had been collected for analysis, such as at the Mayo Clinic, age had no effect on the recurrence rate. On June 19 Hagerty put an end to these speculations by announcing that the president's physicians "have no intention of engaging in controversy with other doctors who have no personal knowledge of the case."

To Snyder it must have been a case of the less said the better. Weeks later on August 29 he held a conference with Heaton, Hagerty, and Dr. Isidor S. Ravdin of the University of Pennsylvania Medical School, who had been a consultant assisting with the operation. The conferees talked regarding publication in a medical journal of a factual report of the operation. "Ravdin strongly in favor, endorsed by Hagerty, questioned by Heaton, and not approved by me. At a later date, Ravdin made arrangements for publication in the Journal of the A.M.A. This action was finally revoked, and all agreed that it would be unwise to publish an article of this type even in a legitimate medical journal."[7]

During the president's Crohn's disease flare-up, Nixon received no new powers because of the incapacity of his chief. It is an interesting political fact that during the president's operation and recovery Nixon behaved carefully in part because the president again was ill. But the more obvious reason was that the Republican convention had not taken place, and he was not yet renominated. Any errors on his part would not add stars to his crown. On the eve of Eisenhower's surgery he was attending a banquet for 250 Young Republicans. The Reverend Frederick Brown Harris, chaplain of the Senate, asked that the group bow their heads in silent prayer. An irreverent photographer took Nixon's picture, standing solemnly with his eyes closed, and it appeared the next day in the *New York Times*. During the banquet reporters noticed Nixon blowing his nose into a handkerchief several times. He leaned over the speakers' table to tell them, with a grin, what he knew they had on their minds: "I know you're not interested in the health of the vice-president, but it's hay fever, not a cold." He assured them that Eisenhower soon would return to the "firing line."[8]

2.

Heaton's Crohn's disease operation on the president created a new medical setup at the White House; it produced the Snyder-Heaton team. The team itself was official. Heaton had seemed to dispose of a longtime problem in Eisenhower's health care, and the president was grateful. Eisenhower designated him as his surgeon a month after the operation, and he thereafter functioned as cophysician to the president. Now Mattingly had to consider the purposes and actions of two political physicians rather than one, and to see if it would be possible for him to remain on the team.

The appearance of Heaton in the White House medical equation, as Mattingly analyzed it, changed some things but mainly brought an ambitious general into a symbiotic relationship with another ambitious general. Heaton had been commanding general at Letterman General Hospital in San Francisco until 1954 when he went to Walter Reed. He was an outstanding surgeon who wanted to be the army's surgeon general. The latter post was to open in 1959. Heaton hence was on the lookout for anything that might interfere with his ambition. He had been unhappy with Snyder's procedure at the White House, which was to make appointments for the president with the various chiefs of professional services and outpatient clinics at Walter Reed without going through his office. He wanted to make the selections of personnel and to greet the president when he came to the hospital. Snyder at first ignored Heaton's requests, continuing to make requests directly to Mattingly and others. Heaton countered by telling his staff to notify him of any requests from Snyder. He was also unhappy with the president's annual evaluations at Fitzsimons in 1953 and 1954 under supervision of Major General Griffin, who also was under consideration for the office of surgeon general. He was put out by Griffin's association with the president and, indeed, disturbed that when the president had a heart attack in Denver he not only went to Fitzsimons but stayed there rather than returning to Walter Reed as soon as it was possible. When the president returned to Washington after his discharge from Fitzsimons, Mattingly rode back to his quarters at Walter Reed with Heaton, and on the way the general began to pump him about Griffin and the care at Fitzsimons. Mattingly gave the general little satisfaction, relating his honest opinion that Griffin and his staff had done a wonderful job. After the operation and Heaton's designation as the president's surgeon, he and Snyder tolerated each other because they needed each other. As Mattingly figured things out, "Heaton needed the support of Snyder and the president to obtain his appointment as the next surgeon general and Snyder needed the surgical expertise of Heaton who the president now accepted as the surgeon who saved his life."[9]

For Mattingly the immediate problem with the team was whether the two doctors were continuing the anticoagulant Coumadin. After the heart attack, at the beginning of the post-discharge period, the prescription from the Fitzsimons cardiological team of White, Pollock, and Mattingly had been an anticoagulant program, which meant keeping a stable level of prothrombin reduction (blood-clotting) of about 30 percent of normal control (normal equals a dangerous level for a patient). At the outset it was clear that prothrombin reduction was quite satisfactory, at about 30 percent. Then the finding of Crohn's disease and the intestinal surgery raised a question about the anticoagulant program, for as a general rule an anticoagulant is troublesome after surgery. Heaton and Snyder believed it might induce intestinal bleeding at the site of the lesions. Too, when the president began his campaign travels Snyder became concerned about accidental injuries or perhaps an assassination attempt. The prothrombin determinations became erratic and at times indicated that Snyder was not administering the drug.[10]

To all of this was added Snyder's "beefing-up" program for the president during the campaign, a disconcerting combination of steroids, endocrine products, and the general's favorite injections of liver extract. Snyder did not give Mattingly a record of, or provide information about, these medications. Sometimes the beefing-up program perhaps helped the Coumadin, other times acted against it.[11]

The result was thoroughly unsatisfactory. Lesions of the skin appeared, conjunctival hemorrhages, and bleeding gums, features that never had occurred prior to the surgery. After the election the general discontinued the beefing-up drugs and decreased the Coumadin. By December 1956, there was evidence of intestinal bleeding and a decrease in the president's normally high hemoglobin with the occurrence of a mild anemia. Mattingly at this point recommended to Snyder and Heaton that they either discontinue the anticoagulant or maintain better control. He hoped for consultation with experts in the field of anticoagulants. They did agree to evaluation and monitoring by Colonel William S. Crosby, chief of hematology at Walter Reed, but Snyder continued with the administration of Coumadin at an ineffective level.[12]

During a cardiological evaluation at the White House on May 1, accompanied by Snyder and Heaton, there was a sort of dispute between the outsider and the two insiders. At this time the president had nearly recovered from a siege of bronchitis and just returned from a vacation at Augusta where he had played golf. The latter was probably on his mind when he suddenly asked Mattingly if the cardiologist thought he could fly to Denver to join his friends there for golf at the Cherry Hills Golf Club. Mattingly continued to believe from previous observations that Eisenhower's blood pressure increased at high altitudes, and he knew the president would immediately play golf without a period of acclimatization to the higher altitude; so he gave a firm answer of "No." Eisenhower was displeased. Mattingly was awaiting an outburst when the president replied, "Tom, I will not go. You are the only one around here who has the guts to tell me something which you know I will not like but which you know is not good for me." Heaton and Snyder looked at each other but said nothing. Later, during return to Walter Reed, Heaton said, "You did not have to be so damned emphatic!"[13]

Independence sometimes has its rewards. Unknown to Mattingly, the president already had sent a personal letter to the secretary of the army suggesting him for promotion to brigadier general. Promotion came at the end of October 1957. The new general had mixed feelings. It pleased him greatly that the president had so expressed his appreciation. At the same time it disappointed him because eventually it would result in his assignment to command or staff, which would limit the opportunity to continue teaching and training in cardiac clinical and research activities.

All the while Eisenhower that summer and autumn of 1957 was encountering one domestic and foreign problem after another. It may well have been the most ill-starred time of his presidency, even worse than the Suez crisis of the autumn of 1956 when things boiled up and down rather quickly. In 1957 things boiled and boiled with one crisis coming down a little just as another went up.

The location for the president's summer vacation was all right, everything considered, and he enjoyed himself there. He had vacationed at Newport, a place that Mamie heartily disliked, in a house on the grounds of the Naval War College that was not entirely satisfactory; it was not a large house and was dank and humid. The salt air did not please Mamie, who was subject to asthmatic attacks. He himself enjoyed the nearby golf links and the somewhat remote situation from Washington—it was not so easy for Washington officials to fly up to Newport as compared to, say, Gettysburg. He perhaps also looked back in his mind's eye to his initial choice of a service branch. In 1910–1911 while living in Abilene, he actually had sought to go to Annapolis rather than West Point, and only his age, together with the fact that the appointing Kansas senator could not choose service branches for would-be cadets and had to make appointments to a general list, prevented it. Perhaps at Newport the minuses (Mamie's dislike) were outweighed by the golf and a certain nostalgia for the navy.

But the attractions of Newport were hardly enough to balance the distractions of, if only to mention one event, Governor Orval E. Faubus of Arkansas who was arguing over the integration of the high school in Little Rock. Eisenhower had accepted the Supreme Court decision of *Brown v. Board of Education of Topeka* and reluctantly was willing to enforce it. If Faubus would have behaved, all would have been well. He did not behave but came to see the president and promised to be good. Back in Arkansas he immediately took up the cause of his racist environment, and it was necessary for the president to send in regular troops of the U.S. Army. The whole situation was a mess.

Then the Russians launched their "Sputnik" satellite and nicely stirred up the international waters. At the time of Suez, Eisenhower had been furious with the Soviets for threatening the United States with their intermediate ballistic missiles. Doubtless the Soviets had no intention of carrying out the threat—nor could they (their missiles could not reach the United States)—but the president was angry. He told Snyder that if he were a dictator he would tell the Soviets that if they "moved a finger" he would drop the United States's entire stock of nuclear weapons on them.[14] His temper did not rise that high during the summer and autumn of the next year, but the Sputnik business was hard to take. The problem was that the lofting of a satellite did not show the United States far behind the Russians in the so-called space race. The Americans in 1954 had miniaturized the warheads of their H-bombs, which made it possible to send up hydrogen bombs without using enormous missiles. The United States hence had abandoned its programs for developing huge missiles. The Soviets had not been able to miniaturize, had the big missiles on hand, and so threw up Sputnik for the propaganda advantage. The result in America was a volume of criticism of the administration, frequently of the president, for failing to understand Soviet superiority.

Faubus's pretensions and Soviet pretensions were driving Eisenhower into a blue funk. Everyone seemed to want something from him:

> The developments of this year have long since proved to me that I made one grave mistake in my calculations as to what a second term would mean to me in the way of a continuous toll upon my strength, patience, and sense of humor. I had expected that because of the Constitutional amendment limiting a president's tenure to two terms, I could rather definitely in a second term be free of many of the preoccupations that were so time consuming and wearing in the first term. The opposite is the case. The demands that I "do something" seem to grow.[15]

On August 28 Snyder wrote how Ike had had a "rough morning" in the office with Mutual Security Administration problems, that is, weapons for NATO, with civil rights, and the like. On October 9 it was "a short morning, but a tense one with Arkansas and Soviet satellite problems, and his Press Conference." On October 10 the president had breakfast with His Excellency Komia Gbedemah, the finance minister of Ghana, "to adjust a misunderstanding of the exclusion of this man from a Howard Johnson restaurant on a prior day" (the minister had been refused service in a restaurant in Delaware). It had been the previous Friday that the Soviets had launched Sputnik. Queen Elizabeth II and Prince Philip arrived for a state visit on October 17. October 25 Snyder wrote in his diary of "the mounting tension of the past few weeks." The president's heart, he said, had showed some skips but otherwise doing "very well." On November 5 Eisenhower came into the White House private area fussing because he could not get things done; he was disturbed because, he said, he could not get a satisfactory speech writer to help with a speech for the following Thursday evening. On November 19 while in Augusta, he worried Snyder with another declaration about the presidency and his health. According to Snyder's diary:

> Returned to quarters [after golf]. BP 140/90 pulse 90 and again showed about 8 to 10 p.v.c.'s per minute. After five minutes, BP

130/86 pulse 82 with 1 to 2 p.v.c.'s a minute. The president again, as he has on a number of occasions in the past, accused the doctors of letting him in for something that he was not physically competent to handle. He stated that the doctors said he would be perfectly all right if he didn't allow tensions to affect his health, and then he commented: "How in the hell can anyone carry the load of the presidency without permitting the tensions to affect his physical self?"[16]

Six days later came the stroke.

3.

What happened to the president shortly after noon on November 25, 1957, was a strange experience, known only to individuals who have undergone it. For a moment he felt that he was in the world but not of it. That morning everything had been fine, and he had welcomed King Mohamed V of Morocco for a state visit with all of the panoply necessary to make a suitable impression on a visiting potentate. He had met the king at the airport, and after introductions the king and the president mounted the reviewing stand to witness the parading of the military honor guard, went down from the stand to inspect the guard, returned for an official welcome of the king to the United States, with a response by the king, followed by presentation of the keys to the city of Washington. The motorcade then departed for Blair House and passed down Pennsylvania Avenue with a file of Marines at attention on each side of the street, and secret servicemen watching out for the president and also ensuring that some visiting Moroccan who was unfriendly to His Majesty would not take a shot at him. All this accompanied by a great banner stretched across the avenue proclaiming the city's enthusiasm for the king. These formalities over, and with the prospect of a state dinner that evening, the president sought to get some work done. He was sitting at his desk looking over papers for signature when it happened:

As I picked up a pen to begin, I experienced a strange although not alarming feeling of dizziness. . . . I became frustrated. It was difficult for me to take hold of the first paper on the pile. This finally accomplished, I found that the words on it seemed literally to run off the top of the page. Now more than a little bewildered, I dropped the pen. Failing in two or three attempts to pick it up, I decided to get to my feet, and at once found I had to catch hold of my chair for stability. I sat down quickly and rang for my secretary. As Mrs. Whitman came to my desk I tried to explain my difficulty—and then came another puzzling experience: I could not express what I wanted to say. Words—but not the ones I wanted—came to my tongue. It was impossible for me to express any coherent thought whatsoever. I began to feel truly helpless.[17]

Mrs. Whitman sent for the president's assistant, Andrew Goodpaster, and Eisenhower tried to dictate to him but could not make himself understood. Meanwhile she had sent for Snyder, who quickly saw that his charge had dropped his spectacles and could not find them. Once the doctor got him to bed the president kept repeating the name "Jones," and Goodpaster, still present, would say, "W. Alton Jones?," and the president would say with difficulty, "No, Jones," and attempt to express himself further. Later, after the president got some sleep, he conversed with Lieutenant Colonel Roy E. Clausen, a neurologist from Walter Reed, and was able to repeat "Methodist Episcopal" but could not say "round the rock the ragged rascal ran." After the doctors left the president, he got out of bed and walked out through the hallway into Mrs. Eisenhower's room. Snyder then told him he could not attend the state dinner that evening, and he said, "If I can't go to that dinner, this spells the end of it for me. We'll be farmers from this time on." As Snyder was getting him back into bed he said, "Did I have a small . . . small . . ." but could not utter the word he wanted. His physician asked him if he meant "a small stroke," and he said, "Yes."[18]

When the president suffered the stroke, Snyder called Mattingly and there was another squabble. Not having examined the president, the cardiologist was reluctant to offer an opinion but said he thought a small cerebral embolism was the most probable cause. Then he raised the issue of prothrombin time. Prior to the stroke he had seen from blood samples that prothrombin determinations were normal or near normal, that is, dangerously high, indicating that Snyder was giving little of the drug. During this period a small news item in the press by Hagerty showed that "the president was taking the anticoagulant only at intervals." Snyder doubtless was the press secretary's source. Mattingly told Snyder over the telephone that he should administer Coumadin with a better reduction of time than during the past year. Snyder bristled, and Mattingly dismissed the issue by saying that he needed a current status of the time and after he had opportunity to examine the president he would give further advice. He made plans to examine the president the next morning.

In the meantime Snyder and Heaton had called in civilian neurologists, Francis M. Forster of Georgetown University, H. Houston

Merritt of Columbia, and James F. Hammill, also of Columbia, who quickly corroborated the fact that the president had suffered a stroke.

The night of the stroke the president had been scheduled to attend the state dinner, and Mrs. Anne Wheaton, acting for Hagerty, who was out of the country preparing for a NATO conference scheduled for Paris the next month, explained his absence by announcing that "the President suffered a chill and the doctors have ordered him to bed." Pressed by reporters, she said Eisenhower did not have a fever and was resting comfortably under mild sedation. Snyder, Sherman Adams, John Eisenhower, and his mother decided that Mamie would carry on with the dinner that evening. This was agreed in consultation with the president. As Snyder put it, otherwise they would have to excuse the president's absence from the dinner with a statement of a more serious illness than a chill induced by exposure during the morning ceremonies. A full day after the stroke, word went out that the president had suffered a cerebral occlusion.

Seeing the president on the day after the stroke, November 26, Mattingly had the opportunity to observe what had taken place. He found the heart unchanged. No significant arrhythmia and no history of such had preceded or occurred during the stroke, except for infrequent premature beats. He saw no evidence of obstructive lesions—hurts or injuries—in the carotid arteries. Maximum blood pressure during the period before, during, and after the stroke was 160 mm Hg systolic, which obviated pressure as a cause for transient cerebral ischemia (short-term blockage of an artery) and/or hemorrhage from hypertension. The prothrombin determination revealed 80 percent of normal control, an altogether inadequate level of reduction.[19] Mattingly wanted it at 30. The purpose of thinning the blood was to avoid the lodging of emboli, foreign materials (a bit of arterial wall or a small blood clot from a roughened artery or diseased heart), in the arteries of the brain, which would temporarily or permanently block them and thereby halt the functions of nearby tissues.

The stroke ran its course rather quickly, as agreed by the neurologists whom Snyder and Heaton called in. Only a slight speech impediment remained. They concluded that there had been an occlusive vascular lesion but did not know where. Their finding suggested the "small terminal branch of the middle cerebral artery supplying the left side of the brain and the speech center." They considered hemorrhage not the cause and favored occlusion or spasm. They agreed that a cerebral embolus from the heart could have been a cause. The senior neurological consultant, Dr. Merritt, agreed on continuation of the anticoagulant therapy.

Mattingly believed the probable cause of the stroke was a thromboembolism, with the thrombus coming from the heart and lodging in a small artery of the brain. Snyder and Heaton in a press report omitted any reference to an embolism as the probable cause and even included a statement that "the present symptoms have no relationship to the previous heart attack." That of course also denied the possibility of an aneurysm giving off emboli. And it let the generals out of any delinquency for failing to administer sufficient quantities of the anticoagulant Coumadin.

This was not quite the end of developments accompanying the stroke episode. After the stroke the president determined to show that he was not like President Wilson and began working on papers while still in bed. On Thanksgiving Day he attended church services with Mrs. Eisenhower. On Sunday he made it known that he would preside over a cabinet meeting on Monday. He meanwhile had motored to Gettysburg, and the arrangement was for members of the cabinet to fly in to Camp David by helicopter.

The calling of the cabinet meeting had something to do with Vice-President Nixon, whom the president wanted to hold at arm's length. Nixon on November 26, the day after the stroke, had said carefully that there was no indication of delegating any of the president's powers. This pronouncement was published next day, November 27, and duly speculated upon. The president on November 30 read an article in the *New York Times* illustrative of how Nixon was taking over (so Snyder wrote in his diary), and about fifteen minutes later said, "Howard, there can't be two Presidents in the United States. I think I'll go down to the Cabinet Meeting Monday morning." Snyder said he thought this was rushing it, but the president said he would not have to be there long. By evening he said he was sure he could attend without harm to himself.

Snyder, concerned if not alarmed, discussed this proposal with Hagerty, who called Sherman Adams. The latter insisted that Snyder get the consultants to the farm to persuade the president not to attend the cabinet meeting.

I told Sherm that it would not be good judgment to ask the consultants to come to the Farm because it would create an impression through press reports that something had gone wrong with the

> President which required me to call in the consultants to handle. I
> also stated that this would be more irritating to the President than
> his attendance at a short Cabinet session. This ended the discus-
> sion concerning this matter.

Snyder told the president that he, the president's personal physician,
thought it was all right to hold the cabinet meeting so long as Eisenhower would not become impatient with any hesitancy of speech that
might develop or, if impatient, would not allow it to irritate him.[20]

When Secretary of State Dulles heard there was to be a cabinet
meeting with the president in attendance, he too became concerned at
what seemed faulty judgment after a stroke. President Wilson had dismissed his uncle, Secretary Lansing, in a fit of childishness after the
stroke of 1919, and Dulles saw ominous parallels. The day before the
cabinet meeting he called Vice-President Nixon, and the two men discussed the possibility of declaring Eisenhower incompetent. Then they
let the matter rest. That was fortunate, for if Eisenhower had ever learned
of this conversation he might have followed the Wilsonian precedent.[21]

Afterward there seemed to be no hard feelings between the president and Vice-President Nixon (whom he at first had thought was
considering himself a rival president of the United States). Eisenhower
told his vice-president that the main problem with the stroke had become transposition—that instead of saying tomorrow he was saying
yesterday or vice versa—and he could not remember some words, such
as thermostat. He had to point to one on the wall and ask Sergeant
Moaney what it was, and when Moaney answered it came back to him.
Nixon told him he was a man whose mind always went much faster
than his mouth and that most people reversed the situation. The president laughed and said it reminded him of the joke about the politician
who could be counted on to have his mouth open and mind closed.[22]

An interesting legal result came from Eisenhower's stroke in terms
of avoiding a serious political collapse of control in the event Eisenhower again became ill. In February 1958, Eisenhower gave Nixon a
letter that encompassed an agreement whereby in case of a coma or
similar circumstance Nixon could determine whether he, the vice-
president, should assume the duties of the president. According to the
letter, Eisenhower alone would decide when he was ready to resume
his office. Presidents Kennedy and Johnson made similar agreements,
until the Twenty-Fifth Amendment in 1967 made them no longer necessary.

On December 1, 1957 (the president's stroke was on November 25), Snyder called Mattingly, who now faced a new danger. Snyder's query on December 1 was nominally over the prothrombin determination, which was only fair, a reduction of 50 percent of normal control. He wanted further directions for administration of the Coumadin. (Ten days later the prothrombin time had come down to 34 percent, the first time it had been near an ideal therapeutic level in six months. This showed him following the recommended dosage.) His real interest, however, was the NATO conference in Paris from December 13 to December 20. Eisenhower wanted to attend. Snyder thought it was all right and began pushing Mattingly, ever so thoughtfully, into giving his consent.

Working with Heaton, Snyder arranged a meeting of the neurological consultants for December 10 to examine the president. He told Mattingly he was going to have the meeting but did not invite any advice. Nor did he ask Mattingly to attend the examination, probably fearing that Eisenhower would ask the cardiologist's opinion directly, as the president had done before, and Mattingly would give his honest judgment.

Snyder and Heaton thereupon pulled another "fast one." They went ahead with the meeting of the consultants, who after the examination dutifully agreed that the president's recovery to date was such that it permitted him to attend the Paris meeting. The two major generals arranged an immediate press release reporting the agreement. They had asked Mattingly and the chief of medicine at Walter Reed, Colonel Francis W. Pruitt, to participate in the release, and both had demurred. The brigadier general and colonel considered the conference travel an unnecessary hazard to the president's health. They feared a repeat embolization. The release did not include Pruitt's name, but it did include Mattingly's.

From that point onward to his retirement in August 1958, Mattingly believed he was no longer a member of the Snyder-Heaton team.

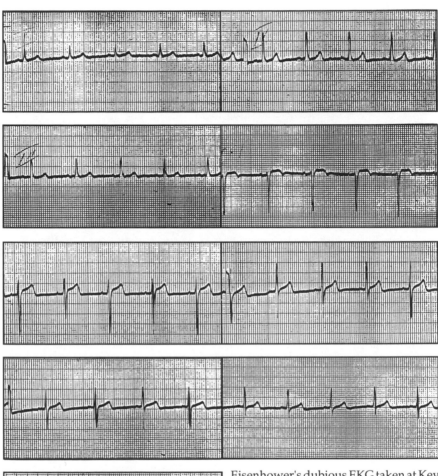

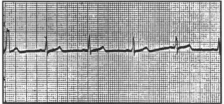

Eisenhower's dubious EKG taken at Key West right after his probable first heart attack in 1949. All photos in this section courtesy Dwight D. Eisenhower Library, Abilene, Kansas.

Eisenhower, when he was still ill, about to throw the first ball at the Washington Senators opening game in April 16, 1953.

Out on the sun deck at Fitzsimons General Hospital, October 26, 1955.

Doctors' press conference, Gettysburg, December 17, 1955. *L to r:* White, Walter R. Tkach (assistant White House physician), Mattingly, and Snyder.

Arriving in Washington, November 11, 1955, from Denver. *L to r:* John Eisenhower, the president, and the vice-president.

A gaunt Eisenhower leaves Walter Reed, June 30, 1956, after recovering from the Crohn's disease operation. He had lost fifteen pounds.

General Heaton liked to welcome Eisenhower to Walter Reed.

After the second major heart attack in 1965, the former president frequently was at Walter Reed. Talking with President Johnson, May 12, 1966.

7
Aftermath

J ust as the heart attack had not been the end of things, so the
Crohn's disease operation and the stroke were not the end either.
Three years remained of Eisenhower's second term, and it was
necessary to watch him carefully to see that his health took no dire
turns. His doctors constantly had to fear the worst, although they
sought to put a bold face on affairs and declared to anyone who would
listen that the president's health was all right—even better than that.
Fortunately, they did not use McIntire's bromide of 1944–1945 that he
was as well as anyone his age. Day after day, month after month, they
hoped against hope that nothing would happen, that his fragile cardiovascular system would hold up until January 1961.

Somehow the president survived. He not only survived his second term but lived another eight years. How he managed to do this is
impossible to know. Franklin Roosevelt some years before had said
while watching the movie about Woodrow Wilson's illness, that he,
Roosevelt, was not going to let anything like that happen to him. As he
discovered, matters were not quite that simple. But Eisenhower, like
the thirty-second president of the United States, possessed a great
deal of resolution, and in some way his resolve, his steely ability to
"take it," together with sheer luck and with an assist, he might have
said, from Providence, enabled him to defy the statistics that his brother
Milton so thoughtfully had kept from him.

1.

In assaying Eisenhower's health during his last years in the presidency, it is possible to see several ways of behavior, none of them new,
that did not make his life any easier, that did not assist the peculiar
chemistry that was taking him through two terms and into retirement.
For one thing he continued, but his recent illnesses notably increased,
his lifelong concern for his health. After November 1957 it turned into
hypochondria. Some of his concern for possible illness must have related to his family's propensity to develop cardiovascular problems.
Part came from upbringing, the need to achieve, which often pushed
him to the physical limit and beyond. Then there had been the wor-

risome military duties of the 1930s and 1940s. Throughout the 1930s he worried about his health as he confronted MacArthur, who might have given fits to any officer working directly under his command. In the 1940s it was the grand series of responsibilities during and immediately after the war, and in the last part of that hectic decade, among other problems, his increasing political prominence as an active non-candidate. Once he entered the presidency it was one concern after another, each imposing upon his nervous energy. But then beginning in 1955, it was a crisis over his health each year. In this regard he now really had something to worry about, so it was understandable that it was much on his mind.

Blood pressure readings caught his attention. Here part of the trouble was that General Snyder was taking half a dozen readings a day, which might have concerned anyone. Probably Snyder had his own reason for taking so many—the general could not easily forget that during the two months in Denver prior to the attack he probably had taken almost no readings, nor had he watched Eisenhower during the crucial twenty-seven holes on September 23, 1955. Another part of the trouble was Eisenhower's labile blood pressure, its ups and downs as, say, good news gave way to bad. When on September 19, 1958, American scientists launched an Atlas missile carrying a four-and-a-half-ton satellite, the president's blood pressure was a wonderful 128/76. It went up during the months when Sherman Adams was in trouble over taking free hotel rooms and a vicuna coat from a Massachusetts textile manufacturer in tax trouble; Snyder sighed in relief when Adams turned in his resignation. But whatever Snyder's assurances on making frequent blood pressure checks, or his explanations of Eisenhower's labile pressure, they did not suffice for the president. Eisenhower considered each reading a possible sign of danger. The doctor was reduced to subterfuge: "I usually knock off 8 or 10 points on the systolic, if it is more than 132, in commenting to him."[1]

Eisenhower often took his own pulse and told Snyder one time that as he was listening to a boring report he "unconsciously" put his hand on his wrist and noted the irregular rhythm. Snyder's answer was that the president had had an arrhythmatic heart for years, and this was nothing new. Doubtless, however, the president knew Snyder's limited abilities in cardiology and was not quite sure of this response.

After the heart attack anything pertaining to his heart fascinated the president, and one time he came close to something important. One day—not long after the attack when he was recuperating at Gettysburg—Mattingly had been out and inadvertently left a statement of the results of an EKG. Eisenhower pounced on it and saw the remark that said a good deal more than he suspected: "Extensive anterior wall and lateral wall infarction." He asked Snyder about it, and the president's physician had "considerable difficulty" assuring him that the statement did not indicate anything more than all the doctors had announced in Denver.[2]

Headaches, which might be allied to cardiovascular problems, bothered him, and this was one of the reasons the president said he took his own pulse. Snyder worried, probably unnecessarily, that Eisenhower might not tell him of headaches. In this regard the president may have read too much about the danger of strokes. After his own stroke, he complained to his physician that for several days he had had a "feeling of dullness." He said he did not know where the headaches came from—sometimes in the back of his head toward the neck.[3]

Sometimes Eisenhower felt a shortness of breath, which could be a bad sign. Snyder thought it was due to overeating. The president loved to eat, and he wolfed his food, which made things worse. If in a good mood or the food attracted him, he could eat enormous quantities. He liked to cook breakfasts for friends, and one morning several weeks after the stroke Snyder saw him eat ten cornmeal griddle cakes with maple syrup and plenty of beef sausage. Another time after a golf game and a shower, he sat down for a snack. He had two cups of tea with a full packet of sugar in each, plus three slices of cold beef with three or four large pieces of New York State sharp cheese, and three whole slices of white bread. He polished off the sandwich with an entire bottle of horseradish. When he ate like this his weight went up. He liked to hold it at 172 pounds, his West Point football weight, and when it moved to 178 the difference bothered him. It might well have made him think he was short of breath.

Eisenhower stewed so much about shortness of breath that Snyder began to worry—the hypochondria was in a sense catching. The doctor began to watch for signs and probably interpreted normal behavior as ominous. One August day in 1959, the president and George Allen and Snyder started out in a farm vehicle along Nevins Boulevard, named for Brigadier General Arthur Nevins who was the president's farm manager, and Eisenhower sounded the cattle call on the car. From everywhere the beasts appeared, galloping in. The president then did something to strip the brakes, and the three had to walk back to the house. Midway, Eisenhower stopped and pointed ostentatiously at something, and Snyder was sure he did this in order to rest.

All the while, and in addition to the hypochondria, the president continued to indulge his temper whenever and wherever it pleased him. Snyder worried most about Eisenhower's sudden flarings of temper, which could be awesome. Prior to the heart attack the president had blown up every time he wanted to, many times, every fifteen minutes according to his special counsel, Bernard Shanley, afterward his appointments secretary, who had an office next to the oval office and was keeping a diary. For a while after the heart attack, when the doctors, Shanley thought, must have spoken to him about his temper, he was completely different. "I was amazed how much under control he had gotten himself through the whole next month. Never once did he blow, as he did so often, prior to his illness."[4] But then Shanley left to run for the senate in New Jersey, and soon Eisenhower was behaving just as before. Dr. Snyder, also a diarist, could not relate what happened in the oval office, but he saw plenty of presidential temper on other occasions. It could arise over the most minute of problems. One day the doctor canceled the president's dinner menu of spare ribs and sauerkraut and substituted broiled steak, string beans, and boiled potatoes. Eisenhower was unhappy and let Snyder know it. Another time it was the removal from his table of a salt shaker. Snyder told Charles the butler to remove the regular shaker to see if the president would insist upon having it. Charles did what he was told for the noon meal. The president called Charles to bring a shaker of regular salt. Charles that afternoon consulted Snyder, who said to give him back the salt. Charles forgot to tell the waiters for the evening meal, and the president had no salt. "When the tray was served without a shaker of regular salt, the President went into a rage. He called me on the telephone, and with much profanity wanted to know what the hell I was doing. We had a very short telephone conversation and that was the end of it."[5] The next morning Mamie mentioned the episode to Snyder and said she was sure the president was going to have a stroke.

The presidential golf game was a likely focus of wrath if anyone did the wrong thing, and Snyder seemingly did often. One time Eisenhower parred on the first and second hole and birdied the third. Snyder walked up and said, "My God, two pars and a birdie on the first three holes!" The president retorted, "Keep your Goddamn mouth shut, Howard." Sure enough, he made a bad drive on the next hole and got a double bogie. He growled at the caddie, "Too Goddamn bad you have to have people around who shoot off their mouths." Another time he played well on the first game, but by the seventeenth green he was doing abominably. He made a bad explosion shot out of the trap and Snyder yelled, "Fine shot!" He became livid with rage and shouted back, "Fine shot, hell, you son of a bitch," and threw his wedge at the doctor. The staff of the club fortunately wrapped itself around Snyder's shins and the heavy iron wedge missed him; otherwise he would have had a fractured leg. The president apologized perfunctorily and said, "Oh, pardon me."[6]

In addition to all the worries that surrounded a president who was not in good health and knew it, and enjoyed losing his temper, was the awkwardness of his relations with Mrs. Eisenhower. The two of them really were fond of each other, and they had been with each other for a long time. But the relationship was edgy. Whose fault it was might have been beside the point. The truth was that they did not always get along.

Eisenhower felt that his wife, deeply concerned about his health, was trying to boss him around, which perhaps she was. He had never liked anyone interfering with his own plans, whatever they were, and the slightest effort on his wife's part to change things could send him into a paroxysm. One time it was a question of going to Secretary of the Treasury Humphrey's plantation in Thomasville, probably the president's favorite place for hunting. He expressed his decision to Mamie at lunch, and she sought to persuade him to wait a day or two. He "flew off in a rage" and went to his dressing room and remained all afternoon. Mamie became alarmed because, she thought, he might have a stroke.[7]

She worried constantly about him. After arriving in Thomasville she "stormed" at Snyder and Humphrey for allowing the president to sit in the bright, warm sun without his cap.[8] Her usual thought, communicated usually to Snyder, was that each evening when the president went to bed he was very tired. Whenever the blood vessels on his temples stood out, she worried. When Ike drank two or three Scotches, she pointed out, they stood out—but then Snyder noticed that the night before when he had had no Scotches they stood out. Moaney told her it was from practicing golf too much. But when the president did not practice golf and spent the evening painting, they stood out. Snyder, who did not always take Mamie seriously, wrote in his diary that she was in a quandary as to why the blood vessels stood out.

Mamie worried about everything. While the president was sitting down drinking beer she went over and turned down his lip and said, "See, Howard, how purple it is."[9] Dick Flohr, the chauffeur, tied the president's shoes because Mamie said it was bad for him to tie his own shoes. In October 1960 Mamie wanted Snyder during the campaign to tell the president he should quit speaking and working for Nixon—that he "might pop a cork."[10] One time she suggested that Snyder put the president on the liver and B-12 shots that she had been getting. Snyder asked the president if he would like them and Ike said, "Oh, I don't give a damn." Snyder arranged for him to have a shot.[11]

The months and years thus gradually passed with Snyder trying to deal with a patient constantly worrying about himself, subject to rages over small things, irritable over his wife's well-meaning efforts to help him. Life with President Eisenhower was by no means the smiling, gracious, easy experience that the average American citizen thought it was.

2.

In view of the stresses the president lived with when in the White House or Gettysburg or even in Thomasville, it was fortunate that in one respect during his last year or so in office he seems to have learned how to relax. It is entirely possible that a principal factor in ensuring his survival until the end of his term was his willingness, indeed eagerness, to travel around the world. In the winter of 1958–1959 his secretary of state, Dulles, took ill again from the cancer that first appeared late in 1956, and died in May 1959. Perhaps as a substitute for Dulles, who had become a noted world traveler, and for Dulles's successor, Christian Herter, who because of arthritis walked with crutches, the president decided to be a world traveler. He decided to get out of the perennial routine of receiving visitors, which was time-consuming and taxing, as each visitor considered the visit as his opportunity to ask the president something or inform the president about something, or both. He doubtless remembered his receptions in Allied capitals in earlier times—the travels in Europe after V-E Day, as chief of staff and head of NATO. He may have remembered, if ruefully, the suggestion from Dr. White that he be a world ambassador for peace. He embarked on an extensive goodwill tour of twenty nations around the world, traveling three hundred and twenty thousand miles in late 1959 and 1960. His first visit in August through September 1959 was to Germany, England, France, back to Scotland, and then to the United States.

Early in December he left for Italy and moved on to Turkey, Pakistan, Afghanistan, India, Iran, Greece, Tunisia, France, Spain, and Morocco. From February through March 1960, it was Brazil, Argentina, Chile, Uruguay, and Surinam. In May, France and Portugal. In June, the Philippines, Taiwan, Okinawa, Korea, and home via Hawaii.

The trips should have been vastly fatiguing, but he enjoyed them thoroughly. They were enough—the travel and assorted activities—to exhaust a young and healthy individual. For a person seventy years of age with multiple health problems, they were an extraordinary achievement. He experienced no cardiovascular problems and less frequent elevations of blood pressure.

In the course of the travel he probably inaugurated what became known as the imperial presidency, which proved easily possible in the time of jet planes and television. Audiences everywhere saw his progress through the many countries, if not with Mrs. Eisenhower then with his attractive daughter-in-law, Barbara Eisenhower. It was every bit as regal as the nineteenth-century progresses of kings and emperors.[12]

Dr. Snyder worried about the president's blood pressure, and on February 24, 1960, wrote: "I believe the toll of the Bonn, Germany, etc. trip and the Europe-Asia-Africa trip is beginning to show. I am going to have to watch his blood pressure carefully." Nothing happened and the president went on to his later trips.

One of the accompaniments of the trips was a sizable consumption of alcohol, and it is barely possible that this indulgence of the imperial presidency had medicinal value. Dr. Snyder seems to have thought so, although his training in the consumption of alcohol doubtless had started in the Philippines, which had driven many of the army's soldiers to drink. But then Snyder did believe that a good drink would not hurt anyone, and evidently Eisenhower believed the same. The president seems to have set the pace by first making a short visit to Acapulco in February 1959. There upon arrival he had a drink in his room with the Mexican officials, and there were more while on board a yacht in the harbor, and drinks again at dinnertime. The hotel was built into cliffs and at dinner the presidential party watched folk dances on the promontories a hundred feet below their tables. They also saw spectacular diving from the promontories at a height of about 135 feet. Snyder reported the president "reasonably well lubricated by 2300 hours" when he invited Ann Whitman, Olive Marsh, his son John, and the doctor into his apartment for more glasses of Scotch and water.

By this time, Snyder wrote, "The old boy was feeling no pain."[13] Next evening Eisenhower sat in his room drinking with Milton, John, Ann, and Andy Goodpaster until arrival of the president of Mexico, Adolfo Lopez Mateos, whom he much admired, and that called for a two-presidents drink before departure for the airport. Snyder's observation for this second night was that "he was pretty well lubricated."[14]

The first visit abroad, not to Mexico, in the cycle of visits of 1959–1960 was to Bonn to see Adenauer. Crowds cheered and it was a great welcome. Snyder found the president at the embassy. "Oh Howard," he said, "thank God you are here." With that, according to the doctor, he absolutely fell into his chair, completely exhausted. "He reached for a double Scotch; he knocked off several."[15]

During the subsequent visit to England, the queen cooked dropped scones for lunch while the president drank at least two Scotches. Later that afternoon, after dressing for dinner, there were a few more and during and after dinner several wines and brandy. During the evening the president sat between the queen and the queen mother "and he really had the time of his life. He talked his head off."[16] It must have been that way during the entire series of trips, save for one or two countries that had subscribed to their own versions of the Eighteenth Amendment.

In between trips he sandwiched a visit by Nikita Khrushchev, which at one point turned into a medical discussion. According to the omnipresent Snyder, "In talking about the medical research centers in the United States, Khrushchev said he didn't understand why we needed them, that people in Russia got along well without all that kind of business; and, in fact, there was one person now alive in Russia at the age of 150. Mrs. Eisenhower retorted, 'I don't believe that!', to which Khrushchev replied, 'I don't either.' "[17]

3.

In such ways the last year or so passed with the president feeling that with the imminence of retirement he had almost made it. When the time came it must have been a relief.

During this final period in his presidency, and perhaps from seeing doctors all the time, also from making his own sometimes shrewd, other times uninformed, guesses about what was going on with his health, Eisenhower was none too charitable about the way his doctors had treated him. He arranged a theory in his own mind that very much irritated Snyder: when he had had the heart attack in 1955 he had been made the subject of experiments by White and Pollock who wanted him to get out of bed on the fourth day and sit in a chair. (This was a form of therapy advocated by the renowned Boston cardiologist, Dr. Samuel A. Levine.) They had done this too soon, Eisenhower believed, and hence his slow recovery from the heart attack. They had fallen under the spell of Levine, and it was a bad spell. One time he expressed himself irritatedly to Al Gruenther on this score while he and Al and Snyder were sitting in the White House's east hall.

> He apprised me of the fact that as Presidential Physician, I should have intervened and prevented carrying out of the instructions of White and Pollock. He stated that as President of the United States, he should not have been subject to any experimentation on the part of the cardiologists. He further emphasized that inasmuch as there was a difference of opinion regarding treatment, this matter should have been brought to his attention so that he could have made the decision. He said that no one should have gambled with the life of the President of the United States in connection with the treatment of his cardiac illness, and that the most conservative of doctrines should have been endorsed.

Al asked whether it would have been wise to present such a critical problem to the president in the early stages of a very serious, indeed critical, illness. The president snapped that he was called upon constantly to make decisions in critical matters as president of the United States, and therefore, he should have made this one.

Snyder did not make any material comments. "Had I done so, I am sure it would have caused an explosion in the President's blood pressure, and one of my main purposes is to conduct my associations and advice to the President in a manner which will assist in reducing, certainly not in elevating, his blood pressure." Snyder did mention the operation for Crohn's disease, and said that physicians treating the president were handicapped by the very fact that he was president, and had he been some ordinary individual they would have operated immediately instead of waiting for many hours and finally operating in the early hours of the morning, a full twenty-four hours and more after the attack.

The president made light of the delay, returned to criticism of White and Pollock, and by implication if not words said he hoped he would never see either of them again. He blamed them for what he believed to be a larger scar in his heart than he would have had, if they had kept him in bed.

Eisenhower's belief that Snyder should have intervened prompted Snyder to set down privately his own version of who intervened. In Denver, the cardiologists had charmed the president, Snyder wrote. Indeed, Eisenhower had ignored him, his personal physician, during the heart attack. "It seemed that I could have been a piece of furniture so far as he was concerned." Ike had put him on the same level as Mamie, which evidently was not a very high level. "I represented, under the circumstances, something familiar, as did his wife."[18]

Mattingly fortunately did not come within these presidential strictures, for at Fitzsimons in September, October, and November of 1955 the Walter Reed cardiologist had recommended taking things easy, *festina lente*. Eisenhower did not understand the whole of Mattingly's logic, the near certainty of an aneurysm. Still, he knew that Mattingly wanted him to move slowly.

Having retired, Mattingly was no longer at hand in the last years of the presidency. Eased out of crucial decisions affecting the president, his judgments finessed, he may not have minded. He remained the president's cardiologist—Eisenhower was very fond of him—and saw the president once in a while, but for the most part he was gone. Retirement from the army had much to do with it; thereafter, he could only be a civilian consultant. He also became very busy with other things. From 1958 to 1962 he was director of medical education for the Washington Hospital Center, from 1962 to 1967 chairman of the department of medicine at the Center, and from 1967 to 1968 coordinator of the metropolitan Washington regional medical program for the District of Columbia Medical Society.

During his last months in uniform and subsequent years, Mattingly could have been excused for going public with his point of view that differed so markedly from that of the powers that be. Much to his credit he refused. During the period between the Crohn's disease operation and the stroke he said nothing. Afterward he carefully bit his tongue. At Snyder's request on December 22, 1957, a technician went to the White House to obtain blood for prothrombin time. It was again up to 64 percent of normal control. Mattingly received no information as to current dosage of the Coumadin, and Snyder apparently was uninterested in recommendations for a subsequent schedule, as the president had made it to Paris and back without problems. On February 5, 1958, Snyder called, the first time since December 22, and in the meantime had not asked blood studies for the prothrombin determination, not apprised Mattingly of the anticoagulant administration, and not even asked advice or a cardiological evaluation. The purpose of the February call was to relate that the president had a dental problem and probably would have an extraction, and he desired advice about anticoagulants during such surgery. Mattingly set out a schedule and agreed to follow the president during the extraction, which was to be at Walter Reed.

Public curiosity about the president's health continued unabated. Reporters were everywhere. Mattingly's position sometimes was difficult in the extreme. He had a sharp reminder of that fact during a trip to a medical convention in Boston.[19] He had received an invitation to be the keynote speaker at the annual heart fund drive of the Massachusetts Heart Association, which he had joined when at the Harvard Medical School and Massachusetts General in 1949 and 1950. The invitation was for February 5, 1958, and he had forgotten about how the press had clamored for information after the stroke incident. He did not give it a thought until his plane landed at the Boston airport and he heard over the loudspeaker, "General Mattingly, you are wanted at the airport lobby. The press is waiting for you." Realizing what he was about to confront, and fortunately having all his luggage in hand, he went straight for the airport exit and boarded a bus going into town. Not in uniform, he knew he would be safe except for some *Boston Globe* reporters whom he hoped would not be on hand. When he arrived at the Somerset Hotel and stepped off the bus a big sign greeted him, "Welcome General Mattingly," and there was a red carpet to the hotel entrance. Then he saw a group of people waiting at the registration desk. He went straight to the elevator, got off several floors up, found a phone, and called the registration desk and asked that a porter bring the room key; he would meet him there. Shortly after entering the room he received a call from the reporters saying, "We missed you. Can we come up or would you come down and talk with us?" His answer was an emphatic "No, unless you wish to talk about the Heart Association and its drive. That is what I came here for and that's all I will discuss." They finally gave up, saying they would see him at the meeting and dinner. There they honored his wishes and neither mentioned the president nor asked anything about the stroke, Crohn's disease, or heart attacks. In his speech he made no reference to the president. His reason for dodging the reporters was that if he had had to refer to the stroke incident he would have given his honest opinion as to the probable cause.

Snyder and Heaton never formally agreed to the idea that the stroke was probably an embolus from intracardiac thrombi. But they followed Mattingly's advice as to subsequent anticoagulant therapy better than any time since the gastrointestinal surgery in June 1956. After a few uncertain weeks in the winter of 1957–1958, the prothrombin time was more stable and satisfactory.[20]

Heaton in 1959 received appointment as surgeon general of the army, and became a lieutenant general.

As in his presidency, Eisenhower's years of retirement saw ups and downs of health. In the initial years of 1961 to 1965, his health was good. It was strangely true that he managed to fulfill the guess of Dr. White at the time just after the heart attack of 1955, that he had ten good years ahead of him. They were really not so good, and yet fairly good, considering his basic condition. But beginning in 1965, with another heart attack, his medical condition went downhill in a hurry; he was afflicted with one thing after another. He spent the last eleven months of his life in Walter Reed, dying on March 28, 1969.

In his final years he looked almost as good as formerly, albeit somewhat gaunt, and if a visitor did not realize that he could at best manage the distance between a chair and bed, or very short walks down the hall, and that when he waved at well-wishers from his hospital window, the gesture itself was a considerable effort. If a visitor did not sense this debility, it might have seemed that affairs physically were not too bad. Mentally he was keen until near the end, and he published the first volume in what he hoped would be a more informal memoir than his presidential memoirs. *At Ease*, published in 1967, took him back to his early years and to people he had known. He had much more to say and tried hard to prepare for another publication in 1967 and 1968 when his condition rapidly was worsening. The publication was not made.[21]

Could any medical procedure have given him more life, or a better life during these last years? After the heart attack in 1965, Mattingly approached Heaton, who then had sole responsibility for Eisenhower's care, because Snyder had retired and was in poor health. He suggested a ventriculogram and coronary artery arteriogram to see if cardiac surgery could repair the aneurysm before more serious complications developed. He had talked over the possibility of such studies with Dr. Mason Soanes of the Cleveland Clinic, a pioneer in their performance. He recommended to the army surgeon general that Soanes do the studies. Never convinced that the patient ever had an aneurysm, Heaton told Mattingly to "forget it, Eisenhower was doing well and why rock the boat?"[22]

Because of Heaton's refusal to look into studies and possible surgery there was not much more Mattingly could do, as he now was only a civilian consultant. Heaton did accept his recommendation of assignment of his former resident and associate, Colonel Loren F. Parmley, as chief of the department of medicine at Walter Reed. A well-trained and experienced cardiologist as well as internist, Parmley could help Eisenhower who was beginning to have complications of congestive failure and arrhythmias. Admittedly, there was a gradual progression of the basic coronary artery disease. There was a series of heart attacks. On August 16, 1968, he suffered his seventh attack, considering the attack of 1955 as his first. That same day his heart went into ventricular fibrillation, and he was shocked into recovery. Between August 16 and 24, this happened fourteen times; on August 17, he was defibrillated four times. He died, in effect, fourteen times. Thereafter the fibrillation stopped. All the while there were operations—gall bladder surgery became necessary in 1966; bowel and bladder surgery in February 1969. Pneumonia and pulmonary embolism and multiple heart attacks then constituted the coup de grace.[23]

The cardiologist continued to believe that development of the ventricular aneurysm with the 1955 heart attack and the predictable complications of congestive failure, arrhythmias, and thromboembolism constituted the basic cause of illness and death. The repeated heart attacks near the end of Eisenhower's life were quite probably from thrombi given off by the aneurysm.

The autopsy lent support to this diagnosis. The radiologists over the years never made a diagnosis of aneurysm, even during the last years of Eisenhower's life and with X rays of the heart just prior to death. Mattingly had observed that paradoxical pulsations did not occur in radiological studies but were present on palpation of the chest wall in 1968. In the 1980s, techniques of ventricular angiocardiography and bidirectional echocardiography made exact diagnosis possible. This was too late for Eisenhower. The autopsy, however, both in appearance and postmortem X rays, demonstrated extensive calcification in the fibrous wall and in the retained thrombi. It proved a longtime presence of an aneurysm and thrombi. Mattingly attended the demonstration of the autopsy findings, and the pathologist expressed an oral opinion that the aneurysm's probable development dated back to 1955. The pathologist did not put this opinion in the written report.

8
Kennedy, Reagan, and Bush

The present pages have considered Eisenhower's medical care with attention to the precedent of Roosevelt and the three cover-ups that preceded it. There is perhaps no reason to draw conclusions generally about presidential illness. And yet the information now available on Eisenhower is so detailed, despite the missing records, and so close, one must assume, to the truth, that if anyone wished to go from the particular to the general, the case of Eisenhower constitutes the best foundation.

Let it be said that after Eisenhower there were two more cover-ups of presidential illness. The case of President John F. Kennedy involved in part a denial by himself and his assistants and relatives that he suffered from Addison's disease, which is a failure of the immune system. Until Kennedy's own lifetime the disease had been fatal. Its name had lodged in the public mind as equal to cancer, even though its incidence was not nearly as large. Then modern medicine produced not a cure but a treatment for stabilization and control. Kennedy, however, feared that if word got out that he was an Addisonian it might affect his political career.[1]

Perhaps this part of the Kennedy cover-up came largely out of his concentrated, almost absurdly dedicated, effort to achieve the presidency. Nothing, just nothing, should get in his way. His father, Joseph P. Kennedy, had groomed the eldest son, Joe Kennedy, Jr., for the presidency up until World War II. But Joe died in the war; he volunteered for a hazardous mission, and his plane blew up shortly after takeoff. The second son, John, took his place. Up the political ladder he went, step by step, to the House of Representatives, then the Senate. In 1956 he tried valiantly for the vice-presidential nomination during the second nomination of Stevenson and missed only because Stevenson, to Kennedy's private fury, opened the vice-presidential nomination to the convention. After nomination in 1960 the still young senator from Massachusetts, who would become the nation's youngest elected president, was bound that nothing would keep him from the great prize. He was in a very narrow race with Vice-President Nixon. The last thing he needed bandied about was that he had Addison's disease.

Kennedy chose to lie about it, explaining that he suffered from malaria picked up in the Pacific during the war, or (so his spokesmen announced) that even though he did have Addison's disease, it was not the "classic sort." "No one who has the real Addison's disease should run for the presidency, but I do not have it."[2] By "classic sort" the spokesmen sometimes explained that Addison's disease was caused by the effects of tuberculosis upon the adrenal glands. The stories about malaria during the war were of course nonsensical; malaria had nothing to do with his adrenal condition. The talk about his having Addison's disease, but not the classic sort, was a double confusion. It used the word *classic* in a narrow medical sense, meaning a case that had not been treated and had entered its final stages. It also gave the impression that one could obtain Addison's disease only through tuberculosis. After the near abolition of tuberculosis, the incidence of the disease discovered by Dr. Thomas Addison in 1855 had much diminished, but it did not disappear. Cases turned up in which for some reason, perhaps inheritance, individuals still suffered a failure of their immune systems.

The writers Joan and Clay Blair, Jr., eventually blew the lid off this Kennedy deception, although it required thirteen years after the president's death (they published their book, *The Search for JFK*, in 1976). They used common sense to find out what was the cause of Kennedy's malady so obvious in the 1940s. They knew that after a trip to London in 1947 he had come back aboard the *Queen Mary* accompanied by a nurse who had flown to London. He was taken in an ambulance to LaGuardia Airport, removed on a stretcher, and flown on a chartered plane to Boston where he entered the New England Baptist Hospital. He had put himself in the care of the Lahey Clinic, which maintained operating rooms and a block of patient rooms in the hospital. He had been to the clinic before, for treatment of a back problem. The Blairs discovered that Dr. Elmer C. Bartels had seen Kennedy both for the back problem and for whatever he had come down with in London. Inquiry to the clinic revealed that Bartels had retired to Osterville on Cape Cod. They sought him out, and without the slightest hesitation Bartels told them everything he knew, which was a great deal. The back problem, he said, was congenital; it had nothing to do with injuries playing touch football, or anything else for that matter. As for the Addison's disease, Kennedy had it; clinical and other tests confirmed it. Bartels could not remember the exact treatment he prescribed, but it probably was standard: desoxycorticosterone acetate (DOCA), devel-

oped in 1939, together with cortisone when it became available a decade later. The doctor had obtained excellent results, although Kennedy's condition thereafter, like that of all Addisonians, required careful attention, such as daily oral doses of cortisone and reimplanting
DOCA pellets in his thigh every three months.

Dr. Bartels's statements to the Blairs constituted proof of Addison's disease. If any more was needed, it became available as a se-
quence to Kennedy's back operation in New York in 1954. By this time
the then senator was suffering intensely from his back, and the Lahey
Clinic back specialist refused to operate because of Addison's. Even
with the new treatment, Addisonians were in danger if they underwent too much mental stress or physical exertion, and risked infection
from an operation of any sort, even a tooth extraction. The backaches
nonetheless were so intense that the senator felt he should take the
chance, and inquiry in New York turned up a surgical team willing to
perform the operation, what was known as a double fusion—lumbosa-
cral fusion together with a sacroiliac fusion. The operation took place
on October 21. It was a success medically, probably saving the patient
from life in a wheel chair, but a very bad experience physically. Bartels
had gone down to New York and warned Kennedy of the danger of
infection. As feared, Kennedy nearly died of infection, and a priest
gave last rites. In an oral history, the *New York Times* reporter Arthur
Krock testified that Kennedy's father came to his office, said his son
was dying, and broke into tears. Young Kennedy was in the hospital
four months. But—and this was the second proof of Addison's disease—because an operation had taken place on an Addisonian the
New York surgeons in the November 1955 issue of the American Medical Association's *Archives of Surgery* published an article on the operation and the patient's survival. In accord with usual medical practice
they omitted the patient's name. The description and everything else
about his medical condition fitted Kennedy exactly.[3]

Until the Blairs published their book, little came of the 1955 article. This was fortunate for Kennedy, who not long after its appearance
began his ascent to the presidency. At that time the American public
was highly sensitive to the issue of presidential health, for Eisenhower
had had his heart attack in 1955. Americans knew a good deal less
about Eisenhower than they thought, but as the 1960 presidential campaign came closer they were much concerned about the health of the
candidates. Reporters sought out leads on whether Kennedy was more
healthy than Nixon or vice versa. For Kennedy supporters it was a

time for caution. If anything emerged proving their candidate lacking in vigor, he would be in great trouble; news either of Addison's disease or his exceedingly delicate back might have denied him the presidency. But Kennedy forces overstressed the health of their photogenic young candidate, and in the course of it allowed him to intimate that one of his competitors for the Democratic nomination, Lyndon Johnson, had had a heart attack, which was true enough (in 1955). The presidency, Kennedy said, demanded "the strength and health and vigor of . . . young men." That same day Johnson supporters struck back and remarked that Kennedy had Addison's. A Johnson partisan, Mrs. India Edwards, said "several doctors" told her this and she was revealing it because she "objected to his muscle-flexing in boasting about his youth." Only quick lying by Kennedy supporters quieted everything. In 1961 the Washington bureau chief of the Gannett newspapers turned up the *Archives of Surgery* article and sent a story to chain papers. This, too, could have been unfortunate, for if confirmed it would have raised a question about reelection. Again, nothing happened. In 1967 an inquiring physician, Dr. John Nichols, reopened the issue in the *AMA Journal,* relating that the article *had* to be about the president.[4] Reporters did not notice the Nichols article. By then Kennedy was dead.

The Kennedy case has been ventilated now, thanks to the Blairs, also the Kennedy biographer Herbert S. Parmet. The latter picked up the story where the Blairs left off (their book did not take Kennedy into the presidency). The Blairs dealt with Addison's disease. Parmet stresses the back problem as it continued into Kennedy's thousand days as president and how it led to another part of the Kennedy cover-up.

The physician whom Kennedy chose to attend him when he entered the White House was Dr. Janet Travell of New York, who had proved exceedingly helpful during the campaign when the Addison's disease issue had arisen. Trained as an internist but having developed a reputation as a pharmacologist, no expert on Addison's disease, she made a campaign statement about Kennedy's malady that was inexcusable, that ducked the issue and was nothing but a thinly veiled prevarication. Probably for that service alone she received as a reward the appointment as the president's personal physician.

Meanwhile, she had been treating him for his back problem. Two of her treatments were all right, a rocking chair and a corset. The third was not all right: injections of anesthetics, notably procaine, at trigger points of the body referring pain to other areas. It was, to say the least, a temporary therapy, as the anesthetics wore off and the patient needed

Kennedy in a rocking chair, as Dr. Travell prescribed. Courtesy John F. Kennedy Library.

another injection. Moreover, the body could become tolerant to the drug, and narcotics would be the next need.

Dr. Travell's injections created a crisis in the president's health care, and Parmet has set it out in luminous detail. The president had become addicted to Travell's shots. He was taking them two or three times a day. His back was getting no better ("completely unrehabilitated," said a back specialist who saw him at this time). Upon the recommendation of a physician who was assisting at the White House, Rear Admiral George G. Burkley, Kennedy began to receive physical therapy by an ethical New York physician, an orthopedic surgeon, Dr. Hans Kraus, who came down to Washington almost daily and treated the president in the White House gym next to the swimming pool where there would be no question of what he was about. The presidential back quickly improved by at least 50 percent. Burkley and Kraus and an associate, Dr. Preston A. Wade, thereupon decided they would have to get Travell off the case, and took a heroic measure to do so. In December 1961, a "summit conference" assembled in Palm Beach, including Burkley, Kraus, Wade, and Travell. Wade first examined the president, whereupon all of them joined the president and told Travell, in the presence of Kennedy, that she could no longer have anything to do with the president. She nominally remained his personal physician and was later visible at Hyannisport, assisting the president's wife with a pregnancy. In the summer of 1963, Admiral Burkley became "physician to the President of the United States." It was a situation somewhat like those of Drs. McIntire and Bruenn, Drs. Snyder, White, and Mattingly.

Nor was Addison's disease and the continuing back problem—White House spokesmen for the most part denied the latter, otherwise played it down—the end of the Kennedy medical cover-up. After Kennedy's assassination an autopsy was held at Bethesda, and Burkley endorsed an autopsy report that scandalously made no mention of Addison's disease. Nearly a year later, the editor of the *AMA Journal* asked the navy for information about the late president's adrenal glands, and the inquiry went to Burkley, who did not respond.

All this said nothing of Kennedy's recourse to the well-known New York society doctor, Max Jacobson, who in 1975 lost his license for manufacturing "adulterated drugs consisting in whole or in part of filthy, putrid and/or decomposed substances." Jacobson may have been the worst of all doctors who saw presidents of the United States, even from the beginning in Washington's time. He was much in evidence during Kennedy's meetings with President Charles de Gaulle in Paris and Chairman Khrushchev in Vienna in 1961. Kennedy and his wife may have seen him at least once a week, sometimes three or four times weekly, during their entire residence in the White House, and by one account asked him to move into the mansion. Known as Miracle Max and Dr. Feelgood, Jacobson looked like a mad scientist with his thick dark hair, horn-rimmed glasses, and fingernails black with chemical stains. He dispensed amphetamine "pep pills," better known as "speed," to such patients as Eddie Fisher, Truman Capote, Alan Jay Lerner, and Tennessee Williams. He also gave injections of the above-mentioned indeterminate ingredients. One of his nurses described him as "absolutely a quack."

> Max was totally off the wall. When he gave an injection he would just spill the contents of his medical bag on the table and rummage around amid a jumble of unmarked bottles and nameless chemicals until he found what he was looking for. . . . Max was out of his mind. . . . And because he was injecting himself with the stuff, his speech often became slurred. It was difficult to understand him at times. My father, who was a psychiatrist, made me quit the job because he feared that Max might begin to inject me.[5]

In the annals of presidential medicine the Kennedy case is bizarre. The full story possibly has not emerged. Perhaps it never will.

Kennedy, incidentally, had been full of sangfroid when he chose Lyndon Johnson as his vice-presidential running mate. He did it entirely because he wanted to get Johnson out of the Senate, so his friend Mike Mansfield would be majority leader. His aides were furious, for Johnson's assistants had raised the issue of Addison's disease. Especially irritable was Kenneth P. O'Donnell, who after the senator announced that he had called Johnson by phone and Johnson had accepted, asked in a burst of anger if Kennedy realized that should he die, Johnson would be president. Kennedy's reply was telling: "Let's get one thing clear. I'm forty-three years old, and I'm the healthiest candidate for President in the United States. . . . I'm not going to die in office. So the Vice-Presidency doesn't mean anything."[6]

The treatment afforded President Ronald Reagan during three medical episodes, his attempted assassination in 1981, the confrontation with colon cancer in 1984–1985, and prostate surgery in 1987, is similarly difficult to analyze, as again the information made public has not been such as to give full understanding of what the nation's oldest president, otherwise in extraordinarily good health, underwent. At the time of the president's shooting by a deranged young man in March 1981, he was rushed to the George Washington University Hospital and from all accounts received the best of treatment. It does appear, however, that he may have been more seriously wounded than was announced, and this in itself constitutes a cover-up. As to the momentary succession, an unpleasant melee took place. Vice-President Bush was aboard Air Force II, and Secretary of State Alexander M. Haig, Jr., asserted that he, Haig, was in charge. During these discussions, if such they were, a White House staffer, Richard G. Darman, later a high official of the Bush administration, locked up papers on the succession prepared by the president's counsel, Fred Fielding, so they would be unavailable.

Another probable cover-up occurred during the president's illness with colon cancer. His physician removed a benign polyp from his intestine in 1984, which nonetheless was a danger sign. When a large cancerous polyp appeared the next year and an operation became necessary, there was an almost national outcry with many physicians asserting that he should have had better and quicker treatment. What had happened made no medical sense—just like Snyder's announcement of Crohn's disease for Eisenhower in June 1956. The cancer of 1985 could not have grown in one year. In 1992 an article in the *New England Journal of Medicine* related a study showing that sigmoidoscopies undertaken every ten years may be nearly as efficacious as more frequent screening.[7] In some cases such spacing could be risky; it is possible for colon cancer to appear within three years. But, and here was the point with Reagan in 1984 and 1985, not in a single year. What almost obviously had happened in 1984 was that the sigmoidoscopy had been ineffective, presumably because the president had not been sufficiently prepped with enemas. The doctors must have decided it would be better not to bother him with a reexamination. They must have been terribly embarrassed the next year.

There was a possible cover-up in 1985 but a surefire cover-up in 1987. Discussion of the president's colon problems in the media may have so disturbed the president's wife that when the prostate surgery became necessary two years later she arranged for a team of Mayo surgeons to come to Washington and perform the operation, after which they repaired to Rochester, Minnesota, and the public had no opportunity to ask them about the operation. Explanations came only from the president's press secretary.

Questions more recently have been raised about President Bush's health and health care. In May 1991, his physician discovered an irregular heartbeat, arrhythmia, after Bush had been jogging. The president spent three days in the hospital during which rumor made the rounds. His personal physician, Dr. Burton J. Lee III, eventually diagnosed Graves' disease, an overactive thyroid. Lee heard from many members of his profession about his failure to order a thyroid test as part of the president's annual checkup, before he took ill, also the slowness, once the president was hospitalized, with which he made his diagnosis of a common problem for a patient with arrhythmia and no history of cardiovascular disease. The commentaries annoyed him no end. A specialist in lymphomas at Memorial Sloan-Kettering for thirty years, he was not about to take them lying down. "We were second-guessed instantly on every single thing we did in handling his Graves' disease, and by experts at the big medical schools, none of whom were on the scene," he told the *New York Times* medical reporter, Dr. Lawrence K. Altman. "Now," he added, "doctors ought to know better than that." With near total lack of diplomacy Lee told Altman, "Where the hell do they think I went to medical school?" But, he added, "I write very polite letters back to everybody and say, yes I am aware of these things."[8]

President Bush's care came under fire again in January 1992 when during a visit to Japan he most embarrassingly collapsed in the midst of a dinner at the residence of Prime Minister Kiichi Miyazawa, and threw up the contents of his dinner in the prime minister's lap. The affair was being televised, and the throwing up was televised, and after an initial hesitation Japanese and American stations showed the full tape in all its details. Dr. Lee had attended the dinner. "I could see it coming forty seconds before it happened," he said. "I saw his face go absolutely dead white. He looked like a curtain coming down! I was out of my chair and trying to get to him before he went, but I did not get there in time."

Dr. Lee made no excuses for his handling of the Tokyo attack. Some physicians thought it a transient episode of a Stokes-Adams attack, when the heart beats extremely slowly. Lee said he had heard the suggestion. "Most doctors feel I should have brought him to a hospital, or should have done this or that." But the diagnosis was gastroenteritis. "I had been living with President Bush for twelve days. I know when he is having a serious problem and not having one."[9]

About the same time it became known that the president's physician was prescribing the drug Halcion, a sleeping pill that sometimes produces adverse side effects. The writer Benjamin J. Stein, an insomniac and one-time user of Halcion, published a witty commentary entitled "Our Man in Nirvana": "When Halcion hits you," he wrote, "it's as if an angel of the Lord appears in your bedroom and tells you that nothing is important, that everything you were worried about is happening on Mars and that nirvana, Lethe and the warm arms of mother are all waiting for you."[10]

There was a debate over how many Halcion pills the president was taking. At one point Dr. Lee said the president had not taken a pill for at least a week before he collapsed in Tokyo. A reporter said the president remarked a few hours before the collapse that he had taken half a Halcion the night before. The doctor refused to discuss the matter, saying it was a closed incident. Here, however, the embattled Dr. Lee probably deserved a break. In recent years almost any sleeping pills, prescription or over-the-counter, have been better than the old barbiturates, which indeed are habit-forming and terribly difficult to stop. The present-day American market for sleeping pills is huge and lucrative (one of three Americans has sleeping problems), and manufacturers have not hesitated to bad-mouth the wares of their competitors. Halcion may not be as bad ("better than heroin") as Stein wrote.

Bush came up for his annual physical two months after the Tokyo and Halcion episodes, and it was difficult to know what to make of it, at least as reported in newspaper accounts. Dr. Lee announced his charge in perfect health, which was reassuring. The story was on the first page of the *New York Times,* where ordinarily it would not be; that was not reassuring. Obviously it was a sensitive public issue. Moreover, the talkative Lee spent much time relating to his reporter, Dr. Altman, how busy the president was, and how much the nation's chief executive needed a vacation. The statements cascaded, one after another. No place he "can go for a few days of peace and quiet so his engine can come back in balance from the incredible pace that he normally keeps." Bush "handles stress far better than the rest of us," and yet "the stress of the job has to get to him, and it is my job to see that it does not get to him in a way that it is bothersome to him in his functioning." Again: "It's a major problem. If the stress level builds up too high you start not becoming as effective as you were." The doctor's prescription was "to try to find a place where the man can get some privacy." "You have to get away, to relax, to get a change of pace, to let your hair down, come out in old clothes without someone taking a telephoto picture of you, to be able to swear a little if you shank a shot on the golf course, and this guy does not have many opportunities to do that." Perhaps it was the ease with which two doctors can converse, or that Altman, a good writer, had a poor copy editor, or simply that Lee likes to talk. The president's personal physician may have been trying to tell his charge or the American people something by relating it in the paper. Or offer a warning in case something happens.[11]

The ambiguity of Bush's serial illnesses raised further questions about his vice-president, J. Danforth Quayle, the handsome, young, wealthy former senator from Indiana. He had been a mediocre student at De Pauw University, a marginal applicant for law school at Indiana University in Indianapolis, a soldier in the Indiana National Guard at the time of the Vietnam War, and as vice-president was promptly tagged with an unbelievable collection of jokes about maladroit behavior (such as studying Latin before making a tour of Latin America). Newspaper reporters hated him. One of them analyzed his basic flaw as "a kind of emptiness." The same writer said he was constitutionally incapable of thinking on his feet. Another spoke of his chance to prove that "beneath his bland, shallow, programmed exterior is something more than a bland, shallow, programmed interior."[12] To observers, Quayle did not seem a likely successor in case the presidency should be vacated by ill health or death.

Is the nation to go through the toils of another succession crisis, perhaps with another cover-up, in the 1990s? The question, then, is what to do about a messy situation in regard to presidential illness that has gone on for nearly a century, ever since the cover-up of Cleveland's operation in 1893. The answer has appeared in a thoughtful little volume, cited occasionally in this book, by Dr. Edward B. Mac-Mahon and Leonard Curry, an account published without fanfare a few years ago.[13]

In a final chapter, "Looking to the Future," MacMahon and Curry put their fingers on a problem with the Twenty-Fifth Amendment, passed in 1967, which supposedly resolved the issue of presidential disability. The amendment designates the vice-president meeting with the cabinet to decide on presidential disability, and in case Congress does not want the cabinet to participate in the decision it can designate another group or body; in the event that the president contests removal, Congress decides. In some future difficulty, they relate, the awkwardness will not come over the extremes of presidential disability—an accident that is obviously disabling, or the slipping of an ill chief executive into a coma. The trouble will be in the gray area between where a future president will refuse to recognize his own incapacity and his personal physician will back him up, exactly as happened with Wilson and Admiral Grayson. Or if the president did not suffer from a stroke, as in Wilson's case, suppose he became mentally unbalanced, as one might argue was true of President Nixon?

In such an instance one wonders if the vice-president would have the nerve to raise an issue of disability; it might look like an attempted coup. Moreover, cabinet members are presidential creatures and one wonders if they too would show enough nerve to unite with, say, an independent-minded vice-president and make a determination. In 1919–1921, Vice-President Marshall, a decent man, did nothing about Wilson's illness. The cabinet did nothing. Nor did—and it was an amazing performance—Congress. The private papers of cabinet members and congressional leaders are alive with their opinions, their irritabilities about being kept in the dark, and their hatred of the president for deceiving them. Yet they did nothing.

Nor would it be wise to believe that the power of the press would somehow protect the country if another Wilson situation arose. It does not seem likely that the willingness of journalists to investigate can be counted on to ferret out presidential disability that would not be obvious, easily discernible. The press in Wilson's time was hardly as omnipresent, certainly not as sharply inquisitive, as it has become. Neither in numbers nor investigative skill did it match the reporting of later generations. Still, in Eisenhower's era, the heyday of modern journalism, of presidential press conferences with hundreds of reporters, and televised press conferences, too, the reporters did not pick up on the awkwardnesses of the president's illnesses. Dr. Snyder managed to carry on without serious challenge from reporters. All this said nothing about the next presidency when the Kennedy assertions about Addison's disease and the presidential back found enough journalistic believers to blanket the media.

When Eisenhower in February 1958, not long after his stroke, gave Nixon a letter instructing him what to do in case of the president's disability, the letter said little about the Wilsonian precedent; it mentioned, together, the "cases of Garfield and Wilson," but the latter instance referred to the first month after the stroke, not the months thereafter when the partially recovered president refused to give up his office. Milton Katz of the Harvard Law School had written the president about such a contingency, and in reply Eisenhower admitted he had not tried to "handle a case where the President might insist that he was able to discharge the duties of his office." Similarly, he refused to face what might happen when a physically (or mentally) ill president decided he was capable of reassuming his duties. In both instances the president "would be the first judge."

Eisenhower believed that if a president became incompetent and insisted on holding office, "he would be certain to do things that would expose him to impeachment proceedings."[14] But impeachment is a very slow procedure, as became evident in 1973 and 1974 when Congress was moving in that direction.

The gray area is the problem. And the way to break through this area, so MacMahon and Curry relate, is to appoint the president's personal physician by and with the consent of the Senate, as are other high officers of government. There is, incidentally, precedent for confirming White House officers in that the president's economic advisers and his budget directors are subject to congressional approval. Confirmation would make the president's physician subject to interrogation by the legislative body that confirmed him or her. In such a situation, an ill president and his personal physician would be very cautious about departing from the truth. There doubtless is no foolproof arrangement against another cover-up. The president's physician might turn out to be a congenital liar, backing a president who himself is a congenital liar. The possibility, however, is unlikely, and in its unlikelihood resides as much safety as one can hope for within a constitutional system.

NOTES

1. Cleveland, Wilson, and Harding

1. An alert reader may notice that I have passed over the possible cover-up of President Chester A. Arthur's Bright's disease—an almost inevitably fatal kidney affliction in adults. If there was a cover-up here, Arthur did it himself. Garfield's successor unfortunately was never clear about when he discovered his disease. It is entirely possible that he learned of it in 1882, well before the end of his term in March 1885. Presumably he would have kept quiet about it because his position as president already was insecure: he had been "elected" by Garfield's assassin, who shouted at the time he shot the president that he did the deed to make Arthur president (Arthur belonged to a different faction of the Republican party). Moreover, because there was no vice-president his illness or death would have raised questions about his successor. See Thomas C. Reeves, *Gentleman Boss: The Life of Chester Alan Arthur.* Arthur lasted a year and a half after he left the presidency. He made no large effort to secure a second term.

2. The cry of sixteen-to-one was only the latest manifestation of the currency issue, which, like reconstruction, civil service, and the tariff, had afflicted American politics since the Civil War. Its earlier version was advocacy of "greenbacks"—the war's paper currency unbacked by gold until 1879. For a while, debtors hoped to inflate the currency by not taking greenbacks out of circulation or issuing more. The war created many debtors, and any contraction of the currency was bound to hurt them. The federal government found itself pushed and pulled by debtors and creditors and pursued a double policy that both contracted and added to the currency. Meanwhile, increasing industrialization and immigration created reasons to inflate the currency. Nothing happened until the Sherman Silver Purchase Act, which was grossly inflationary. It passed during the so-called Billion Dollar Congress, the first Congress to appropriate $1 billion. Someone asked the Speaker of the House, Thomas B. (Tsar) Reed, about the expenditure, and he retorted that the United States was a billion-dollar country. Critics suggested that the Harrison administration, which had gained office because of electoral votes and did not have a popular majority, was ready to embarrass the Democrats when they won the next presidential election.

3. William W. Keen, "The Surgical Operations on President Cleveland in 1893," 25. Keen's article is the source for quotations hereafter without attribution.

4. M. G. Seelig, "Cancer and Politics: The Operation on Grover Cleveland," 376. Dr. Bryant made this remark about Keen to Erdmann, from whom

Seelig obtained it. At that time Erdmann was still active in the practice of surgery in New York.

5. Bryant to Lamont, June 28, 1893, box 81, Daniel S. Lamont Papers.

6. Allan Nevins, *Grover Cleveland: A Study in Courage*, 530. Like Seelig years later, Nevins interviewed Erdmann, who furnished many details.

7. Edward B. MacMahon and Leonard Curry, *Medical Cover-ups in the White House*, 44.

8. A sarcoma originates in nonepithelial tissue, a carcinoma in epithelial.

9. Nevins, *Grover Cleveland*, 531–32.

10. The president's confidential secretary in 1893, Robert L. O'Brien, was editor of the *Boston Herald* in 1917 when Dr. Keen's article appeared in the *Saturday Evening Post*, and eight days later, September 30, revealed how the reporters had solved their news problem by fixing on a single account. "It would be a mistake to suppose that it was an easy matter to keep this affair from the newspapers of the country, with all the light that beats on the presidential throne," he wrote. Keen quoted O'Brien extensively in *The Surgical Operations on President Cleveland in 1893*, a little book that republished the *Saturday Evening Post* article. The *New York Times* stories appeared July 7–8, 1893.

11. Diary entry of July 23, 1893, Charles S. Hamlin Papers.

12. Dr. Jones was the family physician of Commodore Benedict and Andrew Carnegie. One day in August, Edwards was on his way home when Jones saw him and said he had important news. He said the nation narrowly had escaped having Vice-President Stevenson as president, and related the details of the operation and how he had learned them. He told Edwards he was free to use the story. Edwards in 1917 read Keen's article in the *Saturday Evening Post* and wrote him, describing Jones as his "intimate friend of many years." He confessed also to "the newspaperman's desire to be the first to publish important news;—what we call a 'beat.'" His letter of September 12, 1917, is in a scrapbook concerning the operation, kept by Keen, in which he placed letters and clippings—everything he could assemble. He and his grandson, Dr. Walter Freeman, gave the scrapbook to the library of the College of Physicians of Philadelphia in 1926. Joseph M. Miller, "Stephen Grover Cleveland," 528, relates Edwards's explanation in the *Philadelphia Press* of September 26, 1917. For the denials of Lamont and Davis in 1893, see Nevins, *Grover Cleveland*, 533.

13. See box 81, Daniel S. Lamont Papers.

14. Dr. Seelig in his paper of 1947 sought to pursue the question of cancer but came to no secure conclusion. He found Cleveland's death certificate unsatisfactory, crediting the former president's demise to "heart failure, complicated with pulmonary thrombosis and oedema." This after an illness of a single day. He printed a copy of the death certificate. At the time the three attending physicians, one of them Bryant, stated, "Mr. Cleveland for many years had suffered from repeated attacks of gastrointestinal disease. Also that he had long standing disease of the heart and kidneys" ("Cancer and Politics," 374–75). Seelig inquired of Cleveland's widow, by then Mrs. Frances Preston, who wrote him relating her lack of information on "the doctors' side of it all." She concluded: "I never knew what it was, but it must have been the same

deadly enemy, internally. The doctors have all gone. No one really knows. I was close to the suffering and distress of mind and body and could be thankful when the relief came" (376). Erdmann told Seelig he knew Cleveland died of intestinal obstruction but did not know if it was a malignancy; if the latter it must have been a second primary tumor, not metastatic from the tumor of the jaw operated on fifteen years before. Actually Cleveland quite possibly died of cancer. Dr. William C. Lusk performed a postmortem and evidently told the dentist Dr. Gibson that he found extensive carcinoma in the intestines; so Gibson told Keen in 1916. Lusk, however, would not divulge details to Keen without consulting Mrs. Preston. Keen wrote the latter, but apparently she did not want to pursue the matter. Keen's interview with Gibson of September 14, 1916, and his letter to Mrs. Preston of September 25 are in the Keen scrapbook. For investigations of recent times see Charles L. Morreels, Jr., "New Historical Information on the Cleveland Operations," 542–51—Morreels was the first researcher to have access to the Keen scrapbook—and John J. Brooks, Horatio T. Enterline, and Gonzalo E. Aponte, "The Final Diagnosis of President Cleveland's Lesion," 1–25. For verrucous carcinoma see Lauren V. Ackerman, "Verrucous Carcinoma of the Oral Cavity," 670–78, and Frederick T. Kraus, and Carlos Perez-Mesa, "Verrucous Carcinoma: Clinical and Pathologic Study of 105 Cases Involving Oral Cavity, Larynx and Genitalia," 26–38. Ackerman defined the carcinoma in the above article.

15. Diary entry, October 15, 1919, Chandler P. Anderson Papers.

16. It is impossible to know for certain the details of Wilson's medical history. All records disappeared years ago. The records of de Schweinitz were burned in the 1950s. The internist Alfred Stengel, whom Wilson visited in 1906, passed his records to his son, who burned them. Wilson appears to have consulted the neurologist Francis X. Dercum, whose records were destroyed under the terms of Dercum's will. Many places in Wilson's medical past necessarily remain opaque. By far the best reconstruction of Wilson's medical history is Edwin A. Weinstein, *Woodrow Wilson: A Medical and Psychological Biography.*

17. Cary T. Grayson Diary, September 26, 1919, copy in offices of the Papers of Woodrow Wilson, Firestone Library, Princeton University. Courtesy of Arthur S. Link, editor of the Papers.

18. "No one is satisfied that we know the truth, and every dinner table is filled with speculation. Some say paralysis, and some say insanity. Grayson tells me it is nervous breakdown, whatever that means" (Franklin K. to George W. Lane, December 1919, in Anne W. Lane and Louise H. Wall, eds., *The Letters of Franklin K. Lane: Personal and Political,* 330).

19. Joseph P. Tumulty, *Woodrow Wilson as I Know Him,* 443–44. Tumulty seems to have remembered almost too well, but surely the gist of what happened appears here.

20. Close to Arthur Walworth, May 7, 1951, box 1, Arthur Walworth Papers. "At any rate I never saw the President during those months until a day or two before I resigned. I just had nothing to do, and I got awfully tired of doing nothing. Mrs. Wilson apparently ran the whole show during that period."

21. David F. Houston, *Eight Years with Wilson's Cabinet: 1913 to 1920* 2:70.

22. "The Facts about President Wilson's Illness," Irwin H. Hoover Papers.

23. Ray Stannard Baker, *American Chronicle*, 469.

24. Memorandum by Ray Stannard Baker of a conversation with Axson, September 2, 1931, Ray Stannard Baker Papers.

25. The Stuart issue had more to it than met the eye. The former head of the War Industries Board, Bernard M. Baruch, had reason to arrange the dismissal of Stuart, who earlier had placed a dictograph machine in the apartment of an acquaintance of Baruch, in belief that she was a German spy (she also had been acquainted with the German ambassador). Franklin D. Roosevelt, then assistant secretary of the navy, and his cousin Alice Roosevelt Longworth, daughter of former President Theodore Roosevelt, had helped arrange the placement of the machine. Stuart had given the recordings to Secretary of War Newton D. Baker, no friend of Baruch, who refused to give them up. Baruch worked through his friends Tumulty and Grayson to get Stuart sent home, but Grey's refusal to dismiss Stuart summarily and his demand of proof presented a quandary, for any attempted proof of Stuart's remarks at parties might cause the major to reveal Baruch's liaison. Wilson, now aroused because of the claim of Stuart's indiscretions, solved the quandary according to his own lights by refusing to see Grey.

26. The following pages rest on MacMahon and Curry, *Medical Coverups*, together with Rudolph Marx, *The Health of the Presidents*, 323–36; Francis Russell, *The Shadow of Blooming Grove: Warren G. Harding and His Times*, 588–92; Robert K. Murray, *The Harding Era: Warren G. Harding and His Administration*, 438–51; and Eugene P. Trani and David L. Wilson, *The Presidency of Warren G. Harding*, 177–78. The papers of Dr. Charles E. Sawyer, copies of which are in the Harding Papers of the Ohio Historical Society, contain little about Harding's final illness but show the closeness of Sawyer to the Harding family. Especially valuable is Edgar E. Robinson and Paul C. Edwards, eds., *The Memoirs of Ray Lyman Wilbur: 1875–1949*, 378–84, which includes a personal memorandum dictated by Dr. Wilbur a day or so after the president's funeral. Wilbur was one of the five physicians attending the president.

27. Harding to Sawyer, March 15, 1916, roll 262, Harding Papers. (Note: Rolls of the Harding Papers contain numbered frames, but numbers in roll 262 are unreadable.)

28. Edmund W. Starling and Thomas Sugrue, *Starling of the White House*, 189.

29. S. N. Behrman, "Hyper or Hypo?," 24.

30. Sawyer to Florence K. Harding, January 24, 1916; to Harding, June 20, 1922, roll 262, Harding Papers.

31. Starling and Sugrue, *Starling of the White House*, 200.

32. Robinson and Edwards, *Memoirs of Ray Lyman Wilbur*, 379.

33. August Heckscher, *The Memoirs of Herbert Hoover: The Cabinet and the Presidency, 1920–1933*, 250.

34. Charles E. Sawyer, "Reminiscences of Warren G. Harding," frame 337, roll 248, Harding Papers.

35. Ray Lyman Wilbur, "The Last Illness of a Calm Man," 64.

36. Robinson and Edwards, *Memoirs of Ray Lyman Wilbur*, 379–81.

37. Ibid., 381.

38. This may have been the point in diagnosis that convinced Dr. Samuel A. Levine of Boston's Peter Bent Brigham Hospital that Harding had had a heart attack. "I felt so firmly about this," he wrote, "that I suggested to Doctor Harvey Cushing, the celebrated brain surgeon, who was surgical chief at my hospital, that we should telephone Doctor Sawyer. . . . After thinking this over, Doctor Cushing replied that it was not our business and we should not interfere" (Russell, *Shadow of Blooming Grove*, 589).

39. Lawrence K. Altman, "Discovery 60 Years Ago Changed Doctors' Minds on Heart Attack Survival," *New York Times*, December 10, 1972.

40. James B. Herrick, "Clinical Features of Sudden Obstruction of the Coronary Arteries," *Journal of the American Medical Association* 59 (December 7, 1912): 2015–20.

41. Robinson and Edwards, *Memoirs of Ray Lyman Wilbur*, 383–84.

42. For the letter see below, p. 178.

43. Gaston B. Means, *The Strange Death of President Harding*.

44. Mrs. Harding may well have been in heart failure. According to Dr. Wilbur, after the president's funeral exercises in the Palace Hotel in San Francisco, he was standing in the room before the coffin had left the room when Mrs. Harding came in and "joined me where I was standing at the window in order to watch the funeral procession leave the hotel. We stood there for over half an hour looking out across Market and up Geary Street. As my hand was on her left arm to steady her I could feel her enlarged heart beat against the back of my hand" (Robinson and Edwards, *Memoirs of Ray Lyman Wilbur*, 382).

2. Roosevelt

1. For Roosevelt's declining health the most recent accounts are Bert Edward Park, *The Impact of Illness on World Leaders*, 221–94, and Kenneth R. Crispell and Carlos F. Gomez, *Hidden Illness in the White House*, 75–159.

2. Jonathan Daniels, *The Man of Independence*, 230.

3. Charles E. Bohlen, *Witness to History: 1929–1969*, 206.

4. Edward J. Flynn, *You're the Boss*, 179.

5. Harry S. Goldsmith, "Unanswered Mysteries in the Death of Franklin D. Roosevelt," 899–908.

6. *New York Times*, October 15, 1985, and February 19, 1986. A good deal more, mostly relating to the Lahey Clinic, was involved in Mrs. Strand's suit. From the clinic's beginning, Dr. Lahey billed patients according to ability to pay, and as business manager Mrs. Strand made up the bills. She became a formidable presence at the clinic and among other actions installed a typing pool to take dictation from staff surgeons, placing her own people in the pool so that no correspondence escaped her attention. She put relatives on the payroll. At one point she installed herself as director of the clinic, until removed—because she was not a physician—by the trustees. Within weeks of the end of his life in 1953, Dr. Lahey gave Mrs. Strand a lifetime contract to the amount of $50,000 a year, at that time a very large income. Lahey had been drawn into an argument with his successor as director, Dr. Richard B. Cattell, and believed

he was protecting Mrs. Strand. The trustees sought to settle this awkward situation and in 1962 awarded Mrs. Strand a life income that with other payments cost more than a half million dollars. All this is in the very interesting volume by the clinic's third director, Herbert Dan Adams, *The Knife that Saves: Memoirs of a Lahey Clinic Surgeon*. For the Roosevelt memorandum by Dr. Lahey, see Dr. Adams's book, 217–19.

7. Interview by Brenda L. Heaster with Dr. Bruenn, April 21–22, 1989, 8–9. Dr. Goldsmith's theory of a melanoma has had a long history. Its first reference in the literature is probably an article in *Modern Medicine*, March 6, 1961, 211, by Dr. F. M. Massie, recounting a St. Louis medical meeting in 1949. At this meeting, surgeons from Walter Reed General Hospital in Washington presented a paper on treatment of malignant melanoma and illustrated it with slides and specimens, all of which contained hospital serial numbers save a section of brain with a large metastatic melanoma bearing only a date, April 14, 1945—the day Roosevelt's body arrived in Washington from Warm Springs. Unfortunately, the Massie article is impossible to find; one must rely on a summary by Dr. Hugh L'Etang, *The Pathology of Leadership*, 93. Several periodicals have borne the name *Modern Medicine*. The only likely one for the issue and page L'Etang cites contains an advertisement. L'Etang was not concerned by the fact that everyone around the late president testified there was no autopsy, nor that a surreptitious autopsy would be conducted at Walter Reed when Roosevelt's records were at Bethesda, nor that Massie would publish an article a dozen years after hearing such a sensational paper. The present writer discovered another article by Massie, on a different subject, indicating that he lived in or near Kentucky; an inquiry to the Kentucky Medical Association revealed that he died in 1985. Dr. L'Etang's book nonetheless fitted loosely with what Dr. Pack related about Dr. Lahey's memorandum; this in the lecture to Dr. Goldsmith and colleagues at Memorial Sloan-Kettering. Recently, the president of the American Association for the History of Medicine, Dr. Robert P. Hudson of the University of Kansas Medical School, delivered a paper based on the Goldsmith article that inquired whether Roosevelt's illness fitted a diagnosis of melanoma. One should add that in addition to reinforcing the clinical analyses of Drs. Goldsmith and Hudson, the L'Etang book persuaded Dr. Bruenn to publish an article (below, n. 8) the same year.

8. Howard G. Bruenn, "Clinical Notes on the Illness and Death of President Franklin D. Roosevelt," 579–91.

9. In a file of miscellaneous medical records of the president in box 66, Halsted Papers, are the above-cited readings together with the following: 184/108, March 29, 1944; 202/102, P.M. 198/98, April 9; 196/94, P.M. 200/104, April 10; 192/96, P.M. 204/100, April 11; 200/102, P.M. 204/98, April 12; 198/100, P.M. 202/98, April 13; 206/100, P.M. 200/96, April 14; 208/102, P.M. 196/100, April 15; 215/102, P.M. 206/120, April 16; 216/120, P.M. 206/116, April 17; 220/120, April 18; 218/120, P.M. 204/104, April 19; 212/108, noon 210/98, P.M. 190/100, April 20; 234/126, 210/116, 218/120, P.M. 214/120, 220/114, April 21; 214/120, 210/114, P.M. 208/110, April 22; 214/118, P.M. 212/114, April 23; 222/122, P.M. 220/116, April 24; 224/116, P.M. 214/106, April 25; 214/112, P.M. 222/110, April 26; 222/118, P.M. 210/114, April 27; 224/124, P.M. 230/120, April

28; 196/112, 236/120, 220/118, P.M. 236/112, 210/110, April 29; 210/110, 206/104, P.M. 208/114, 234/120, April 30; 220/116, noon 210/110, P.M. 210/106, 210/112, May 1; 216/116, 226/112, P.M. 240/130, May 2; 210/118, P.M. 220/120, May 3; 218/120, 210/116, P.M. 216/118, May 4; 210/108, P.M. 202/104, May 5; 206/106, May 6; 204/118, May 8; 208/114, May 9; 206/110, May 10; 210/106, May 11; 206/108, P.M. 184/96, June 1; 220/106, P.M. 198/98, June 2; 206/110, P.M. 188/88, June 3; 198/100, P.M. 186/94, June 4; 194/98, June 5; 210/122, June 6; 208/110, June 7; 220/128, June 8; 208/104, June 9; 202/104, June 10; 212/114, June 11; 210/120, June 12; 200/106, P.M. 194/96, June 13; 216/118, June 14. Dr. Bruenn's article relates that during the Quebec Conference trip in September readings ranged from 180/100 to 240/130, that a reading of November 18 was 210/112, that during a trip to Warm Springs that began November 27 his pressure after swimming rose to 260/150. At the end of March 1945, blood pressure readings were ranging widely, from 170/88 to 240/130. Park, *Impact of Illness*, 248, cites P. Beeson, W. McDermott, and J. Wyngaarden, *Cecil's Textbook of Medicine* (Philadelphia, 1979), 1203, that individuals with pressure exceeding 160 systolic and 95 diastolic run a threefold risk of coronary disease, fourfold for congestive heart failure, sevenfold for stroke. The comment about diastolic pressure and the third term is from the author's interview with Dr. Bruenn, February 16, 1992, Riverdale, N.Y.

10. "In accordance with the routine decided on, I parked my car before the White House every morning around 8:30 and went to the President's bedroom for a look-see. Neither the thermometer nor stethoscope was produced, there was no request for a look at the tongue or a feel of the pulse, and only rarely was a direct question ever asked. Finding myself a comfortable chair, I sat a bit while breakfast was being eaten or the morning papers looked over. A close but seemingly casual watch told all I wanted to know. The things that interested me most were the President's color, the tone of his voice, the tilt of his chin, and the way he tackled his orange juice, cereal, and eggs. Satisfied on these points, I went away and devoted the rest of the day to my own affairs" (Ross T. McIntire and George Creel, *White House Physician*, 63–64).

11. Interview by Brenda L. Heaster, 2.

12. Bruenn, "Clinical Notes," 580.

13. Interview by Brenda L. Heaster, 36–37.

14. Dr. Bruenn, interview by Jan Kenneth Herman, entitled "The President's Cardiologist," *Navy Medicine* 81, no. 2 (March–April 1990): 11.

15. Ibid., 8.

16. Interview by Brenda L. Heaster, 41.

17. Jerry N. Hess, Robert G. Nixon Oral History, 1970, 56–59.

18. The day that Roosevelt died, "I talked with Admiral McIntire and he said that this was a complete shock to him—it was something absolutely new and came as a complete surprise. The president's blood pressure was all right and had been for some time, and there was absolutely no apparent cause for the stroke" (Thomas M. Campbell and George C. Herring, eds., *The Diaries of Edward R. Stettinius, Jr.: 1943–1946*, 316). When Roosevelt died, the former ambassador to Russia, Joseph E. Davies, hurried over to the White House and saw McIntire, who said the trouble was that FDR lost weight too fast; the presi-

dent had been trying to put it back on but others had prevailed on him to diet (Diary entry, April 12, 1945, Joseph E. Davies Papers). As for the admiral's statements to the press in the spring and fall of 1944: "I did not volunteer these statements but gave them when personally and pointedly queried by the Washington correspondents. They were not 'glowing' in the sense that they painted the President as a perfect physical specimen, but a cautious judgment that he was in 'excellent condition for a man of his age.' *I stand by that judgment today without amendment or apology* [italics in original]. Although he was tired and worn, since he could not be induced to spare himself, every check justified the expectation that he could and would continue to carry the load, barring the unforeseen" (McIntire and Creel, *White House Physician*, 17). "His heart, quite naturally, was our principal concern. Why not? Here was a man of sixty-three, under terrific strain for years, who had been coughing heavily for more than two months in the spring of 1944. Time proved that our fears were groundless, for that stout heart of his never failed, but we could not foresee that this would be the case. As for cerebral hemorrhage, it was and is unpredictable. There are some conditions, of course, in which we think we can predict it, such as extremely high blood pressure and advanced general arteriosclerosis although there is no certainty. President Roosevelt did not have either of these. His blood pressure was not alarming at any time; in fact on the morning of the day he died, it was well within normal limits for a man of his age. I have talked to many excellent pathologists and have yet to find one willing to say that he can tell when a man will have a cerebral hemorrhage or when he will not. The signs that we count on for the condition of the cerebral arteries all denied that the President would have any trouble in that regard. His kidneys and liver functions were normal" (ibid., 239). McIntire never asked Bruenn about the book—the admiral sent him a copy upon publication (Dr. Bruenn, interview with author, February 16, 1992). In subsequent years McIntire held to his story. James A. Farley, the former Democratic national chairman, who had resigned in 1940 because of his opposition to a third term, had written in his diary during the 1944 convention that "anyone with a grain of common sense would surely realize from the appearance of the President that he is not a well man and that there is not a chance in the world for him to carry on for four years more and face the problems that a president will have before him; he just can't survive another presidential term" (Diary entry, July 26, 1944, James A. Farley Papers). On March 5, 1951, he stated this point in a letter to the editor of the *New York Times* ("it was widely known among political leaders that he was a dying man"). The *Washington Star* published a lead editorial the next day, quoting Farley, which led McIntire to a three-column response in the *Star* four days later, repeating what he had said in his book. An article, with a similar burden, appeared in *U.S. News and World Report*, March 23, under title of "Did U.S. Elect a Dying President?"

19. Herman, "President's Cardiologist," 11. For Bruenn's memory of placing a final note in the record, see his letter to Anna Roosevelt, July 18, 1967, "Bruenn, Howard G. 1963–1975," box 8, Halsted Papers. It now seems almost certain that as Dr. Bruenn told Herman, who is editor of *Navy Medicine*, McIntire destroyed the president's medical file. I asked Dr. Mattingly, Eisenhower's

cardiologist, if it were possible that McIntire destroyed FDR's file, and he said it was very possible indeed. In his own experience in the military as a career officer who achieved the rank of brigadier general, he saw many officers over the years (including very well-known ones) and was always struck by the way they moved to protect themselves, and of how they would do almost anything to keep awkward information out of their files. I ventured to Dr. Mattingly that McIntire might have felt a sense of respect for the integrity of files and have put the Roosevelt record back in the Bethesda files. He laughed. (Interview at Davidson, N.C., November 9, 1991.

Over the years, researchers have sought to find Roosevelt's medical file, to no avail. Working together, Jan Herman and I made another attempt. We both had seen the McIntire Papers at the Roosevelt Library and were stuck by the odd, almost embarrassing relationship between McIntire and his collaborator, Creel, in writing McIntire's memoirs. Creel may have initiated the project—this was difficult to know—in hope that a book would prove financially attractive (which it did not). McIntire, on his side, had every reason to bring out a book, as he was receiving a good deal of criticism over his patient's untimely death. But once Creel got to work he found it almost impossible to get any information out of McIntire. Correspondence became acrimonious, with Creel pushing McIntire to give him something to write about, and McIntire making one excuse after another. McIntire seemed to clam up—perhaps embarrassed that he had destroyed the president's medical file, not wishing to take matters further, wanting almost to get out of the project. Creel, a skilled writer, constructed a thin little book almost out of the air.

From all this Herman and I thought it highly probable that McIntire by that time, the winter of 1945–1946, had destroyed the file. Hoping, however, that he had not, we went ahead. Herman ordered McIntire's 201 file from the National Personnel Records Center in St. Louis, thinking that it might show traces of the medical file or somehow offer leads. It is an enormous file, eight inches thick, and contains nothing on his relations with the thirty-second president of the United States. It does have every single order he received, transferring him from ship to ship, hospital to hospital, beginning with the year 1919. The back files of the Bethesda Naval Hospital are now at the center, and we asked for a checking not only under the president's name but under the aliases that McIntire used for Roosevelt's medical tests (it was of course necessary to use aliases, or all sorts of speculation about the president's illnesses would have arisen as records passed from lab to lab). Dr. Crispell of the University of Virginia Medical School uncovered aliases in 1981. There were twenty-three, some of them close in nomenclature: George Adams, John Cash, Roy F. David, Mr. Delano, Mr. Elliott, James D. Elliott, Mr. Ford, G. A. Forkes, Mr. Fox, Ralph Frank, Frank A. McCormack, D. Rhoades, Dan R. Roades, and F. David Roy, to name a few. Nothing turned up. Belatedly we learned that until the 1970s all civilian records in the center were under a ten-year removal rule. We discovered that the center maintains a VIP file in its safe, and we asked for a check of that file under the president's name and the aliases, and again the result was negative. On President Roosevelt's medical records there is, hence, a total absolute blank.

20. Dr. Bruenn, interview with author, February 16, 1992.

21. Bruenn, "Clinical Notes," 583.

22. Keen, aged eighty-four, examined Roosevelt on the third day of his illness—on the second, FDR lost the ability to move his legs. The doctor concluded "that a clot of blood from a sudden congestion has settled in the lower spinal cord temporarily removing the power to move though not to feel." He prescribed massage and predicted that recovery might "take some months." Mrs. Roosevelt added, in a letter to her husband's half-brother, "He also sent his bill for $600!" As Roosevelt's condition worsened the next few days, Keen altered his diagnosis from a clot to a lesion in the spinal cord. James R. Roosevelt to FDR, August 18, 1921, in Elliott Roosevelt, ed., *F.D.R.: His Personal Letters* 2:523–25.

23. Diary entry, March 5, 1945, Jonathan Daniels Papers.

24. Entry of August 16, 1944, in John M. Blum, ed., *The Price of Vision: The Diary of Henry A. Wallace, 1942–1946*, 380.

25. "There is no reason to doubt Mrs. Roosevelt's remark to Morgenthau just after her husband's death that the president had known what was wrong with him and so had she" (Frank Freidel, *Franklin D. Roosevelt: A Rendezvous with Destiny*, 513). Diary entry, May 16, 1944, in Jonathan Daniels, *White House Witness: 1942–1945*, 220.

26. Hess, Robert G. Nixon Oral History, 128, 513. Diary entry, May 16, 1944, in Daniels, *White House Witness*, 220.

27. Diary entry, December 5, Frank C. Walker Papers.

28. For the following maneuvers see Brenda L. Heaster, "Who's on Second?," 156–75. For the vice-presidential nomination in 1944, there is much material in the Harry S. Truman Library, also in the James F. Byrnes Papers.

29. Diary entry, December 22, 1943, Frank C. Walker Papers.

30. Entry for April 23, 1947, in Robert H. Ferrell, ed., *Truman in the White House: The Diary of Eben A. Ayers*, 176–77. For the letters see chap. 5, "God, Man, and the Guru," in J. Samuel Walker, *Henry A. Wallace and American Foreign Policy*, 50–60.

31. Herman, "President's Cardiologist," 9. McIntire's description of this event is unbelievable: "To my consternation it had been arranged for him to speak from the forecastle deck of a destroyer; and, by the time I had discovered it, there was no time to change. A stiff wind was blowing, and there was quite a slant to the deck, two things that called for bracing on his part, and as a result he finished up with considerable pain. Purely muscular, as it turned out" (McIntire and Creel, *White House Physician*, 202). To Dr. Bruenn's knowledge, which had to be expert, the affair at Bremerton marked the only occasion when the president suffered from angina. The president's son James, in a book with Sidney Shalett, *Affectionately, F.D.R.: A Son's Story of a Courageous Man*, 351–52, also in a volume with Bill Libby, *My Parents: A Differing View*, 278–79, recounts that during a visit to Camp Pendleton near San Diego in 1944 the president suffered excruciating pains while in his private railroad car, and that because the berth was not long enough James Roosevelt lifted his father and placed him on the floor where he writhed in agony until the pains gradually went away. James's sister Anna was taken aback by the description. "Mr. Shalett

interviewed me also for this book and . . . during the entire interview he was trying to ferret out something sensational from me. My personal feeling about the whole thing is that if Father was as badly off as Jimmy says that Jimmy was indeed derelict if he did not inform you or Dr. McIntire of what had happened. It is also my feeling that it would have been extremely difficult for Jimmy, by himself, to maneuver Father from his bunk to the floor. . . . Of course, if you were queried about this, and knew nothing of it—that would be sufficient answer. After all, Jimmy writes, 'we considered calling the doctor, then decided against it.' Jim [Anna's husband, Dr. James Halsted] says he supposes the attack was caused by his known gallstones" (Anna Roosevelt Halsted to Howard G. Bruenn, October 24, 1969, box 8, Halsted Papers). In *Affectionately, F.D.R.,* 354–55, James Roosevelt related a similar incident at the time of the fourth inaugural.

32. Crispell and Gomez, *Hidden Illness in the White House,* 110–13.

33. MacMahon and Curry, *Medical Cover-ups,* 91.

34. Anna to John Boettiger, February 7, 1945, "Boettiger, John and Anna, November 1943–February 1945," box 6, John Boettiger Papers. I am indebted to Kathleen Esfahanian who used part of this letter in "A Shadow on the Presidency: Roosevelt's Last Year," (Honor thesis, University of Connecticut, Storrs, 1988), 69–70. In a letter of February 9, Anna intimated to her husband that McIntire knew more about her father's health than was later supposed: "Ross goes nuts because he has nothing to do but 'do' OM's nose night and morning, and worry about some of the things I last wrote you about" ("Boettiger, John and Anna," box 6).

35. William D. Hassett, *Off the Record with F.D.R.: 1942–1945,* 333. See also Elizabeth Shoumatoff, *FDR's Unfinished Portrait: A Memoir,* 117–18.

3. Eisenhower

1. Among the many books on Eisenhower see Herbert S. Parmet, *Eisenhower and the American Crusades,* and Stephen E. Ambrose, *Eisenhower.*

2. Harry C. Butcher, *My Three Years with Eisenhower,* 386, 398–99. These passages from Butcher's headquarters diary remark only that the dispensary doctor had prescribed bed rest. But Butcher did not publish all of the diary, and an unpublished passage for August 17, 1943, relates that after the initial dispensary visit, during which the general was told to rest, he had another checkup, and "his blood pressure was 136—considerably improved. A more thorough checkup with a cardiograph is to be made as soon as convenient." Again on August 25, when he was suffering from an infected toe: "The doctor came to dress it yesterday and found that his blood pressure had risen again" (Principal file, prepresidential file, 1916–52, box 167, Eisenhower Papers). In the eventual examination, taken September 2, 1943, blood pressure was 142/90 ("Copies of All Medical Records," [no. 1], box 1, surgeon general's records).

3. Howard McC. Snyder, draft medical history of Eisenhower, 1946, p. 12, box 11, Howard McC. Snyder Papers.

4. John S. D. Eisenhower, ed., *Letters to Mamie,* 270 (September 4).

5. *Eisenhower Was My Boss*. The second volume, *Past Forgetting: My Love Affair with Dwight D. Eisenhower*, asserted an affair. The author's executor—the book appeared posthumously—assured the present writer that Ms. Summersby had nothing to do with the book, that it was written in the publishing house.

6. [Herbert Brownell], "Brownell Sheds Light on Dewey's Presidential Campaigns," *Miller Center Report: Newsletter of the Miller Center of Public Affairs, University of Virginia* 7, no. 1 (Spring 1991): 2, 5.

7. Chester Bowles, *Promises to Keep: My Years in Public Life, 1941–1969*, 173. For Truman's impatience, see Ferrell, *Truman in the White House*, 264.

8. Nothing in the Harry S. Truman Library in Independence, Missouri, supports Eisenhower's belief. Truman kept an occasional diary, often composed essays concerning political and other problems, and wrote voluminous letters. More information is available on him than on any of his predecessors or successors, but there is no evidence that he sought to put Eisenhower in a hole.

9. Alfred D. Chandler and Louis Galambos, eds., *The Papers of Dwight David Eisenhower* 10:544–45.

10. Howard McC. Snyder, draft medical history, 1949, p. 123, box 11, Snyder Papers.

11. Thomas W. Mattingly and Olive F. G. Marsh, Cardiovascular system, 1:25, Mattingly Papers. The formal title of Dr. Mattingly's history is "The Life Health Record of Dwight D. Eisenhower." Hereafter, it appears as above, with citation to its parts and crediting its several participants.

12. Howard McC. Snyder, draft medical history, 1947, p. 52, box 11, Snyder Papers.

13. Ibid., 1946, 19.

14. Dwight D. Eisenhower, *At Ease: Stories I Tell My Friends*, 354.

15. Mattingly and Marsh, Cardiovascular system, 1:25.

16. Box 1, Snyder Papers.

17. Draft medical history, 1949, p. 128, box 11, Snyder Papers.

18. Ibid., 32. See Omar N. Bradley and Clay Blair, *A General's Life*, 500–501. Eisenhower was working in Bradley's office when the 1949 collapse occurred, so Bradley should have known about it. If Eisenhower went to Walter Reed, he would have seen Taylor. As for the possibility that Taylor did not put anything in the files, "There was a great deal of action by the military in protecting records. Often they would arrange to be seen by private physicians so the result would not get into their records. Else they would try to talk surgeons or other specialists into putting the best appearance on their ills. This was common" (Mattingly, interview with author, November 9, 1991).

At the time of Eisenhower's heart attack in 1955, General Snyder wrote the medical editor of the *New York Times*, Howard A. Rusk, "I have had the President's cardiovascular system observed by electrocardiograph, fluoroscope, etc. several times annually for the past ten years. I had all of these records available for review by the cardiac specialists . . . at the hospital here in Denver" (Snyder to Rusk, September 26, 1955, box 10, Snyder Papers). This was a singular statement, for Mattingly took Eisenhower's records out to Denver, and there were no EKGs between 1947 and 1952, the latter being the year Mattingly first saw Eisenhower.

19. For Leedham, see Mattingly and Marsh, Cardiovascular system, 1:27.

20. Mattingly and Marsh, Cardiovascular system, 1:29.

21. For the press secretary, see Robert H. Ferrell, ed., *The Diary of James C. Hagerty: Eisenhower in Mid-Course, 1954–1955.*

22. Dwight D. Eisenhower, *The White House Years: Mandate for Change* 1:147–48.

23. Mattingly and Marsh, Cardiovascular system, 1:37.

4. Crisis

1. Thomas W. Mattingly with assistance of George M. Powell and Olive F. G. Marsh, Cardiovascular system, 2:31. Years later Mattingly remembered a special reason Snyder might have wanted him to bring the records: they contained a negative history of cardiovascular disease (Mattingly, interview with author, November 13, 1991).

2. See A. Merriman Smith, *Thank You, Mr. President.* An unfavorable view of Smith is in the Robert G. Nixon Oral History, by Jerry N. Hess.

3. Dwight D. Eisenhower, *The White House Years* 1:536.

4. This was the same George Allen who earlier had been secretary of the Democratic national committee.

5. Mattingly with assistance of Powell and Marsh, Cardiovascular system, 2:9–10. Mattingly was unsure that the following hour-by-hour account was contemporary; Snyder might have composed it after the fact, as a justification for his treatment (Mattingly, interview with author, November 9, 1991). To a query concerning the account's innocent nature, he would only restate his uncertainty.

6. Robert H. Ferrell, ed., *The Eisenhower Diaries,* 302. "I reported [to Murray Snyder] that the President had an attack of indigestion. This was only part of the truth, but it was a real truth that he suffered an attack of indigestion the prior afternoon" (Howard McC. Snyder, draft medical history, 1955, p. 16, box 11, Snyder Papers).

7. Snyder to Robert B. Anderson, October 5, 1955, box 10, Snyder Papers.

8. Diary entry, September 26, 1955, box 3, Clarence Randall Papers.

9. E. Grey Dimond, ed., "Paul Dudley White, A Portrait," 506.

10. Mattingly with assistance of Powell and Marsh, Cardiovascular system, 2:34.

11. Paul Dudley White, *My Life and Medicine: An Autobiographical Memoir,* 78.

12. Mattingly with assistance of Powell and Marsh, Cardiovascular system, 2:34.

13. White, *My Life and Medicine,* 182; Oglesby Paul, *Take Heart: The Life and Prescription for Living of Dr. Paul Dudley White,* 163–64.

14. Mattingly with assistance of Powell and Marsh, Cardiovascular system, 2:36.

15. One individual who was not encouraged was Vice Admiral Joel T. Boone, by this time retired and living in poor health in California. His letter of September 26 to General Snyder recalled the death of a president in 1923: "Without contradiction, I believe, I have more of an appreciation of the whole picture than anyone else for I am the only living physician who cared for President Harding throughout his final illness and am one who has suffered a cardiac accident from which even after six months I am having great difficulty in getting rid of left chest pain on too little exertion, digestive disturbances, and if pain occurs I do not sit or better lie down I get dizzy. Standing even for ten minutes brings on pain. It was a strange circumstance that last Saturday I went to San Francisco to have lunch at the Bohemian Club with an older friend. . . . Before lunch we were in the lounge of the Club and I picked up a newspaper when I saw that there was a report that the President was ill suffering with 'indigestion.' I commented that that disturbs me for 'indigestion' can mean anything and I thought back to the early symptoms presented in President Harding's case as we left Vancouver headed for Seattle on the transport *Henderson*. Sometime I will tell you the whole story. I did not wish to cause speculating by my friend and a friend he had with him from Washington so I purposely refrained from mentioning President Harding's illnesses but I felt a strange feeling come over me. There I was in San Francisco again where President Harding was taken from the presidential train and put to bed at the Palace Hotel on a Sunday morning with his life terminated the following Thursday early evening. From the time we arrived until late afternoon of Thursday I never took my clothes off even for a bath and only did then because he had shown definite improvement through Wednesday and Thursday until within a few minutes of death. Our final consultation with all physicians in attendance present was held late Thursday afternoon. A bulletin was prepared for all of us to sign. I felt it too optimistic and requested that it be modified and have a more cautionary note to it. My ideas prevailed and it was rewritten. I said 'we must keep our fingers crossed for I do not believe that we are yet out of the woods.' Two consultants said that they did not believe their services would be needed henceforth. I asked for assurance that the heart specialist would be available on call. I make mention of some of the occurrences and would tell you more in confidence if I were near to talk with you, because I was disturbed to read in the newspaper today that upon leaving Denver good and very able Doctor White, in whom I have great confidence . . . , gave a statement to the press among other things that the president should remain in Fitzsimons for a month and that cases such as his usually could return to more or less normal activity within two months. I hope he did not say that nor that if so it will be a guidepost in directing his recovery. Each case reacts differently than another. Observation of progress and time will only give the answer as to how long recovery will take place. No physician unless he has suffered a cardiac accident can know actually how measured must be convalescence. It must be individualized. Only the patient experiences reaction to effort" (Box 3, Snyder Papers, American Heritage Center).

16. Mattingly with assistance of Powell and Marsh, Cardiovascular system, 2:37.

17. Ibid., 38.

18. White, *My Life and Medicine,* 181. See n. 23 below.

19. Mattingly with assistance of Powell and Marsh, Cardiovascular system, 2:40.

20. "I cannot pass up the opportunity of describing our trip to Denver on the evening of October 21 and arrival in Denver. I left Washington in late evening, boarded the president's plane with Governor Adams, from where we traveled to Boston and picked up Dr. White. The pilot informed us that he would fly slowly so as to arrive in Denver around 7:00 A.M., at which time we could have breakfast, as no plan was made to serve a breakfast on the 'Columbine' on that flight. When we arrived at the Air Force base in Denver the commanding general had been informed that Governor Adams from the White House and Dr. White from Boston were arriving about 7:00 A.M.; he was there to greet them. When it was made known that no breakfast had been served en route, the general was all flustered—and he announced that the only facility open at that hour was a small convenience restaurant for workers at the airport, if we would like to get a bite there. Adams and White accepted graciously. In the restaurant we were informed of the local menu. Hot cakes, etc., were ordered. The general was still apologizing when Governor Adams opened an old, beat-up briefcase and took out a Mason jar of his favorite Vermont maple syrup, which made the hot cakes a royal dish—the Waldorf could not have done better. When the general observed that he was the host, not to New England lords but to two down-to-earth folks, he finally relaxed and enjoyed Governor Adams's good Vermont syrup" (Dr. Mattingly to the author, March 1, 1992).

21. Mattingly with assistance of Powell and Marsh, Cardiovascular system, 2:41.

22. Mattingly, interview with author, November 14, 1991.

23. White's notes are now among his papers in the Francis A. Countway Library, Harvard Medical School. Most of them have been typed up but some are still in his marvelously readable, distinctive hand. They make a stack, for he not merely took notes when in Denver but when called over the telephone by Pollock. The notes begin with his appearance at Denver on September 25 and continue until the president left for Washington on November 11. White evidently could dictate with ease, but anything requiring thought he often wrote out in longhand. September 26 he noted, "I don't like the heart sounds or rather fast pulse ["and many premature beats," he added in his autobiography; above n. 18] but there are favorable points otherwise. The next few days are critical." September 27: "Heart sounds fair, very slight pericardial friction." September 28: "No pain or friction rub, heart sounds soft." Late that evening: "Heart sounds better. No friction or murmurs." September 29: "Heart sounds good. Loud friction rub last night, less friction rub today, presumably because of the stronger heart action." Late that evening: "No murmur or friction rub." September 30: "Heart sounds good—no murmurs or rub." October 1: "Ecg. continues to show N.R. with elevated S-T segments. . . . It seems likely that an associated pericarditis is responsible for the persistent elevation of the S-T segments." October 2: "Very slight but definite rub at the 4th inter-

space. No pain on breathing." October 3: "No rub or murmurs." October 5: "No murmurs or rubs." October 6: Same. October 7: Same. "Evolving ecg indicates large area of infarction which may have extended from original area of a week ago. . . . Meeting in Vt. with Dr. Lepeschkin. After an hour of study of these records, Dr. L. has observed that they indicate the presence of an anterior myocardial infarct probably extending from the anterior edge of the septum over the surface of the left ventricle . . . but that the infarct does not extend actually into the lateral wall. There is a suggestion, however, especially in V3, of extension to the apex and perhaps a little onto the inferior wall of the heart. . . . Dr. L. is strongly of the opinion that this represents the added effect of pericarditis." October 8: "Clinically doing well. Ecg.—slow evolution of pattern of myocardial infarct healing with a large area but not yet clearly definable." October 17: "Dr. Lepeschkin sends the report of his analysis of the ecgs. from Oct. 6 to October 14 inclusive. 1) While during the first 10 days the electrocardiographic counterpart of the healing process appeared delayed, it has now caught up with the time schedule. 2) It must be emphasized that in a wide-chested person the area of this pattern on the chest wall is larger than in a narrow-chested person with the same size of infarction. It is, therefore, probable that the area of this case is smaller than seems to be indicated by the Q5 area of the body surface." October 22: "No murmurs or rub." November 10: "X-ray film today shows a very slight bulge and diminished pulsation just above the apex in the a-p view and anteriorly in the oblique view." Summary: "The pericarditis which was evidenced clinically by the presence of a pericardial friction rub on several occasions during the first week, accompanied by very slight anterior chest discomfort, was a part of the process of infarction and not a complication" (folder 31, box 35, White Papers).

24. The following description is from Mattingly with assistance of Powell and Marsh, Cardiovascular system, 2:43.

5. Second Term

1. In a study published ten years later, when surgical measures for aneurysms had become possible, the Mayo Clinic reported a 73 percent mortality in five years. Thereafter the diagnosis of aneurysms and availability of surgical resection made such troubles much easier to handle, but a study reported in 1982 involving 1,136 patients with left ventricular aneurysms gave a mortality rate at the end of four years of 29 percent. Thomas W. Mattingly, Cardiovascular system, 8:15.

2. Milton Eisenhower was a director of Geisinger Hospital at University Park, Pennsylvania, where he was president of Pennsylvania State University, and the head of the hospital sent him a set of statistics. He at once saw the danger of giving such material to his brother. "It does not seem to me," he wrote Snyder, "to be the kind of information which should be given to the President, but you're the judge of that. Please do with the material whatever you like, and do not bother to reply to this note" (Milton Eisenhower to Snyder, October 31, 1955, box 10, Snyder Papers). Snyder replied posthaste, Novem-

ber 8, "I concur in your opinion that it is not wise to show to the President data with reference to expectancy in cases of myocardial infarction. Your unusually mentally alert brother, as you well know, seizes upon information that appears to bear the stamp of authenticity. He would ponder what 'liability' classification he represents in the several statistical reports sent to you by the Director of the Geisinger Hospital."

3. Thomas W. Mattingly, Doss O. Lynn, and Olive F. G. Marsh, Cardiovascular system, 3:23 n.

4. Eisenhower to George E. Allen, February 10, 1956, "Feb. '56 Miscellaneous (4)," box 13, DDE diary series, Ann Whitman file, Eisenhower Papers.

5. Mattingly to White, December 15, 1955, box 4, Thomas W. Mattingly Papers.

6. Draft medical history, 1955, p. 13, box 11, Snyder Papers.

7. Ibid., 8.

8. Mattingly, Lynn, and Marsh, Cardiovascular system, 3:24.

9. Mattingly, Cardiovascular system, 8:7.

10. Oglesby Paul, *Take Heart,* 170. White read these notes approximately as he had written them. For a verbatim transcript of the press conference see Mattingly, Lynn, and Marsh, Cardiovascular system, 3, addendum 8(b). White's clinical note for the examination preceding the press conference, interestingly, amounted to another hedge of the question of aneurysm: "The scar has evidently held well, of moderate size measuring about 2 cm. in the X-ray film *without distinct aneurysmal dilatation or paradoxical pulse*" (italics added). White Papers. He of course did not read this note at the press conference.

11. Paul, *Take Heart,* 170.

12. Ibid., 169.

13. White, *My Life and Medicine,* 188–89; "White, Dr. Paul Dudley (2)," box 38, administrative series, Ann Whitman file.

14. White to Eisenhower, December 18, 1955, Eisenhower Papers.

15. "White, Dr. Paul Dudley (2)," box 38, administrative series, Ann Whitman file, Eisenhower Papers.

16. Paul, *Take Heart,* 172. "What he wants is facts, and not our philosophy or wishful thinking. He has long learned and taught that you cannot win battles that way. Either you have the ammunition or you do not. His question from us is likely to be—'Have I or have I not a good heart?'—and he would like a yes or no. We know it is not normal and he knows it also. He likewise knows that has happened to many of his officers and staff in the past. He knows, for instance, how soon General Carroll [Brigadier General Paul T. Carroll, presidential assistant] died, nine months after first attack and less than a week after Vice President Nixon foolishly dissertated on the marvelous 'cure' and 'recovery he had made from a heart attack.' He now hears the same dissertations and press reports from people like Martin, Adams, McCann [Kevin McCann, presidential speech writer], etc., who are quoting medical opinions and saying that they are sure that 'he will receive a certificate of health from his doctors'" (Mattingly, Lynn, and Marsh, Cardiovascular system, 3, addendum 5[b]).

17. Folder 14, box 35, White Papers.

18. Milton S. Eisenhower, *The President Is Calling*, 343, 345–47.

19. White to Mattingly, December 28, 1955, box 4, Mattingly Papers; Eisenhower to White, January 14, 1956 in Paul, *Take Heart*, 171.

20. Folder 14, box 35.

21. Paul, *Take Heart*, 171, 173.

22. Mattingly, Cardiovascular system, 8:6–7; Mattingly, interview with author, November 14, 1991.

23. "He did have a right smart attack and has undoubtedly (and confidentially) had a larger area of infarction than might be interpreted from some of the earlier reports at least. Happily we never went into any great detail about the size of the muscle damage. We spoke of the coronary thrombosis itself as moderate and this is, of course, substantiated by the fact that he has symptomatically and otherwise objectively gotten along remarkably well, in fact much better than I would have thought likely on looking at his electrocardiogram. Personally I think we have been rather lucky that he has not had more in the way of unfavorable symptoms or signs up to date. . . . There were two or three signs that have bothered me just a little and I would like your own appraisal of these in particular. His heart sounds have been distant and distinctly weak in my judgment but we haven't said anything particular about them in our reports. . . . It is barely possible that there may have been an extension of the infarction, not of the thrombosis, in that first week. Some of the fringe of ischemic [lacking in blood, anemic] muscle may have been knocked out as we sometimes see it. That may be the possible explanation for the so-called slowness of the evolution of the electrocardiogram during the first ten days" (White to Andrus, October 25, 1955, Mattingly with assistance of Powell and Marsh, Cardiovascular system, 2, addendum 11).

24. Mattingly, Cardiovascular system, 8:6. Snyder's note to Mattingly and the latter's response are in ibid., addenda 4 and 5. Snyder's note, on White House stationery, was quite short: "Dear Tom, Please forgive me for my explosion of temper. No one has more complete confidence in your wisdom and professional judgement than I. I was not questioning that. Howard." The response was four handwritten pages: "Perhaps the difference in my interpretation and that of the radiologist (and other cardiologist) is one of definition of an aneurysm. They apparently insist that 'paradoxical pulsation' be present, a finding in most thin-walled aneurysms which can be easily viewed in fluoroscopy or palpated over the precordium. Such is not always discernible in a thick-walled aneurysm as I believe is present here. From my long experience in cardiac fluoroscopy, follow-up autopsy studies and in recent years by angiocardiography, I am convinced that an aneurysm exists. . . . I really desire *not to be a part of* subsequent press conferences. I find it very difficult not to 'speak my mind' and you and General Heaton (our new conference member) may not like my opinions."

25. Mattingly, Lynn, and Marsh, Cardiovascular system, 3, addendum 6.

26. *New York Times*, February 15, 1956.

27. David D. Rutstein, "Doctors and Politics," *Atlantic*, 32–35. White did not know about the article until shortly before it appeared on August 1. It is

interesting that two physicians associated with the same institutions—Harvard Medical School, Massachusetts General—should have had no relations short of publication, although Rutstein had to know that White would be angry over the article and by not showing it to him he saved him a few months of irritability. Whatever, when the article appeared White indeed was disturbed, and next day wrote Snyder inquiring if he and two associates should jump the gun on a follow-up article they had prepared on an article of 1941 and publish it in newspapers prior to its appearance in the *Journal of Chronic Diseases* in October (David W. Richards, Edward F. Bland, and Paul D. White, "A Completed Twenty-Five-Year Follow-Up Study of 200 Patients with Myocardial Infarction, 214–22). White's letter bore signs of confusion, for just what publication of a technical article might have done to soften the blow of "Dave" Rutstein's article was difficult to say. The article of 1941, cited by Rutstein, had shown that only 30 percent of 162 patients surviving coronaries after the initial four weeks lived for ten years. Furthermore, of the group only one-third could live fully active lives; the authors had arranged three categories in a table, according to recovery: complete, 55 cases; limited by angina, 63 cases; limited by dyspnea (difficult or labored respiration), 44 cases. Paul Dudley White and Edward F. Bland, "Coronary Thrombosis (with Myocardial Infarction) Ten Years Later," 1171–73.

White placed Eisenhower in the "complete" category, for which after ten years there were thirty-one survivors (56 percent of that particular group). Accompanying his letter to Snyder he included a prepared two-page rebuttal of Rutstein that made another arrangement of his thoughts that favored the president: "Finally, statistics of past experience always form only part of the basis for decision in any individual case. No two persons are exactly alike and the physician who practices medicine must base his diagnosis, prognosis, and treatment as much (at least) on the findings in the individual case at the time as on any past experience" (White to Snyder, August 2, 1956, box 11, Snyder Papers). White asked Snyder to consult the president, Hagerty, Heaton, and Mattingly as to whether to pay any attention to Rutstein. In response Snyder said he had consulted all of those individuals (including the president?) and they thought White should take no notice. Snyder to White, August 6, White Papers. Again, Snyder did not want mortality statistics presented to the president.

28. "Feb. '56 Miscellaneous (2)," box 13, DDE diary series, Ann Whitman file, Eisenhower Papers.

29. "Milton felt personally that Dad should not run again; the record of the first four years would be enough to establish him as a great President, and another term might not be worth the risk from many considerations. I decided to put my thoughts down on paper, as I find this device useful in avoiding a mental merry-go-round. . . . At the end of this rather prolix document I recommended his bowing out. Dad—and especially George Allen—expressed admiration of the piece of work, but Dad made no commitment. A meeting Dad held at the White House on the evening of Friday, January 13, 1956, seemed to have the greatest single influence on him. He had gathered a group of men, all of them in the Administration except Milton . . . I do not like to think of

myself as a cynic. But I cannot avoid the visceral feeling that the self-serving element affected the advice Dad received. On the other hand, I wonder what else he would expect from the 'fine group of subordinates' themselves. Of course, even such unanimity, had Dad felt otherwise, would never have swayed him. His colleagues were telling him what, by that time, he wanted to hear" (John S. D. Eisenhower, *Strictly Personal*, 184–85).

30. On this subject the best analysis is by William B. Ewald, Jr., *Eisenhower the President: Crucial Days, 1951–1960*, 170–200. Ewald was a White House assistant in 1954–1956 and worked with Eisenhower at Gettysburg when he wrote his memoirs during the early 1960s. See also Stephen E. Ambrose, *Eisenhower* 2:292–99, 319–26.

31. Conversation between the president and vice-president, June 29, 1954, "Richard M. Nixon (5)," box 28, administrative series, Ann Whitman file, Eisenhower Papers. The president was referring to Nixon's recent Milwaukee speech. "With further reference to remarks about Acheson, the president pointed out that McCarthy had several times referred to the '20 years of treason'—an indefensible statement and urged that by no implication could Nixon be considered saying the same thing."

32. Diary entry, November 11, 1955, box 3, Randall Papers.

33. Milton S. Eisenhower, *The President Is Calling*, 335.

34. Eisenhower to Everett E. (Swede) Hazlett, December 8, 1954, Robert Griffith, ed., *Ike's Letters to a Friend*, 138.

35. Pre-press conference briefing, February 29, 1956, "Feb. '56 Miscellaneous (1)," box 13, DDE diary series, Ann Whitman file, Eisenhower Papers. After the president made his announcement that he, himself, would accept a second term, the first question from the reporters was "would you again want Vice President Nixon as your running mate?" At that point Eisenhower made his pat explanations. *Public Papers of the Presidents: Dwight D. Eisenhower, 1956* (Washington: Government Printing Office, 1958), 266–67.

36. *Public Papers of the Presidents: Dwight D. Eisenhower, 1956*, 287.

37. In the files of the Eisenhower Library is a detailed three-page memorandum of the conversation between the president and vice-president—"Apr. '56 Miscellaneous (1)," box 14, DDE diary series, Ann Whitman file, Eisenhower Papers—that almost certainly is the result of a tape. When the president's aide, Andrew J. Goodpaster, sat in on conversations he initialed the resulting memoranda. The president's secretary, Ann Whitman, usually did likewise. The above-mentioned memo has no initials but is similar to many other memos in the Eisenhower Papers that undoubtedly came from tapes. The historian Francis L. Loewenheim in 1979 first revealed the existence of such taping in the Eisenhower White House. Among the documents he identified was the Eisenhower-Nixon conversation mentioned above, note 31.

38. Griffith, ed., *Ike's Letters*, 138.

6. Two More Crises

1. Apparently there was nothing in Eisenhower's hospital record to show the discovery of Crohn's disease. The record in Snyder's files relates, "The upper GI series revealed no abnormality and the barium enema showed a normal colon." Report of May 12, 1956, signed by the chief of medicine at Walter Reed, Colonel Francis W. Pruitt, box 1, Snyder Papers. Heaton's clinical record of the Crohn's disease attack read, as "previous medical history," that "a barium enema in 1949 revealed a normal colon and did not visualize the terminal ileum. Similar examination in May 1956 revealed a normal colon with radiological involvement of the distal 50 cm. of the ileum. It was the consensus of opinion by the Chief of the Radiology Service, Chief [of the] Department of Medicine, and others that this represented an old burned-out terminal ileitis [Crohn's disease], and it was so diagnosed at that time" (record, August 10, 1956, box 4, Snyder Papers). Snyder years later claimed an agreement not to mention the constriction to the president or anyone by the medical group of Heaton, Pruitt, Mattingly, Lodmell, and himself. The doctors, he wrote, felt that knowledge of this fact would cause the president unnecessary anxiety. This irritated Eisenhower: "The President, afterward, took a great exception to our decision in this matter" (Howard McC. Snyder, draft medical history, 1956, pp. 2–3, box 11, Snyder Papers).

2. David D. Rutstein, "Doctors and Politics," 33.

3. Record of June 22, 1956, box 4, Snyder Papers.

4. Leonard D. Heaton Oral History, by Maclyn P. Burg, October 27, 1975, 43–47, 53.

5. Ibid., 70–71.

6. Rutstein, "Doctors and Politics," 33. Dr. Rutstein was hardly alone in his sharp criticism both of Dr. White's prediction that Eisenhower could have five to ten more years of public service and that a similar politicization of the president's health had taken place in the diagnosis of ileitis without any previous symptoms. The husband of Anna Roosevelt, Dr. Halsted, wrote Dr. White with irritation: "Frankly, Paul, I think it is owed to the medical profession to insist on frankness and honesty in this situation. If I were a Republican I would say the same thing, since many Republican doctor friends are saying exactly this at the present time" (Halsted to White, July 8, 1956, folder 20, box 35, White Papers). Similarly Dr. Philip M. LeCompte wondered "if members of the medical profession have on any other occasion dished out such a combination of misinformation and silly remarks" (*New England Journal of Medicine*, August 2, 1956). The dean of the Harvard Medical School, Dr. George Packer Berry, wrote Rutstein, then vacationing in France, sending a theoretical news release from Gettysburg:

"Gettysburg—Death, as it must to all men, came last night to Dwight D. Eisenhower.

"Press Secretary James Hagerty announced this made no change in plans for November, but rather enhanced the spiritual nature of the administration.

"National Chairman Leonard Hall pointed out that there was no constitutional provision that the President must be alive during his term of
office.

"Major General Howard Snyder, after performing an autopsy, declared
the President was in better organic condition than any other previous
candidate for the presidency.

"Snyder also stated that the cause of the President's death was a second
emergency operation, in which everything was taken out and Sherman
Adams put in."

Berry to Rutstein, August 13, 1956, folder "Atlantic journal," box 76, David D.
Rutstein Papers.

7. Diary entry, August 29, 1956, Snyder Papers. Heaton later did publish
an account of the operation: Leonard D. Heaton, Isidor S. Ravdin, Bryan
Blades, and Thomas J. Whelan, "President Eisenhower's Operation for Regional Enteritis: A Footnote to History," 661–66. In this article Heaton was still
critical of medical colleagues who gave advice concerning the operation: "Comments on the selection of operation arrived by letter and wire from numerous
known and unknown colleagues, many of them surgeons but many of them
from decidedly remote specialties. A professor of preventative medicine, for
instance" (665). The latter reference, of course, was to Rutstein. But it was in
the article that for the first time the commanding general of Walter Reed admitted that he had known a month in advance of the operation of June 1956
that Eisenhower was suffering from chronic ileitis—exactly as Rutstein suspected. Figure 1 of the article is of "Small bowel series showing localized
regional enteritis in the terminal ileum performed on May 11, 1956." The text
also related this fact. There is no explanatory comment.

8. *New York Times,* June 9, 1956.

9. Mattingly and Marsh, General health status, p. 93.

10. In the Snyder Papers, box 6, are prothrombin charts, with times:
November 17, 1955, 32 percent; November 23, 32; November 30, 32; December
10, 30; December 17, 30; December 28, 28; January 11, 1956, 31; January 26, 32;
February 11, 32; February 28, 50; March 12, 26; March 29, 38; April 19, 25;
May 1, 21; May 31, 32; June 12, 100; June 27, 90; June 29, 12; June 30, 20; July 2,
30; July 5, 12; July 17, 40; July 30, 100; August 10, 36; August 21, 30; Sep-
tember 7, 30; September 22, 30; October 9, 40; October 12, 20; October 29, 40;
November 8, 22; November 21, 30; December 19, 36; January 3, 1957, 28;
January 17, 70; February 7, 22; February 21, 60; March 4, 70; March 12, 70;
March 25, 80; April 15, 35; May 1, 36; May 22, 100; July 11, 58; August 15, 76;
October 5, 56; November 26, 80. There was every reason to keep Eisenhower
on anticoagulants. On January 1, 1956, Dr. F. Janney Smith of the Henry Ford
Hospital in Detroit, a nationally known expert in use of anticoagulants for
survivors of acute myocardial infarction, wrote White—who apparently sent
a copy to Snyder—of the results of a five-year study, not yet published. There
were 121 long-term anticoagulant-treated cases with 12 deaths over a five-
year period, and 234 untreated cases with 112 deaths. These were for both
single and double infarcts. Of the single infarct group of 71 treated cases and

186 untreated, the death rate was three times greater for the untreated patients. For the recurrent infarct group (in which Eisenhower probably belonged) there were 50 treated cases and 48 untreated, and the death rate was five times as large for untreated. Of 28 patients who stopped taking anticoagulants, 14 or 50 percent were dead in times ranging from three days to twenty months, this when mortality from the acute phase of recurrent myocardial infarction was around 30 percent. Box 4, Mattingly Papers.

11. The Snyder diary is full of annotations about the beefing-up drugs, especially the liver extract, such as "This noon I gave the President a hypo of Crude Liver with Folvite, 1 cc" (July 30, 1956). Also August 3, 10, 14, 20, 26, 30; September 1, 3, 7, 28; October 2, 5, 15, 30; and November 12, 23. It is possible that liver extract won the election.

12. Many months after the Janney Smith letter of January 1, 1956 (above, n. 10), Snyder wrote White (December 3) that he thought Mattingly satisfied with the Coumadin dosage but would check and get back. January 3, 1957, he had checked and instead of relating the prothrombin times discussed the possibility of changing to Marcumar. Mattingly and Crosby, he said, agreed that there should be no change, "inasmuch as there has been no difficulty in controlling the prothrombin level" (folder 25, box 35, White Papers).

13. Mattingly, Lynn, and Marsh, Cardiovascular system, 3:29.

14. Diary entry, November 5, 1956, Snyder Papers.

15. Diary entry, September 13, 1957, in Ferrell, *Eisenhower Diaries*, 347.

16. Diary entry, November 19, 1957, Snyder Papers.

17. Dwight D. Eisenhower, *The White House Years* 2:227.

18. Diary entry, November 25, 1957, Snyder Papers. The other two sources for the president's behavior after the stroke, in addition to Eisenhower's writings, are Sherman Adams, *Firsthand Report: The Story of the Eisenhower Administration*, 195–98, and John S. D. Eisenhower, *Strictly Personal*, 195–97. Adams has the president saying, "If I cannot attend to my duties, I am simply going to give up this job. Now that is all there is to it" (197).

19. Snyder had written White on November 6 that "there has been no interruption in the Coumadin program in the President's case since it was resumed following the operation of June 1956. Dosage for the past approximate year has been 5 mg. for six days, skipping the seventh" (folder 25, box 35, White Papers).

20. Diary entry, November 30, Snyder Papers.

21. Stephen E. Ambrose, *Eisenhower* 2:438–40. Dulles was of course very sensitive to what had happened to his "Uncle Bert" Lansing, doubtless having heard the story from his uncle's lips more than once. At the time of the president's heart attack he also had called Nixon and brought up President Wilson's illness and "the situation which prevailed when Dr. Cary Grayson and Mrs. Wilson decided what papers the President should and should not see with the result that they literally ran the Government." In September 1955 the two men, Dulles and Nixon, had decided that Sherman Adams would "play the role this time." It was an interesting exercise of nonpresidential authority, somewhat on the same scale as the actions of the personages they spoke of in the Wilson administration. Before deciding on Adams they had

talked about Adams's assistant, Major General Wilton B. Persons, but "agreed he would not be good for this spot." Memorandum of telephone conversation with the vice-president, September 25, 1955, "Telephone Conv. Sept. 1–Dec. 30, 1955, (5)," box 4, telephone calls series, John Foster Dulles Papers.

22. Memorandum by Nixon of a meeting with Eisenhower, December 3, 1957, "Nixon–Vice President Correspondence (8)," box 50, William P. Rogers Papers.

7. Aftermath

1. Diary entry, November 14, 1958, Snyder Papers.
2. Ibid., November 24, 1955.
3. Ibid., December 2, 1957.
4. Shanley diary, January 12, 1956.
5. Snyder diary, January 13, 1960.
6. Ibid., September 1, 1958, and April 11, 1959.
7. Ibid., February 11, 1958.
8. Ibid., February 21, 1958
9. Ibid., July 20, 1958.
10. Ibid., October 28, 1960.
11. Ibid., October 26, 1959.
12. Arthur M. Schlesinger, Jr., *The Imperial Presidency*.
13. Diary entry, February 19, 1959, Snyder Papers.
14. Ibid., February 20.
15. Ibid., August 26.
16. Ibid., August 28.
17. Ibid., September 15.
18. Snyder memorandum, May 13, 1958, box 4, Thomas W. Mattingly Papers.
19. For the following story, see Mattingly, Lynn, and Marsh, Cardiovascular system, 3:34–35.
20. Prothrombin times from charts in box 6, Snyder papers: December 3, 1957, 50 percent; December 5, 76; December 10, 48; December 13, 34; December 17, 38; December 21, 60; December 7, 46; January 22, 1958, 26; February 5, 64; February 13, 60; February 28, 72; March 25, 60; April 25, 50; June 5, 46; July 16, 32; August 14, 58; September 24, 98; October 4, 50; October 30, 30; December 5, 28; December 17, 38; January 15, 1959, 52; February 16, 80; March 17, 50; April 29, 60; May 28, 28; June 24, 34; July 14, 56; August 11, 38; September 17, 48; September 23, 50; October 29, 34; November 30, 52; December 24, 42; February 3, 1960, 36; February 19, 76; February 22, 54; March 18, 46; April 6, 82; April 27, 90; April 30, 36; May 13, 35; June 9, 30; July 16, 25; August 9, 50; September 13, 40; October 14, 45; November 4, 47; January 17, 1961, 50.
21. The Eisenhower Papers in Abilene contain drafts of essays on major military and political figures during and after World War II, often of a dozen

or more pages. Eisenhower drafted and redrafted but could not focus on the writing long enough to put the material together.

22. Mattingly, Cardiovascular system, 8:15–16.

23. Carl W. Hughes et al., "A Review of the Late General Eisenhower's Operations: Epilog to a Footnote to History," *Annals of Surgery* 173 (1971): 793–99.

8. Kennedy, Reagan, and Bush

1. The following account of Kennedy's illnesses relies on Joan and Clay Blair, Jr., *The Search for JFK*, 556–79, and Herbert S. Parmet, *Jack: The Struggle of John F. Kennedy*, 119–24.

2. Arthur M. Schlesinger, Jr., *A Thousand Days: John F. Kennedy in the White House*, 19.

3. James A. Nicholas et al., "Management of Adrenocortical Insufficiency during Surgery," *AMA Archives of Surgery* 71 (1955): 739–40. "A man 37 years of age had Addison's disease for seven years" (739).

4. John Nichols, "President Kennedy's Adrenals," *Journal of the American Medical Association* 201 (July 10, 1967): 129–30.

5. Thomas C. Reeves, *A Question of Character: A Life of John F. Kennedy* (New York: 1991), 295–96. Sometimes Jacobson took patients to his laboratory in back of the office. "There were cauldrons and masses of rocks and things boiling around. It was like science fiction, the colored lights. Then he would show me what he described as uranium, which he put in the vials. Very often the vials had little rocks at the bottom to give energy, he said." Jacobson told patients he was involved in high-level medical research. He told a House committee that he used "ultrasonic bombardment" to make medications, together with a strong magnetic field and the ability of certain minerals and precious stones to regain fluorescence. He said that in 1953 he was coinventor of the laser microscope—that is, seven years before the first laser was developed. The device, he said, was more powerful than the best microscopes in use in the 1970s. Asked why no scientists used the invention, he said that unfortunately his partner was "completely insane" and ran off with the device and had not been heard from since (*New York Times*, December 4, 1972).

6. Kenneth P. O'Donnell and David F. Powers, "*Johnny, We Hardly Knew Ye,*" 192–93.

7. Joe V. Selby et al., "A Case-Control Study of Screening Sigmoidoscopy and Mortality from Colorectal Cancer," *New England Journal of Medicine* 326 (March 5, 1992): 653–57.

8. "Every Time Bush Says 'Ah,' Second-Guessers of His Doctor Cry 'Aha!,'" *New York Times*, February 18, 1992.

9. Ibid.

10. *New York Times*, January 22, 1992.

11. Ibid., March 27, 1992.

12. *St. Petersburg Times:* Mary McGrory, "Quayle has a chance to rise

above his image," January 10, 1992; Mike Royko, "Quayle gears up to bash Cuomo," February 6, 1992.

13. MacMahon and Curry, *Medical Cover-ups,* 164–71.

14. Eisenhower to Katz, April 9, 1957, box 428, official files, central files, Eisenhower Papers.

BIBLIOGRAPHY

Manuscripts

Dwight D. Eisenhower Library, Abilene, Kansas. John Foster Dulles Papers.
———. Thomas W. Mattingly Papers, including "The Life Health Record of Dwight D. Eisenhower."
———. Clarence Randall Diary.
———. William E. Robinson Papers.
———. William P. Rogers Papers.
———. Bernard M. Shanley Diary.
———. Walter Bedell Smith Papers.
———. Howard McC. Snyder Diary and Papers.
———. Surgeon General's (U.S. Army) Papers.
Franklin D. Roosevelt Library, Hyde Park, New York. John Boettiger Papers.
———. Anna Roosevelt Halsted Papers.
———. Ross T. McIntire Papers.
Harvard Medical School, Francis A. Countway Library, Boston, Massachusetts. David D. Rutstein Papers.
———. Paul Dudley White Papers.
Library of Congress, Washington, D.C. Chandler P. Anderson Papers.
———. Ray Stannard Baker Papers.
———. Joseph E. Davies Diary. Davies Papers.
———. James A. Farley Diary. Farley Papers.
———. Charles S. Hamlin Diary. Hamlin Papers.
———. Irwin H. Hoover Papers.
———. Daniel S. Lamont Papers.
Byrnes, James F. Papers. Robert Muldrow Cooper Library, Clemson University, Clemson, South Carolina.
Daniels, Jonathan Diary. Daniels Papers. Southern Historical Collection, University of North Carolina at Chapel Hill.
Grayson, Cary T. Diary. Offices of the Papers of Woodrow Wilson. Firestone Library, Princeton University, Princeton, New Jersey.
Keen, William W. Scrapbook. Library of the College of Physicians of Philadelphia, Pennsylvania.
Sawyer, Charles E. Papers. Reels 248 and 262. Warren G. Harding Papers, Ohio Historical Society, Columbus.

Snyder, Howard McC. Diary and Papers. American Heritage Center, University of Wyoming, Laramie.

Truman, Harry S. Papers. Harry S. Truman Library, Independence, Missouri.

Walker, Frank C. Diary. Walker Papers. Archives of the University of Notre Dame, Hesburgh Library, South Bend, Indiana.

Walworth, Arthur. Papers. Archives of Yale University, Sterling Memorial Library, New Haven, Connecticut.

Interviews

Bruenn, Howard G. Interview with Robert H. Ferrell. Riverdale, New York. February 16, 1992.

———. Interview with Brenda L. Heaster. Riverdale, New York. April 21–22, 1989.

———. Interview with Jan Kenneth Herman. Riverdale, New York. January 31, 1990. "The President's Cardiologist," *Navy Medicine* 81, no. 2 (March–April 1990): 6–13, and full transcript courtesy of interviewer.

Mattingly, Thomas W. Interview with author. Davidson, North Carolina, November 9, 13–14, 1991.

Oral Histories

James C. Hagerty. 1967–1968, by Ed Edwin. Eisenhower Library.

Leonard W. Hall. 1975, by David Horrocks. Eisenhower Library.

Leonard D. Heaton. 1975, by Maclyn P. Burg. Eisenhower Library.

Robert G. Nixon. 1970, by Jerry N. Hess. Truman Library.

Books and Articles

Abrams, Herbert L. *"The President Has Been Shot"*: Confusion, Disability, and the 25th Amendment in the Aftermath of the Attempted Assassination of Ronald Reagan. New York: Norton, 1992.

Ackerman, Lauren V. "Verrucous Carcinoma of the Oral Cavity." *Surgery* 23 (1948): 670–78.

Adams, Herbert Dan. *The Knife that Saves: Memoirs of a Lahey Clinic Surgeon.* Boston: Francis A. Countway Library of Medicine, 1991.

Adams, Sherman. *Firsthand Report: The Story of the Eisenhower Administration.* New York: Harper, 1961.

Ambrose, Stephen E. *Eisenhower.* 2 vols. New York: Simon and Schuster, 1983–1984.

Asbell, Bernard. *When F.D.R. Died.* New York: Holt, Rinehart and Winston, 1961.

Baker, Ray Stannard. *American Chronicle.* New York: Scribner's, 1945.

Behrman, S. N. "Hyper or Hypo?" *New Yorker* 15 (April 8, 1939): 24.

Bishop, Jim. *FDR's Last Year: April 1944–April 1945*. New York: Morrow, 1974.

Blair, Joan, and Clay Blair, Jr. *The Search for JFK*. New York: Putnam, 1976.

Blum, John M. *Woodrow Wilson and the Politics of Morality*. Boston: Little, Brown, 1956.

————, ed. *The Price of Vision: The Diary of Henry A. Wallace, 1942–1946*. Boston: Houghton Mifflin, 1973.

Bohlen, Charles E. *Witness to History: 1929–1969*. New York: Norton, 1973.

Bowles, Chester. *Promises to Keep: My Years in Public Life, 1941–1969*. New York: Harper and Row, 1971.

Bradley, Omar N., and Clay Blair. *A General's Life*. New York: Simon and Schuster, 1983.

Brooks, John J., Horatio T. Enterline, and Gonzalo E. Aponte. "The Final Diagnosis of President Cleveland's Lesion," *Transactions and Studies of the College of Physicians of Philadelphia* 2, no. 1 (March 1980): 1–25.

[Herbert Brownell]. "Brownell Sheds Light on Dewey's Presidential Campaigns." *Miller Center Report: Newsletter of the Miller Center of Public Affairs* (University of Virginia) 7, no. 1 (Spring 1991): 2, 5.

Brownell, Herbert. "Presidential Inability: The Need for Constitutional Amendment." *Yale Law Journal* 68 (1958): 189–211.

Bruenn, Howard G. "Clinical Notes on the Illness and Death of President Franklin D. Roosevelt." *Annals of Internal Medicine* 72 (1970): 579–91.

Burner, David. *John F. Kennedy and a New Generation*. Boston: Little, Brown, 1988.

Burns, James M. *Roosevelt: The Soldier of Freedom*. New York: Harcourt, Brace, Jovanovich, 1970.

Butcher, Harry C. *My Three Years with Eisenhower*. New York: Simon and Schuster, 1946.

Campbell, Thomas M., and George C. Herring, eds. *The Diaries of Edward R. Stettinius, Jr.: 1943–1946*. New York: New Viewpoints, 1975.

Chandler, Alfred D., and Louis Galambos, eds. *The Papers of Dwight David Eisenhower*. 13 vols. Baltimore: Johns Hopkins University Press, 1970–.

Cooper, John Milton, Jr. *The Warrior and the Priest: Woodrow Wilson and Theodore Roosevelt*. Cambridge: Harvard University Press, 1983.

Crispell, Kenneth R., and Carlos F. Gomez. *Hidden Illness in the White House*. Durham: Duke University Press, 1988.

Cross, Wilbur, and John Moses. "My God, Sir, I Think the President Is Doomed!" *American History Illustrated* 17 (November 1982): 40–45.

Dale, Philip Marshall. *Medical Biographies: The Ailments of Thirty-three Famous Persons*. Norman: University of Oklahoma Press, 1952.

Daniels, Jonathan. *The Man of Independence*. Philadelphia: Lippincott, 1950.

————. *White House Witness: 1942–1945.* Garden City, N.Y.: Doubleday, 1975.

Eisenhower, Dwight D. *At Ease: Stories I Tell My Friends.* Garden City, N.Y.: Doubleday, 1967.

————. *The White House Years.* 2 vols. Garden City, N.Y.: Doubleday, 1963–1964.

Eisenhower, John S. D. *Strictly Personal.* Garden City, N.Y.: Doubleday, 1974.

Eisenhower, Milton S. *The President Is Calling.* Garden City, N.Y.: Doubleday, 1974.

————, ed. *Letters to Mamie.* Garden City, N.Y.: Doubleday, 1978.

Ewald, William B., Jr. *Eisenhower the President: Crucial Days, 1951–1960.* Englewood Cliffs, N.J.: Prentice Hall, 1981.

Fabricant, Noah B. *13 Famous Patients.* Philadelphia: Chilton, 1960.

Feerick, John D. *From Failing Hands: The Story of Presidential Succession.* New York: Fordham University Press, 1965.

Ferrell, Robert H., ed. *The Diary of James C. Hagerty: Eisenhower in Mid-Course, 1954–1955.* Bloomington: Indiana University Press, 1983.

————, ed. *The Eisenhower Diaries.* New York: Norton, 1981.

————, ed. *Truman in the White House: The Diary of Eben A. Ayers.* Columbia: University of Missouri Press, 1991.

————. *Woodrow Wilson and World War I.* New York: Harper and Row, 1985.

Flynn, Edward J. *You're the Boss.* New York: Viking, 1947.

Freidel, Frank. *Franklin D. Roosevelt: A Rendezvous with Destiny.* Boston: Little, Brown, 1990.

Gallagher, Hugh C. *F.D.R.'s Splendid Deception.* New York: Dodd, Mead, 1985.

Garraty, John A. *Woodrow Wilson: A Great Life in Brief.* New York: Knopf, 1956.

Giglio, James N. *The Presidency of John F. Kennedy.* Lawrence: University Press of Kansas, 1991.

Goldsmith, Harry S. "Unanswered Mysteries in the Death of Franklin D. Roosevelt." *Surgery, Gynecology and Obstetrics* 149 (December 1979): 899–908.

Griffith, Robert, ed. *Ike's Letters to a Friend: 1941–1958.* Lawrence: University Press of Kansas, 1984.

Hassett, William D. *Off the Record with F.D.R.: 1942–1945.* New Brunswick, N.J.: Rutgers University Press, 1958.

Heaster, Brenda L. "Who's on Second?" *Missouri Historical Review* 80, no. 2 (January 1986): 156–75.

Heaton, Leonard D., Isidor S. Ravdin, Bryan Blades, and Thomas J. Whelan. "President Eisenhower's Operation for Regional Enteritis: A Footnote to History." *Annals of Surgery* 159 (1964): 661–69.

Heckscher, August. *The Memoirs of Herbert Hoover: The Cabinet and the Presidency, 1920–1933.* New York: Macmillan, 1952.

———. *Woodrow Wilson.* New York: Scribner's, 1991.

Houston, David F. *Eight Years with Wilson's Cabinet: 1913 to 1920.* 2 vols. Garden City, N.Y.: Doubleday, 1926.

Hughes, Carl W. et al. "A Review of the Late General Eisenhower's Operations: Epilog to a Footnote to History." *Annals of Surgery* 173 (1971): 793–99.

Keen, William W. "The Surgical Operations on President Cleveland in 1893. *Saturday Evening Post* 190 (September 22, 1917): 24–25, 53, 55.

———. *The Surgical Operations on President Cleveland in 1893.* Philadelphia: Jacobs, 1917.

———. *The Surgical Operations on President Cleveland in 1893 together with Six Additional Papers of Reminiscences.* Philadelphia: Lippincott, 1928.

Kraus, Frederick T., and Carlos Perez-Mesa. "Verrucous Carcinoma: Clinical and Pathologic Study of 105 Cases Involving Oral Cavity, Larynx and Genitalia." *Cancer* 19 (1966): 26–38.

Lane, Anne W., and Louise H. Wall., eds. *The Letters of Franklin K. Lane: Personal and Political.* Boston: Houghton Mifflin, 1922.

L'Etang, Hugh. *The Pathology of Leadership.* New York: Hawthorne, 1970.

Link, Arthur S. "A President Disabled." *Constitution* 4 (Spring/Summer 1992): 5–15.

———. *Woodrow Wilson: A Brief Biography.* Cleveland, Ohio: World, 1968.

———. *Woodrow Wilson: Revolution, War, and Peace.* Arlington Heights, Ill.: AHM, 1979.

McElroy, Robert M. *Grover Cleveland: The Man and the Statesman.* 2 vols. New York: Harper, 1923.

McIntire, Ross T. "Did U.S. Elect a Dying President?: The Inside Facts of the Final Weeks of FDR." *U.S. News and World Report* 30 (March 23, 1951): 19–23.

———, and George Creel. *White House Physician.* New York: Putnam, 1946.

MacMahon, Edward B., and Leonard Curry. *Medical Cover-ups in the White House.* Washington: Farragut, 1987.

Martin, J. S. "When the President Disappeared." *American Heritage* 8 (1957): 10–13, 102–3.

Marx, Rudolph. *The Health of the Presidents.* New York: Putnam, 1960.

Master, Arthur M. et al. "Survival and Rehabilitation after Coronary Occlusion." *Journal of the American Medical Association* 156 (1954): 1552–56.

Mattingly, Thomas W., in E. Grey Dimond, ed. "Paul Dudley White, A Portrait." *American Journal of Cardiology* 15 (January–June): 504–10.

Means, Gaston B. *The Strange Death of President Harding.* New York: Guild, 1930.

Merrill, Horace S. *Bourbon Leader: Grover Cleveland and the Democratic Party.* Boston: Little, Brown, 1957.

Miller, Joseph M. "Stephen Grover Cleveland." *Surgery, Gynecology and Obstetrics* 113 (1961): 524–29.

Morgan, Ted. *FDR: A Biography.* New York: Simon and Schuster, 1985.

Morreels, Charles L., Jr. "New Historical Information on the Cleveland Operations." *Surgery* 62, no. 3 (September 1967): 542–51.

Murray, Robert K. *The Harding Era: Warren G. Harding and His Administration.* Minneapolis: University of Minnesota Press, 1969.

Nevins, Allan. *Grover Cleveland: A Study in Courage.* New York: Dodd, Mead, 1932.

Nicholas, James A. et al. "Management of Adrenocortical Insufficiency during Surgery." *AMA Archives of Surgery* 71 (1955): 737–42.

O'Donnell, Kenneth P., and David F. Powers. *"Johnny, We Hardly Knew Ye": Memories of John Fitzgerald Kennedy.* Boston: Little, Brown, 1972.

Park, Bert Edward. *The Impact of Illness on World Leaders.* Philadelphia: University of Pennsylvania Press, 1986.

Parmet, Herbert S. *Eisenhower and the American Crusades.* New York: Macmillan, 1972.

———. *Jack: The Struggle of John F. Kennedy.* New York: Dial, 1980.

———. *JFK: The Presidency of John F. Kennedy.* New York: Dial, 1983.

Patterson, James T. *The Dread Disease: Cancer and Modern American Culture.* Cambridge: Harvard University Press, 1987.

Paul, Oglesby. *Take Heart: The Life and Prescription for Living of Dr. Paul Dudley White.* Boston: Countway Library of Medicine, 1986.

Peskin, Allan. *Garfield.* Kent, Ohio: Kent State University, 1978.

Reeves, Thomas C. *Gentleman Boss: The Life of Chester Alan Arthur.* New York: Knopf, 1975.

Reilly, Michael F., and William J. Slocum. *Reilly of the White House.* New York: Simon and Schuster, 1947.

Richards, David W., Edward F. Bland, and Paul D. White. "A Completed Twenty-Five-Year Study of 200 Patients with Myocardial Infarction." *Journal of Chronic Diseases* 4 (1956): 415–22.

Robertson, Charles W. "Some Observations on Presidential Illnesses." *Boston Medical Quarterly* 8, nos. 2–3 (June–September 1957): 1–22.

Robinson, Edgar E., and Paul C. Edwards, eds. *The Memoirs of Ray Lyman Wilbur: 1875–1949.* Stanford, Calif.: Stanford University Press, 1960.

Roosevelt, Elliott, ed. *F.D.R.: His Personal Letters.* 3 vols. New York: Duell, Sloan and Pearce, 1947–1950.

Roosevelt, James, and Sidney Shalett. *Affectionately, F.D.R.: A Son's Story of a Courageous Man.* New York: Harcourt, Brace, 1959.

——— with Bill Libby. *My Parents: A Differing View.* Chicago: Playboy Press, 1976.

———— with Sam Toperoff. *A Family Matter.* New York: Simon and Schuster, 1980.

Rosenhouse, Leo. "President Cleveland's Secret Surgery." *Private Practice* 69 (October 1974): 43, 45–47.

————. "White House Doctor." *Private Practice* 4 (September 1972): 57–58, 62, 64.

Russell, Francis. *The Shadow of Blooming Grove: Warren G. Harding and His Times.* New York: McGraw-Hill, 1968.

Rutstein, David D. "Doctors and Politics." *Atlantic* 198 (August 1956): 32–35.

Sawyer, Charles E. et al. "President Harding's Last Illness: Official Bulletins of Attending Physicians." *Journal of the American Medical Association* 81 (1923): 603.

Schlesinger, Arthur M., Jr. *The Imperial Presidency.* Boston: Houghton Mifflin, 1973.

————. *A Thousand Days: John F. Kennedy in the White House.* Boston: Houghton Mifflin, 1965.

Seelig, M. G. "Cancer and Politics: The Operation on Grover Cleveland." *Surgery, Gynecology and Obstetrics* 85 (1947): 373–76.

Shoumatoff, Elizabeth. *FDR's Unfinished Portrait: A Memoir.* Pittsburgh: University of Pittsburgh Press, 1990.

Smith, A. Merriman. *Thank You, Mr. President.* New York: Harper, 1946.

Smith, Carter. "Length of Survival after Myocardial Infarction." *Journal of the American Medical Association* 151 (1953): 167–70.

Sorensen, Theodore C. *Kennedy.* New York: Harper, 1965.

Starling, Edmund W., and Thomas Sugrue. *Starling of the White House.* New York: Simon and Schuster, 1946.

Stevenson, R. Scott. *Famous Illnesses in History.* London: Eyre and Spottiswoode, 1962.

Summersby, Kay (Kathleen Summersby McCarthy-Morrogh). *Eisenhower Was My Boss.* New York: Prentice-Hall, 1948.

Summersby, Kay (Kay Summersby Morgan). *Past Forgetting: My Love Affair with Dwight D. Eisenhower.* New York: Simon and Schuster, 1976.

Trani, Eugene P., and David L. Wilson. *The Presidency of Warren G. Harding.* Lawrence: Regents Press of Kansas, 1977.

Tumulty, Joseph P. *Woodrow Wilson as I Know Him.* Garden City, N.Y.: Doubleday, Page, 1921.

Walker, J. Samuel. *Henry A. Wallace and American Foreign Policy.* Westport, Conn.: Greenwood, 1976.

Walworth, Arthur. *Woodrow Wilson.* 2d ed. Boston: Houghton Mifflin, 1965.

Weinstein, Edwin A. *Woodrow Wilson: A Medical and Psychological Biography.* Princeton: Princeton University Press, 1981.

Welch, Richard E., Jr. *The Presidencies of Grover Cleveland.* Lawrence: University Press of Kansas, 1988.

White, Paul Dudley. *My Life and Medicine: An Autobiographical Memoir.* Boston: Gambit, 1971.

———, and Edward F. Bland. "Coronary Thrombosis (with Myocardial Infarction) Ten Years Later." *Journal of the American Medical Association* 117 (1941): 1171–73.

Wilbur, Ray Lyman. "The Last Illness of a Calm Man." *Saturday Evening Post* 196 (October 13, 1923), 64.

Wold, Karl C. *Mr. President—How Is Your Health?* St. Paul and Minneapolis: Bruce, 1948.

INDEX